Praise for
Distracted

This book will change how you think about education. *Distracted* takes us on a phenomenal ride into a much misunderstood aspect of human learning and finally into the refreshing light that science, literature, philosophy, and history bring. Anyone who cares about learning—their own or anyone else's—should take this journey.

—Ken Bain, author of *What the Best College Teachers Do*

Lang's books have held a place of honor in my library of parenting and education books, and *Distracted* will, too. It is a delightful mash-up of the research and history on attention and learning. I adore this book and will be recommending it to parents and teachers.   —Jessica Lahey, author of *The Gift of Failure*

Distraction didn't begin with digital devices—and it won't end by banning them from classrooms. The human mind has always been a wandering mind. James Lang offers a fresh and hopeful analysis of this enduring problem. This book is an essential primer for helping students learn to cultivate attention.

—Daniel H. Pink, author of *When, Drive*, and
A Whole New Mind

Distracted gives teachers a powerful way to address one of the knottiest problems they face. Lang is an empathetic and knowledgeable guide, and reading this book feels like being in the middle of a conversation with dedicated, supportive, and enthusiastic colleagues. Whether you're new to the classroom or a veteran teacher, *Distracted* is a must-read.

—Kevin Gannon, Grand View University

In order for learning to happen, we need our students to be fully present in the classroom—and we need to be fully present for them as well. This book tells us why we must actively cultivate our students' ability to focus, weaving together compelling and unexpected approaches for addressing the age-old problem of distracted students.   —Michelle D. Miller, Northern Arizona University

Distracted is a must-read for every classroom teacher. Lang makes a compelling argument that "attention is an achievement" and that we should be cultivating "attention renewal" rather than preventing distractions. He presents practical classroom activities for fostering curiosity and community—with the research to back them up. Candid insights on effective laptop policies, inviting students into the conversation, and the role of assessments make *Distracted* an invaluable resource that will change how you—and your students—think about learning.

—Pooja K. Agarwal, PhD, Cognitive Scientist and
Author, *Powerful Teaching*

Attention is a finite and precious resource we are always in danger of squandering. *Distracted* will help teachers and students use it to nourish mind and soul.   —Ian Leslie, author of *Curious*

Attention is an essential part of the learning process. Yet, to those who teach, attention can feel elusive and fleeting. In *Distracted*, James Lang helps us navigate the challenges presented by technologies that bring both a world of information, and the potential for endless distractions, to students' fingertips. Lang encourages us to rethink our attempts to ban anything that may distract learners, and instead, to focus on practices that gain attention.

—Bonni Stachowiak, *Teaching in Higher Ed*

Distracted proves once and for all that the question we face today is not "How do we make students stop looking at their phones during class?" but rather "How can we help students find meaning during class?" Packed with specific, easy-to-implement pedagogical strategies for seizing and maintaining students' academic attention, *Distracted* is an eminently practical guide for increasing authentic student learning in any subject. It will transform the way we think about teaching and learning in higher education.

—Jessamyn Neuhaus, SUNY Plattsburgh

Distracted

Distracted

Why Students Can't Focus and What You Can Do About It

JAMES M. LANG

BASIC BOOKS

NEW YORK

Basic Books
Hachette Book Group
1290 Avenue of the Americas, New York, NY 10104
www.basicbooks.com

Printed in the United States of America

First Edition: November 2020

Published by Basic Books, an imprint of Perseus Books, LLC, a subsidiary of Hachette Book Group, Inc. The Basic Books name and logo is a trademark of the Hachette Book Group.

The Hachette Speakers Bureau provides a wide range of authors for speaking events. To find out more, go to www.hachettespeakersbureau.com or call (866) 376-6591.

The publisher is not responsible for websites (or their content) that are not owned by the publisher.

Print book interior design by Jouve.

Library of Congress Cataloging-in-Publication Data
Names: Lang, James M., author.
Title: Distracted : why students can't focus and what you can do about it / James M. Lang.
Description: First edition. | New York : Basic Books, 2020. | Includes bibliographical references and index.
Identifiers: LCCN 2020015825 | ISBN 9781541699809 (hardcover) | ISBN 9781541699816 (ebook)
Subjects: LCSH: Motivation in education. | Attention in adolescence. | Interest (Psychology) | Effective teaching. | Classroom environment. | Active learning. | Problem-based learning. | Student participation in curriculum planning. | Cognitive neuroscience.
Classification: LCC LB1065 .L348 2020 | DDC 370.15/4—dc23
LC record available at https://lccn.loc.gov/2020015825

ISBNs: 978-1-5416-9980-9 (hardcover), 978-1-5416-9981-6 (ebook)

LSC-C

10 9 8 7 6 5 4 3 2 1

For my father,

who has taught me to pay attention to what matters.

Instructions for living a life:
Pay attention.
Be astonished.
Tell about it.

MARY OLIVER, "SOMETIMES"

Contents

Preface

I FINISHED WRITING this book in February of 2020, one month before the COVID-19 pandemic erupted in the United States. While the book wound its way through the production process, teachers around the world were shifting their courses online on very short notice. Having never taught online before, I had ten days to transform my British literature survey course, which met three times per week in a physical classroom, to one in which our every encounter would be mediated by screens. During those ten day I learned how to record video lectures for my students, write productive prompts for our discussion board, conduct group and individual Zoom sessions, and assign and evaluate student work entirely online. Much to my surprise, I found the exploration of these new teaching practices invigorating. I had been curious about online teaching for several years, wondering how it would compare to the traditional classroom experience. Some of the teaching practices I experimented with in my online course proved very effective for my students; I will continue to use them when I return to the face-to-face classroom.

I suspect many traditional high school and college courses, the kind that meet in physical classrooms filled with human bodies, will undergo a similar transformation in the post-pandemic world.

Our courses will be enriched by our newfound familiarity with tech tools that have been tested and proven effective by online teachers for the past decade or two. As a consequence of this, the devices that we like to blame for distractibility will assume an even more important role in the lives of educators and students. Attempts to remove them from our learning spaces will become increasingly challenging in this world of blended learning environments, in which students are learning through both their devices and the community setting of the classroom. But whatever differences might emerge in the educational world as a result of the COVID-19 pandemic, the core challenge that this book addresses remains exactly the same as prior to the pandemic, and as it will remain for as long as humans teach other humans through formal schooling: cultivating the attention of students in support of their learning.

You'll read much in the pages that follow about how attention contributes to learning, and about how and why distraction gets in the way. If you have been teaching for any length of time, you will have direct experience with this problem in your own classroom: you will have seen students' attention drifting out the window, waning over the course of the day, or disappearing into their phones and laptops. If you have now also taught online, at least temporarily, you will likely have witnessed attention failing and flailing in those environments as well. Perhaps you noticed students eyeing their phones or checking e-mail during your Zoom sessions, or perhaps you were able to surmise this was happening because you were doing precisely the same thing in your departmental Zoom meetings. You might also have complained to your spouse or friends that you were having difficulty concentrating on your work during the early weeks of the pandemic—a reminder that distraction comes in many forms, and not just from our digital devices. We can be as distracted by our fears and anxieties (and other aspects of our nonacademic life) as we can by our phones and laptops. Whenever we are attempting challenging cognitive work, distraction sings to us sweetly, beckoning us into easier and more pleasurable pursuits.

But the education supported by attention brings greater and more meaningful rewards than the temporary bursts of pleasure we can get from our distractions, and it can give us the cognitive tools we need to manage our fears and anxieties during times of crisis. A student comes into my literature course baffled and a little frustrated by the poems I had assigned her to read; we circle our desks and work our way slowly through one of those poems, and then finish with a writing exercise in which I ask her to think about how the poem connects to her own life experience. Through the attention she has given to the class and the poem, she emerges with new insights into humanity's right relationship with the natural world. A student who has no idea what she wants to do with her life hunkers down over an experiment with a lab partner, and finds in those test tubes something so fascinating that it launches her into her major and ultimate career path. While we were all teaching and learning remotely, I watched one of my daughters, who has struggled with anxiety, complete an art class online, working patiently at her charcoal drawings under the occasional online supervision of her teacher. Later in the evenings, I would sometimes find her holding coloring and drawing sessions with her younger siblings in her bedroom, helping all of them find comfort during this crisis through the exercise of their creative faculties.

Digital devices did not create the challenge of cultivating student attention in support of these kinds of life-altering learning experiences. We have been sidetracked in recent years by assertive voices who lay the entire blame for our distractible natures at the feet of our laptops and phones. But to place the blame exclusively there only works if you ignore the architectural features of our brain that make us prone to distraction, or the long history of humans complaining about the distractibility of their minds. Although we have more distractions today than we had in the past—and more powerful distractions in the form of our digital devices—teachers have always wrestled with the challenge of capturing and sustaining student attention in support of their learning. To overcome that challenge, we need to turn our heads *away* from distraction and *toward* attention. Our challenge is not to wall off distractions; our challenge is to cultivate attention, and help students use it in the service of meaningful learning.

This book emerges from my convictions about the essential role of attention to education. It offers many recommendations for how to make attention a priority in your classroom, from the building of community and the design of your course to the structuring of your class period and the development of creative new teaching strategies. I hope that you will find in here a new understanding of the role that attention can play in student learning, new tools for cultivating the attention of your students, and fresh enthusiasm for the task.

April 20, 2020
Worcester, Massachusetts

Introduction

From Distraction
to Attention

IN THE EARLY 1930s, British author E. M. Delafield published a short novel about an English woman whose literary aspirations bumped up against the drudgeries of life with an indifferent husband, two precocious children, and the challenges of everyday household management.[1] It proved such a hit that Delafield produced multiple sequels in the years that followed. In the second installment, *The Provincial Lady in London*, the title character has scored an unexpected success with her own first novel. After its publication, she describes sitting in a literary conference in Europe, struggling to pay attention to the proceedings:

> Literary Conference takes place in the morning. . . . Am sorry to find attention wandering on several occasions to entirely unrelated topics, such as Companionate Marriage, absence of radiators in Church at home, and difficulty in procuring

ice. Make notes on back of visiting-card, in order to try and feel presence at Conference in any way justified. Find these again later, and discover that they refer to purchase of picture-postcards for Robin and Vicky, memorandum that blue evening dress requires a stitch before it can be worn again, and necessity for finding out whereabouts of Messrs. Thos. Cook & Son, in case I run short of money.[2]

The provincial lady's futile efforts to focus on the conference reflect a theme that recurs throughout the novels in the series: the difficulty of sustaining one's attention on a single object of focus. Every few pages, she chronicles conversations or trains of thought that are derailed by interruptions from children, minor household disasters, or the irritatingly random peregrinations of her own thought processes. All of this, it should be noted, occurs almost a hundred years before the invention of the modern devices that we assume are driving our minds to distraction today.

We have been voicing complaints about our distractible human minds for at least as long as we have been talking and writing about them. A wandering mind represented a threat to the ideals of Greek philosophers who viewed ordered, rational thought as the ultimate achievement of the human species. Christian writers who urged their followers to "pray without ceasing" did so in response to minds that seemed too easily distracted from their devotions. Renaissance intellectuals living in crowded European cities complained about the noisy dins that prevented them from study and scholarship. Media technologies drive our contemporary concerns about our attention, but this has been true since at least the nineteenth century. The telegraph, the radio, the television, the computer—as each of these arrived on the scene, they brought with them critics who argued that they were destroying our attention spans, turning us into distractible creatures who could no longer focus on our work, our prayers, our study, or one another. In most of these cases, writers and thinkers suggested that some new development in human history was eating away at our powers of attention or cognition. When it comes to the distractible nature of our minds, the argument goes, we used to be like *that*; now we are like *this*, and we are worse off for it.

The story they tell is a biblical one. At one time, we lived in a prelapsarian state of mental grace, in which we were capable of complete control over our minds, long periods of sustained attention, and the ability to ward off distractions at will. But (so the story goes) our minds have been progressively degraded by our inventions, wearing away at our attentional capacities, making us dumber and dumber with each new technology. For the writers that embrace this narrative, and for the teachers who read and believe it, our task is to reclaim our minds and the minds of our students from the distractions that beset us today. We have only to put away our phones, sit on our meditation cushions, focus our brains *really hard*, and we will eventually get back the minds we have lost. Attention is our state of grace, distraction the original sin. Get rid of the distractions, and attention will naturally return.

I used to share this perspective. It was hard not to, as I heard versions of it from teachers and parents everywhere: our children and students were hopelessly distracted by their devices and could no longer pay attention in school the way they used to. That problem was a microcosm of the larger challenge occurring at all levels of society; children and students were not the only ones whose minds were suffering at the hands of their distracting devices. Everywhere around me, people were using their phones while driving their cars, scrolling through their social media feeds on dinner dates, texting in movie theaters and concert halls and even at wakes and weddings. There seemed no place safe or sacred enough to keep our phones in our pockets. Surely this level of uncontrolled interaction with our digital devices represented a new phase in human history, and perhaps it also was reshaping our brains in alarming ways. So I began exploring the literature on attention and distraction, because I wondered whether it was true, as everyone seemed to assume, that previous generations of students had better focus, more capacity to tolerate boredom and silence, and less distractible natures than the children in our homes and classrooms today. Were the brains of twenty-first-century students fundamentally different from students in the past?

If the answer to that question was an affirmative one, the implications for teachers would be monumental. The work of teaching could be considered, as biologist James Zull has written, "the art of changing the brain."[3] If the brains of our students today turned out to be different from the brains of their predecessors, then perhaps our centuries-long tradition of attempting to change them through classroom education had become irrelevant.

Stewards of Attention

If we have lost the attention of our students, we're in trouble. The cultivation and direction of attention are fundamental tasks of every teacher, from the kindergarten classrooms of an elementary school to the high-tech learning laboratories of the modern university. "Teaching's essential task," writes Yves Citton in *The Ecology of Attention*, "consists in heightening the ability to notice what is remarkable and important in what we are looking at."[4] In every discipline, in every classroom, instructors prepare for and teach their classes by deciding what is remarkable and important in their fields of study. Countless things have happened in the world; the historian identifies the ones that matter for this particular course and trains the attention of her students on them. Human beings behave in a mind-boggling array of different ways; the social scientist notices patterns in those behaviors and creates courses that high-light the ones that deserve our attention. The enormity of the universe stands before us all, with its planets and stars and dark matter and empty space; the astronomer narrows students' attention to the details that explain the origin of the universe or describe futures near and far—from approaching asteroids to the end point of existence. In every discipline, in every classroom, in all of our research, teachers point and explain: if you pay attention to *this*, you will learn something important.

We are worried today that our efforts at directing the attention of students no longer work. The narrative can be spun in different ways: in one version, the students are taking control of their own attention and directing it to places the teacher has not pointed to, such as their phones or laptops. In another, the attention of our students has been hijacked by sinister forces, preyed upon by app designers and social media moguls, and those forces are directing the attention of students in irresponsible, meaningless ways. In either case, the problem remains. Teaching fails when we can no longer focus our students' attention. Michelle Miller, a cognitive psychologist who writes at the intersection of learning and technology, has argued that teachers could think of themselves as "stewards of students' limited stores of attention."[5] In the twenty-first century, our stewardship seems to falter and fail, besieged by the onslaught of screens and devices that call out to our students constantly.

Too many faculty and educational institutions have responded to this onslaught by attempting to wall off the classroom from digital distractions, banning phones and laptops in the vain hope that students will pay attention if they don't have access to their screens. In November 2017, the economist Susan Dynarski published a *New York Times* essay entitled "Laptops Are Great. But Not During a Lecture or a Meeting," in which she explained why she banned all electronic devices from her college classroom. Dynarski argued that the rationale for such a seemingly drastic action rested on "a growing body of evidence [that] shows that, overall, college students learn less when they use computers or tablets during lectures. They also tend to earn worse grades. The research is unequivocal: Laptops distract from learning, both for users and for those around them."[6] In support of this claim, Dynarski pointed to studies like the ones we will consider in Chapter Two, which demonstrate that digital distraction in the classroom can hurt student learning. She also linked to a highly publicized study that suggested students learn better from taking notes by hand than they do from typing on laptops.[7] Considering the power of handwritten notes along with the benefits of an environment free of digital distractions made the solution clear for her: ban devices from the room. Her essay sparked a lively debate in higher education, as faculty argued with one another about whether we should solve the problem of distracted students by banishing laptops and digital devices from our lecture halls, seminar rooms, and laboratories.

I serve as both an English professor and the director of the Center for Teaching Excellence at a smallish liberal arts university in Massachusetts. At the teaching center, we provide programming and resources that help faculty reflect upon and improve their teaching. Our work is enhanced by a group of student fellows, who meet with us every month to help take the pulse of teaching and learning on campus. They also write essays for the center's blog. Just around the time Susan Dynarski's piece appeared, I published on our website a thought-provoking essay by one of the fellows, Jessica Ferronetti, a senior who was preparing for a career as a high school Spanish teacher. The essay began with a striking story about an experience Ferronetti had while doing her preservice teaching at a local high school:

> This past fall, I was standing up in front of a class of freshmen and sophomores, teaching them a lesson on stem changing

verbs in the present tense in Spanish. I glanced at the clock and decided it was time for their closure activity. I asked the students to please take out a piece of paper for the closure activity as I was going to collect it to gather evidence of assessment. The students didn't move. I asked them again to take out a piece of paper, and one timid hand rose up. "Señorita, we don't have any paper. We don't carry notebooks."[8]

What Ferronetti learned from the conversation that followed was that the district in which she was teaching was working to ensure that every student had a Chromebook or an iPad, and that students were increasingly doing all of their work on these devices, including in class. She concluded her essay by noting that she knew many professors had mixed feelings about allowing technologies in the classroom, but that these polices were setting up a conflict between what students had experienced in their education up to that point and what they would encounter in their college courses. "Students are increasingly becoming dependent on their iPads and laptops in a world where technology is so easily accessible," she explained. "These students will start appearing on college campuses across the country soon, expecting to be able to use all of this technology in class. Teachers and professors must be ready to work with them." You can find evidence of this in almost any K–12 classroom you might care to visit. From kindergarten through high school, our future students are learning on electronic devices.

One could argue that we should just push Dynarski's solution down into the K–12 realm as well, banning devices from classrooms everywhere, from kindergarten through graduate school. But this approach would mean abrogating our responsibilities as educators. We prepare students not only for the future, but for the world in which we are all living now. In the present, they are using their devices to get information, find directions, access music and videos, apply to college, communicate with their teachers, and more. In the future, they will be pursuing careers in which they rely on laptops, tablets, smartphones, or some not-yet-invented technology to facilitate their work, even as those devices will offer them continuous distractions. They will also be using their devices to manage their personal lives: to get driving directions, manage their household while on vacation, communicate with distant children, parents, and friends, and discover and pass along news. Part of our work as educators has to include helping them understand how to navigate their digital environments safely and effectively. It seems strange to me that we would ask students who are immersed in technology outside of school, and will be immersed in it throughout the rest of their lives, to come to our classrooms and work in a technology-free bubble during their school years.

Derek Bruff is the director of the Vanderbilt University Center for Teaching and the author of two books on the use of technology in the college classroom. Our students, he noted in a recent interview on digital distractions, are "going to have to graduate and get jobs and use laptops without being on Facebook all day."[9] Their employers are not going to ban laptops from their desks, or force them to put their smartphones away. Screens, and their potentially distracting powers, have become an inextricable part of the education process, the twenty-first-century workforce, and the personal lives of an increasing majority of humans.

For all of these reasons, which we will consider in greater detail in Chapter Two, I am convinced that we need more nuanced responses to the problem of distraction than laptop or device bans. The evidence adduced by writers like Susan Dynarski is real and unequivocal; digital distraction in the classroom hurts the learning of our students. Everyone teaching today has likely seen this play out. The students whose eyes are glued to their laptop screens, or who are texting furtively throughout class, are often the ones who struggle the most. I know that enough of us are speaking to students about the problem of distraction that they likely know they should pay attention in class, and yet they don't. But they are not unique in that respect. I expect you will have no problem envisioning times and places in which the urge to distract yourself interferes with your work: checking Twitter instead of grading, texting during committee meetings, watching YouTube videos instead of writing. We are all guilty of these behaviors, even when we know they might be hurting the quality of our work or setting us up for misery later, once we finally turn our attention to the tasks we need to complete. Our distractions—and particularly our digital distractions—call to us convincingly these days. To begin the process of turning down the volume, we need at least a basic understanding of their appeal. What makes digital distractions so difficult to resist, for us and our students?

The Pull of Distraction

In *The Distracted Mind: Ancient Brains in a High-Tech World*, neuroscientist Adam Gazzaley and psychologist Larry Rosen address the thrall of digital devices by inviting us to consider the situation of an early human in a grasslands environment.[10] What would have helped our ancestors survive, in order to pass along the features of an evolving brain structure to future generations? Envision this ancient progenitor moving across a natural landscape with an extended family group, in search of the components of life that we still need today: food and water sources, potential mates, shelter. In addition to these elements of the environment he was seeking to discover, there were others he had to avoid: predators, dangerous landscapes, rival groups. What helped him find what he needed and avoid what would hurt him was a brain that had different capacities for attention. On the one hand, he most certainly needed the ability to focus on elements that would ensure his survival. That focusing capacity would have facilitated tracking and hunting, or the kind of deliberate thinking that would have allowed him to retrace the steps of the group toward shelter or water after a long absence. It would have enabled him to attend to his family group and to build or find shelter.

But even while he was using his focused attention to achieve these objectives, it would have been unwise for our ancestor to stay too focused. He also needed the capacity to remain open to potential surprises in the environment, including anything that might hurt or help him. If he attended too closely and exclusively to the tracks of a tasty animal, for example, he might find himself becoming lunch for a different animal. If he focused completely on seeking shelter, he might miss the flash of fur that indicated a possible food source had just unexpectedly arrived in his vicinity. However much focused attention might have benefited our ancestor, too much would have ultimately hurt him. What would have been most helpful to our ancestors, then—and what they have passed along to us today—is the ability to focus and pursue a goal in a sustained manner, *and* the ability to remain open to novel movements or developments in the environment that provide crucial survival information. In order to survive, in other words, the brain needed to be easily distractible.

I don't want to place too much weight on an imagined evolutionary scenario—because the next thing you know, we're inventing paleo diets—but some version of this history would help explain the attention systems that we still carry in our brains today.[11] The dual nature of our attention is not exclusive to humans, either; it may be a fundamental feature of the architecture of the animal brain. In a talk based on his book *The Master and the Emissary: The Divided Brain and the Making of the Western World*, psychiatrist Iain McGilchrist invites us to consider the spectacle of a bird pecking at dirt and grit in search of seeds: "It's got to focus very narrowly and clearly on that little seed and be able to pick it out against that background. But it's also, if it's going to stay alive, it's got to actually keep a quite different kind of attention open. It's got to be on the lookout for predators, or friends . . . whatever else is going on."[12]

McGilchrist argues that the attention systems of most animals take two forms: one enables us to focus, while the other remains in a state that he describes as "broadly vigilant," meaning open to whatever novelty might arise in the environment. If you have a furry creature living in your house, as I do, this will likely seem familiar. When my dog Finn eats his food, he's zoned in pretty tightly on it. But if someone knocks on the door while he does so, he turns immediately and searches for the intruder. The work of McGilchrist and other scientists who write about attention makes clear that our complex attention systems, capable of focus but open to distraction, are as inseparable from us as our five-fingered hands or four-chambered hearts.

But one aspect of our attention systems seems especially characteristic of primates, including the primates in your classroom: not only do we notice novelty in the environment, but we actively seek it out. Sources of novelty—like a flash of fur or the gurgle of a nearby stream—provided our ancestors with useful information and contributed to their ongoing understanding of the environment. Because the acquisition of such information benefited survival, the brain evolved to search continually for it. Gazzaley and Rosen explain that biological mechanisms that rewarded our ancestors for finding new information still exist in us today, as they do in some of our primate cousins:

At our core we are *information-seeking creatures*, so behaviors that maximize information accumulation are optimal. . . . This notion is supported by findings that molecular and physiological mechanisms that originally developed in our brain to support food foraging for survival have now evolved in primates to include information foraging. . . . Macaque monkeys, for example, respond to receiving information similarly to the way they respond to primitive rewards such as food or water.[13]

Our desire to scan the environment for new information, the authors argue, forms such a fundamental part of our attention systems that it parallels our desire for basic needs. We get a burst of satisfaction from identifying a new bit of information, just as we do from a cool glass of water on a warm summer day.

Modern Problems

Gazzaley and Rosen ultimately describe us as having "ancient brains in a high-tech world," and from that phrase we see our modern dilemma. We have brains that have the capacity for concentrated attention in the pursuit of our goals, but that are also designed to search continuously for novelties in our environment. The students who come into our classrooms, for the most part, do not need to notice or seek out novelty in order to survive. Shelter comes in the form of their bedrooms or dorm rooms, food comes packaged in the supermarket or served in the dining hall, and potential reproductive partners live next door. Even though we no longer depend on our information-seeking brains to ensure our survival in many aspects of our lives, those brains still do what they evolved to do: seek new information. But now our students have information dispensers always at their fingertips, beckoning and calling to them at every turn.

We might not think about the phones of our students as information-dispensing machines when they are using them to watch YouTube videos, but that's simply because we are judging the information they are dispensing as meaningless. Viral videos may well be useless for the pursuit of academic goals, but that doesn't mean they're not information. Those social media accounts that students find so enticing are absorbing for a reason: they provide users with an ongoing stream of new data about what's happening with their friends, family, and the world around them. Phones and laptops are perfectly designed to draw and hold the attention of an information-seeking brain, especially because they offer frequent and varied bursts of novelty. Nothing new on Twitter? Check Instagram. Instagram tapped out? Try YouTube. On my phone or laptop I can sit for hours and never run out of novel sources of information, each of which has been built to push new content in front of me constantly, in the form of scrolling and feeds. Our ancient brains love every minute of it.

That our devices have become so effective at this solicitation of my attention is no accident, as we can see from the work of someone like Nir Eyal, a former video-game designer who wrote a book teaching companies how to grab the attention of consumers. "As infinite distractions compete for our attention," he writes in his book *Hooked: How to Build Habit-Forming Products*, "companies are learning to master novel tactics to stay relevant in users' minds."[14] Reading through the book and its footnotes, one finds well-informed references to the scientific research on attention. The designers of our new technologies have made themselves experts in attention and have a wealth of new scientific research at their disposal. They can operate in ways that were not accessible to earlier attention-catching technologies. The television sought to grab my attention, but it could only do so once I turned it on. The phone in my pocket is designed to always be on and within reach, and it does everything in its power to say, "PAY ATTENTION TO ME, JIM!!!!" It buzzes with phone calls and text messages, it plays an annoying melody when someone wants to FaceTime, and when I pull it out of my pocket to check the time it shows me all of the people who *like* me, dammit, whether they are doing so on Instagram or Twitter or Facebook. Sometimes it tells me it needs an upgrade, or it offers me tips on how it can play an even bigger role in my life through some new app.

While some of this comes to me freely, much of it carries costs, either hidden or explicit. In *The Attention Merchants: The Epic Scramble to Get Inside Our Heads*, Tim Wu traces the historical pathways that capitalism has helped to pave toward increasingly distracting digital technologies, from the rise of newspaper advertising in the nineteenth century to today's apps and devices. As the popularity of books like Nir Eyal's would attest, capturing our attention brings big dollars to corporations who can do it successfully, and the competition for our attention drives innovation and effectiveness. "The game of harvesting human attention," Wu writes, "and reselling it to advertisers has become a major part of our economy."[15] When smart people with big bankrolls want to grab our attention, they work with increasing effectiveness at doing so. They entice us with badges and certificates, draw us into games and competitions, reward us with stickers and levels, promise us better health, connect us to potential friends and mates, and more. To turn away from these potential distractions of our digital devices and focus on academic pursuits that demand hard cognitive work requires increasing effort—and increasingly smart strategizing on the part of teachers.

Emphasizing Attention: Three Principles

This is a hopeful book, in which I will argue that such smart strategizing can have a powerful impact on the attention we seek to cultivate in our classrooms. But we will not succeed in teaching today's students unless we make a fundamental shift in our thinking: away from *preventing distraction* and toward *cultivating attention*. The human brain is an eminently distractible organ. We thus are fighting a losing battle if we try to solve the problem of attention by eliminating distractions. Banning devices from the room still leaves pencils for doodling, windows to stare through, coughing and sniffing humans to irritate us, and the endless chaotic swirling of our thoughts. Instead, we need to think about how the learning environments that we build for students can be safe and supportive spaces in which they are inspired, encouraged, and rewarded for directing their attention toward the hard work of learning. Reorienting our thinking away from distraction and toward attention opens up an entirely new way of approaching the problem. It shifts the debate away from the use or disuse of specific technologies, or technology in general, and asks us to reevaluate basic assumptions we make about the nature of our teaching. If we are willing to think with careful and open minds about the research standing at the crossroads of attention and pedagogy, I believe that we can discover teaching approaches that push us into exciting and creative new territories, both for ourselves and our students.[16]

That doesn't mean, however, that we educators don't need to evolve our work as a result of the explosive growth of personal technologies; we do. Thanks to the speed with which they dispense novel information to us, today's digital devices are highly potent tools for distraction. The time that students spend on their devices is shaping their behavior at school and work, and their beliefs about themselves, the world, and the responsibilities that we bear toward them. They are developing habits of living and thinking that are worth questioning, and that may prove resistant to change. The time they spend with their devices may also be reshaping the way they interact with the human beings around them and impacting their mental health.[17] Those of us who teach have to account for all of these possibilities and be prepared to do what teachers have always done: consider the education our students need in both present and future, and work together to determine how we get them there. As I will argue, one of the most fundamental challenges for educators today is helping students use their attention to support their learning in an age when distractions are more potent and numerous than they have ever been. If we want to do that successfully, we need to recognize three fundamental truths about attention in education. They represent the most important ideas I hope you will take away from this book.

First, **attention is an achievement.** Our students are distracted for the same reasons we all feel distracted these days: because we have easily distractible minds, because attention is difficult, and because our devices make it even more difficult. Teachers tend to assume that attention represents the norm, from which distraction constitutes a falling away. But this characterization of our minds is both incorrect and disempowering. As we shall learn from philosophers and writers in Chapter One, the normal state of our brains might best be characterized as distracted or dispersed, from which focused and sustained attention arises in certain specific contexts. In *Cognition: Exploring the Science of the Mind*, Daniel Reisberg offers an admirable description of this view:

> We need to think of paying attention as an *achievement*, something that you're able to do [and not that you do effortlessly]. Like many other achievements (e.g., doing well in school, staying healthy, earning a good salary), paying attention involves many elements, and the exact set of elements needed will vary from one occasion to the next. In all cases, though, multiple steps are needed to ensure that you end up aware of the stimuli you're interested in, and not pulled off track by irrelevant inputs.[18]

Introduction: From Distraction to Attention

Attention is an achievement, and a difficult one at that. Sustained periods of attention in the classroom arise like islands from the ocean of distraction, in which we all swim on a regular basis. The achievement of attention comes from multiple parts of our brain and requires coordination between those parts.[19] The focus we seek to cultivate in our classrooms represents an especially difficult form of attention, because of the hard cognitive work we are asking students to do in the presence of multiple possible distractors, from other bodies in the room to wandering minds and alluring devices.

The second point is that **attention remains achievable**. Even in this distracting era, human beings remain perfectly capable of paying attention in non-digital contexts, even if they don't do it as consistently and frequently as we would like. They spend minutes and hours and whole days locked into playing or watching sports, pursuing hobbies, reading and writing, traveling off the grid, exercising, and working on difficult projects. In the classroom, we can find equally diverse examples of students paying attention: they concentrate on quizzes and exams, participate in discussions, take notes on lectures, engage in in-class activities, do field and lab work, and more. Since we can find plenty of examples of humans in general and students specifically paying attention, we know that attention is achievable. Our students remain capable of focusing their attention, sustaining it, and blocking out distractions. They can attend to you, to one another, and to the course material when the conditions are right. All of the factors that go into that are complex, and not all of them are under your control. Sometimes attention flags or never arises because students are hungry or tired, or because they are in the midst of emotional turmoil or trauma. We should therefore not expect perfect attention in our classrooms, since we can't (and shouldn't) control all aspects of our students lives. But we also should not give up hope.

Putting the first two points together leads ineluctably to the third: **if we wish to achieve attention in the classroom, we must cultivate it deliberately**. The achievement of student attention requires deliberate and conscious effort from the teacher. We won't get students' attention by scolding them, at least in the long term. We won't get it from simply hoping for the best. We won't get it from going about our business in the front of the room and letting them fend for themselves out there in the seats. We'll get attention when we establish it as an important value in our courses and consider how we will help students cultivate and sustain the forms of attention that help them learn.

Audience and Scope

In the pages that follow, I'm going to offer you plenty of models for what it looks like to think and teach with a deliberate focus on attention. Those models arise partly from my observations of dozens of classrooms—high school and higher education—during the two years I spent researching and writing this book. In every classroom I visited, I kept a close eye on the students in the room and noted when they seemed to perk up and tune in, as well as when they seemed to slump in their chairs and sneak off-task. I observed how students' attention waxed and waned according to the structure of the class, the variety and nature of different activities, and even the timing and placement of these activities. During that same time period, I searched continuously for good ideas for cultivating attention in the educational literature, everything from teacher blogs and podcasts to the latest books and journal articles on effective teaching practices. I compared what I read in those places and observed in live classrooms with the more theoretical and scientific research on attention and distraction. I also observed when people paid attention in contexts outside of school. I tried to understand what drove people into activities that sustained their attention and what principles we could derive from those activities and bring back into the classroom.

This process of developing the ideas for the book will help clarify its audience. The teachers who will see the most immediate potential application for its ideas are college and university faculty, followed very closely by secondary-school teachers. Although my work addresses higher education faculty most directly, I also work regularly with future high school teachers at my institution and have given multiple workshops for secondary-school teachers over the past several years. I have found much common ground in the challenges faced by higher education and secondary-school teachers, and significant overlap between the teaching strategies that prove most effective for our students. Middle and elementary school teachers should also find useful strategies here, although there may be developmental issues for younger students that differentiate their challenges from those of teaching teenagers and emerging adults. Readers should also notice from my description of the research process that this book focuses primarily on the cultivation of attention in face-to-face classrooms. The challenges for online students are overlapping but distinct. Still, I hope online teachers will find food for reflection on attention and distraction, as well as opportunities for translating some of the recommended strategies into their teaching practice. I hope all readers, including administrators or parents who might not be directly involved in classroom teaching, will come to find the challenge of attention as fascinating as I have, and will consider this book as a spur for their own creative thinking about the cultivation of attention in the digital age.

Of course, some percentage of our students face specific obstacles to attention in the classroom, including those who might be diagnosed with attention disorders and students who struggle with anxiety or other conditions that make focusing difficult in an academic environment. Although I do not address directly the unique challenges of working with these populations, the pathways I have chosen toward attention in Part Two are ones that should have a beneficial impact on all learners in the classroom, whatever level of attention they bring. Indeed, as will be clear in places throughout the book, some of the specific recommendations I make in Part Two come from conversations with teachers who work with students with these special challenges or from reading or hearing the perspective of those students.

As you will see in the chapters of Part Two, teachers in classrooms of every kind, teaching students of every kind, are embracing and meeting the challenge of thinking creatively about attention. I invite you to join them in that creative work. As you read this book and reflect upon your own experiences with attention (or lack thereof) with students today, you should ask yourself this core question: What captures the attention of my students? Your answer will provide you with the best models you can create for reinvigorating your teaching with attention, whether your context is the physical classroom or online or some combination of the two. In her book *The Power of Mindful Learning*, Harvard psychologist Ellen Langer argues that "when we are distracted, we are attracted to something else. From this perspective very different questions come to mind: What is so attractive about the alternative stimulus? What can we learn from that attraction?"[20] You will devise the best possible answers to these kinds of questions if you ask and answer them with a group of peers. Get together with your friends on the faculty, with the members of your department, with a book group, or with the team at your center for teaching and learning. Organize or participate in a discussion, and share with one another what you have learned about attention from your on-the-ground experiences. I had multiple opportunities during the writing of this book to present ideas to faculty on other campuses, and I always posed to them the same questions that I am encouraging you to ask yourself: What is happening in your classroom when students *are* paying attention? And what you can you learn from those moments?

Attention has a strong social component; when we turn our gaze in some new direction, other eyes follow. My ultimate goal is to turn the gaze of more teachers to the challenge of attention, and in so doing provide an opportunity for us all to think and talk together about how to help and support student attention in an age of distraction.

Conclusion

Joanna E. Ziegler was an art historian at the College of the Holy Cross in Worcester, Massachusetts, before her untimely death at the age of sixty. In an essay for a collection entitled *Becoming Beholders: Cultivating Sacramental Imagination and Actions in College Classrooms*, Ziegler described a striking assignment she gave to students in her art history courses. The students had to leave campus every single week and make a visit to the nearby Worcester Art Museum in order to spend time in front of the same work of art for thirteen consecutive weeks. They wrote a new paper on that same work every week, describing what insights they had developed with each viewing. This slow unfolding led them, Ziegler explains, "from personalized, almost narcissistic responses to descriptions firmly grounded in the picture."[21] As they learned to train their attention on a work of art, that attention brought them insights. They saw more clearly, developed new ideas, and wrote creatively about what they observed.

The important point about Ziegler's experiment to me is that she believed that sustained attention was an important value to cultivate in her students. So—instead of simply lamenting its disappearance, criticizing students for their distractibility, or scapegoating their digital devices—she designed an assignment that helped them develop it. Ziegler was right in believing that attention deserves our attention; our students won't learn without it. We can throw up our hands in the face of our devices, wish that the kids these days paid more attention than they used to, or ban technologies from the room in the vain hope that sustained attention will suddenly blossom in response. A better solution would be to join teachers like Ziegler in recognizing that the challenge of attention in learning is a deep and historic one. It requires us to address it directly and think creatively, in conversation with one another, in order to help our students stay attentive to their learning, and to one another, in the age of distraction.

part one

THEORIES OF DISTRACTION

1

A Brief History
of Distraction

OUR FEARS ABOUT the distractibility of students exist within the context of larger social fears about increasing distractibility in the digital era. With screens available everywhere now, even on watches and glasses, we wonder whether our devices are doing permanent damage to our attention. We tend to express that fear most vocally in relation to our children and students, perhaps because we see them so frequently interacting with their screens in ways that seem trivial to us: texting one another, watching videos, tracking celebrity social media feeds. But most adults I know also fear, or at least wonder about, the extent to which distraction might harm our attention. A couple of years ago, while visiting another campus, I had dinner with an administrator in his mid-sixties, and the topic of attention and distraction arose. "I can't seem to pay attention anymore like I used to," he said, shaking his head sadly. "I can barely get through a few pages of a novel before I find myself checking my phone." The resignation in his voice struck a chord with me, as it seemed to capture well the dominant tone of our current conversations about distraction and attention. Something has been lost, and we regret it; we know the identity of the culprit, but we are helpless in the face of its power. Two assumptions buried within that administrator's statement underpin this story of attention lost: the first is that we once had a greater ability to pay attention; the second is that our devices are to blame.

Before we turn specifically to the challenges of attention in education, then, it would be useful to put our assumptions about attention and distraction into a broader historical context. As we shall see, rumors about the recent death of attention have been greatly exaggerated. We can trace concerns about our distractible minds just about as far back as we can trace the development of written philosophical, religious, and literary texts. The history of human reflection on the problem of attention encompasses writing from both Western and Eastern traditions; works of ancient philosophy and sacred scripture; novels, poetry, and nonfiction; instruction manuals for polite behavior; and screeds against new technologies. We need to acknowledge this history before we consider how to address our contemporary educational concerns, because it can shape both the intensity and nature of our response. When we recognize the extent to which anxiety about distraction has a long history, we can dial back the sense of panic that infects much of today's discourse about students and their short attention spans. But we can also acknowledge that today's technologies are presenting some particularly complex new challenges to our students—and to ourselves.

Wandering Minds and Fly-Catching Lizards

Considerations of the problem of distraction date at least back to Greek and Roman antiquity. In the *Ethics*, Aristotle argued that distraction arises from a clash between activities which are more and less pleasant to us. "People who are passionately devoted to the flute," he explains, "are unable to pay attention to arguments if they hear someone playing a flute, since they enjoy the flute-playing more than the activity that presently occupies them." Thus we are distracted away from challenging tasks (such as attending to arguments, paying attention in class, or grading papers) when we encounter the prospect of something more pleasing (such as listening to music, chatting with a friend, or checking Twitter). In a following passage, Aristotle explains that the problem can arise not only from the potentially pleasant nature of the distraction, but also from the unpleasant or boring nature of the experience we are having: "When we are [only] mildly pleased with things of one sort, we do things of other sorts; for instance, people who eat snacks in theaters do this most when the actors are bad."[1] In this statement we get not only a description of Aristotle's theory of distraction, but also a glimpse of the challenges that ancient theaters faced in the form of their distracted audiences (a problem to which we will return in greater detail in Chapter Five). But we see even in these earliest writings about distraction the dual nature of its power over us: we can be pushed toward distraction by unpleasant or difficult experiences (listening to arguments, watching bad theater) and pulled toward it by the prospect of something more pleasing (listening to flutes, eating snacks).

The Latin theologian Augustine of Hippo, who penned the *Confessions* in the late fourth century, offered less of an analysis and more of a lamentation of the distractions that beset our mind. For Augustine, as for many religious writers, the proper focal point should be God; he was thus disturbed by the inability of the human mind to stay focused on prayers. In the *Confessions*, he bemoans the ways in which his contemplation of God and truth could be broken by the smallest and most everyday distractions:

How is it that when I am sitting at home a lizard catching flies, or a spider entangling them as they fly into her webs, often-times arrests me? . . . When this heart of ours is made the depot of such things and is overrun by the throng of these abounding vanities, then our prayers are often interrupted and disturbed by them. Even while we are in thy presence and direct the voice of our hearts to thy ears, such a great business as this is broken off by the inroads of I know not what idle thoughts.[2]

In the same chapter of the *Confessions*, Augustine explains that he can try to structure his life in order to minimize distractions: for example, he can avoid going to the circus to watch dogs chasing rabbits. But even his best intentions and efforts won't stop his attention from being diverted if he sees a dog chasing a rabbit while he's out taking a walk. No matter how we try to corral our disobedient attention toward higher matters, it will defy us in the end.

We find these same laments about our distractible minds in the religious and wisdom traditions of other cultures. Huston Smith and Philip Novak explain in *Buddhism: A Concise Introduction* that the core insight of the Buddha was the impermanence of all existence; our failure to reconcile ourselves to this impermanence represents the source of our suffering. That impermanence applies not only to the physical objects of this world that come and go, but to the thoughts and emotions that spin incessantly through our mind. In Smith and Novak's summary of the insights of the Buddha, "Every mental and physical state is in flux; none is solid or enduring. . . . We have little control over our mental states and our physical sensations, and normally little awareness of them."[3] Practitioners of Buddhism begin their journey toward a more mindful existence by acknowledging what the Buddhist tradition often refers to as the "monkey mind"—jumping, swinging, and howling in unceasing motion. That monkey mind, subject to constant distraction and wanderings, represents the starting point for the long and arduous journey toward enlightenment.

From the monkey mind to the blissful state of enlightenment, from fly-catching lizards to contemplation of God: the ancient texts of attention and distraction put the two terms in a clear hierarchy, with attention above and distraction below. Attention enables us to contemplate the truth, to focus on what matters, to achieve peace and wisdom. Distraction scatters the mind, deters us from right thinking and behavior, and brings unhappiness. We speak about attention and distraction in these same terms today, as we admonish our children and students to pay attention at the dinner table or in the classroom. We feel Augustine's unhappiness and irritation when we are distracted by trivial matters—pulled in many directions, true to the Latin roots of the word *dis-traction*, which means to drag something apart. We chide ourselves for the hours we spend on our phones, knowing that we might have spent that time in more productive ways: in study or scholarship, in exercise or prayer, in conversation with our children, parents, or friends.

These ancient texts establish another important binary, though—one that is essential to understanding our contemporary concerns about distraction. We see in the range of early writing about attention that we are subject to both internal and external distractions. For the Buddhist, the source of the problems lies within us. Minds jump and wander, disobey and distract; no matter how hard we work to harness and sustain our attention, it slips from our grasp. But Aristotle and Augustine point out that our susceptible minds are also drawn from their focus by external forces. Flute players, lizards, and spiders intrude on our attention and pull it away from the places we wish it to be. The English poet and cleric John Donne, writing in the early sixteenth century, describes in a funeral sermon the way that his efforts at attention to prayer are beset by these twin demons of internal and external distraction:

I throw myself downe in my Chamber, and call in, and invite God and his Angels thither; and when they are there, I neglect God and his Angels for the noise of a Flie, for the rattling of a Coach, for the whining of a doore; I talke on in the same posture of praying; Eyes lifted up, knees bowed down; as though I prayed to God; and, if God, or his Angels should aske me when I thought last of God in that prayer, I cannot tell: Sometimes I find that I had forgot what I was about, but when I began to forget it, I cannot tell. A memory of yesterday's pleasures, a feare of tomorrows dangers, a straw under my knee, a noise in mine eare, a light in mine eye, an anything, a nothing, a fancy, a Chimera in my braine, troubles me in my prayer.[4]

Given all of the distractions that Donne describes—from the noise of a fly to the straw beneath our legs (external distractions), from our memories of yesterday to our fears for tomorrow (internal distractions)—it begins to seem miraculous that we are ever capable of sustained attention of any kind.

Theorists of attention will continue to express concern about both internal and external causes of distraction right up to the present day, but in eighteenth-century Europe a new formulation of the relationship between internal and external distraction emerges, one that raises a scary prospect.

Coffeehouse to Computer Screen: The Destructive Power of Distraction

That lovely hot beverage that you might be enjoying as you read these words, the source of so much energy and delight among students and teachers alike, first became popular in the Ottoman Empire in the sixteenth century. It was discovered by Europeans through both travel and trade, and was promoted for its stimulating qualities and for its many reputed health benefits. The first coffee-house in England was opened in 1650 at Oxford University, thus initiating a long and still vibrant association between learning and coffee. The first coffee shop in London opened just two years later, and then coffeehouses spread with startling speed throughout the English capital. Fifty years later, there were more than two thousand coffeehouses in London. They became sites of leisure, political discussion, and commercial work. The insurer Lloyd's of London originated in a coffee shop, as did an early version of the London Stock Exchange. These buzzing sites of social, commercial, and political interaction drew people together in major cities across England and beyond, including Vienna, Paris, and Amsterdam.[5]

The manic atmosphere in the coffeehouses created energy and excitement, but at the same time drew the concern of intellectuals who feared that it was interfering with the ability of coffeehouse patrons to put their heads down and focus on serious work. Tom Standage, author of *Writing on the Wall: Social Media—the First 2,000 Years*, cites the words of an Oxford don in 1677 who argued that "solid and serious learning" was declining as a result of people wasting their days in coffeehouses.[6] A lawyer from Cambridge had made the connection between coffeehouses and a decline in focus slightly more specific a few years earlier: "Who can apply close to a Subject with his Head full of the Din of a Coffee-house?"[7] The rise of the coffeehouse—and the concerns raised by these scholars about its role as a new source of distraction—echoes the fears of Augustine and John Donne about the ways in which external distractions can intrude on thinking.

In eighteenth-century discussions of the coffeehouse, a new-found focus on the problem of distraction raised a dreadful prospect: sustained exposure to external distractions can degrade our internal capacities for attention. Isaac Watts was an English clergyman and writer of Christian hymns, including that Christmastime classic "Joy to the World." In 1727, he published a self-help book for freethinking folk called *The Improvement of the Mind*, and in it he cautioned readers that spending too much time in distraction-filled environments would eventually create an easily distractible mind:

> Do not choose your constant place of study by . . . the most various and entertaining scenes of sensible things. . . . A variety of Objects, which strike the Eye or the Ear, especially while they are ever in motion or often changing, have a natural and powerful tendency to steal away the mind too often from its steady pursuit of any subject, which we contemplate; and thereby the Soul gets a habit of silly curiosity and impertinence, of trifling and wandering.[8]

The use of the word "habit" in this passage reflects a fear that what we have previously acknowledged as an unhappy feature of the mind—its tendency to wander away in spite of our wishes—can be exacerbated or made more permanent by too much time spent in the company of external distractions. In other words, the more time you spend being distracted, the more you will become an easily distractible person.

The formulation that we see in Watts's book has become the dominant way of theorizing the problem of distraction, right down to the present day. Writers will no doubt continue to reflect upon and lament the internal wanderings of their own minds, echoing eighteenth-century writer Samuel Johnson's remark that "with or without our consent . . . the mind will break, from confinement to its stated task, into sudden excursions."[9] But this problem seems much less pressing to writers as we progress into the twentieth century and beyond. The locus of concern rests more and more squarely, with each passing century, on the newly developed technologies or media that steal our attention, chip away at our cognitive powers, and destroy our ability to pay attention to one another. A 1906 cartoon from the British magazine *Punch* depicts two well-dressed late Victorians seated under a tree, facing away from each other, each staring at a telegraph receiver on their lap. "These two figures," the caption reads, "are not communicating with one another. The lady receives an amatory message, and the gentleman some racing results." The figures, mesmerized by their quaint devices, bear an uncanny resemblance to students today, sitting under a shady tree on the quad, transfixed by the phones in their hands.[10]

The specific fear of external technologies diminishing attention capacities arises again with the arrival of the radio. As this new device found its way into people's homes in the 1920s and '30s, according to historians Luke Fernandez and Susan J. Matt, "many grappled with the meaning and place of the radio in their mental lives. Could they take in all it had to offer without sacrificing other mental powers? Was it a force of enlightenment or a source of distraction and dissipation?" A diary writer from the time notes that she "spent a stupid and useless morning at home did not even get the papers read. The radio interferes with my intellectual life very much."[11] Note the connection here again from short- to long-term: the concern is less about the "stupid and useless morning" than it is about the ability of such mornings to destroy her "intellectual life." The more she listens to the radio, with its short bursts of entertainment, the less she can pursue an intellectual life of sustained thinking.

Both radio and its successor, television, raised special concerns about their impact on young people and their developing brains. In the late twentieth and early twenty-first centuries, those concerns included a special focus on the ways in which screen exposure could negatively impact the attention spans of young people. In 2004, a research study appearing in the journal *Pediatrics* presented data showing a correlation between high rates of television viewing among very young children and rates of attention deficit hyperactivity disorder (ADHD) diagnoses at age seven.[12] "This study," explained the lead author in a news release, "suggests that there is a significant and important association between early exposure to television and subsequent attentional problems."[13] Two years later, the same journal published a second essay calling these findings into question. Using a different set of research tools to approach the issue, a pair of researchers found that "effect sizes for the relationship between television exposure and symptoms of ADHD were close to zero and not statistically significant."[14] But the media had jumped on the original study and broadcast its findings widely, cementing the proposition in the minds of the public that too much attention to screens could cause permanent damage to the attention spans of children.

And who could forget the ongoing panic about whether video games are destroying our attention spans? Michael Z. Newman documents the ways in which the rise of video-game culture in the 1980s "prompted educators, psychotherapists, local government officeholders and media commentators to warn that young players were likely to suffer serious negative effects."[15] Those negative effects of course included the ability to pay attention. As recently as 2010, news outlets were covering an alarming study, also published in *Pediatrics*, that showed that video games could be destroying the attention spans of children.[16] "Playing video games may make it harder for some children to pay attention in school, a new study suggests," reads the opening sentence of a Canadian news report on the study.[17] What the study actually revealed was that children who spent more than two hours per day on video games and television were more likely to be flagged by teachers as having attention problems. The caveats were buried in the article: there was no way to determine whether the video games were causing the attention-span problems, and in fact the causality could just as easily have run in the other direction—it could have been the case that children with attention problems were more likely to gravitate toward video games. Or perhaps there was no meaningful connection at all—the real culprit might have been the fact that children were gaming beyond their bedtimes, and lack of sleep was creating the attention problems reported by the teachers.

Contemporary Concerns

With all of this historical context in mind, we can now take a fresh look at the arguments being made by contemporary critics of distraction, like Nicholas Carr. Carr's best-selling book *The Shallows: What the Internet Is Doing to Our Brains*, a finalist for the Pulitzer Prize in 2011, points the finger at the internet and the devices that enable it: computers, tablets, smartphones. But the underlying logic is the same as the one articulated by Isaac Watts: too much time spent in the company of distractions ultimately changes who we are—for the worse. Carr posits the existence of a "linear mind," one that can proceed logically and deliberately from one thought to the next, that is being slowly supplanted by a more scattered version of itself: "Calm, focused, undistracted, the linear mind is being pushed aside by a new kind of mind that wants and needs to take in and dole out information in short, disjointed, often overlapping bursts—the faster, the better."[18] As previous writers have argued, Carr posits that this change occurs because of the way external forces—coffee shops, telegraphs, radios, television screens—continually draw our attention in multiple, divided ways. "The division of attention demanded by multimedia," Carr writes, "strains our cognitive abilities, diminishing our learning and weakening our understanding."[19] Carr tells a story of innocence lost, or perhaps innocence deliberately destroyed. When our brains were living in simpler times, they worked in simpler ways: slower, more focused, more attentive. Now that they are living in highly distractible times, they are becoming highly distractible organs: shallow, surface oriented, in constant search of novelty and distraction.

Carr's presentation of this argument seems more convincing than those previous iterations because it incorporates a well-established principle of neuroscience: neuroplasticity, or the ability of our brains to adapt, grow, and evolve throughout our lifespan. We have plenty of evidence that both external circumstances and internal mental activity can alter the landscape of our brains in substantive ways. When the brain encounters a situation over and over again, and responds to it in the same way, it strengthens neural pathways that are new or slightly altered from the existing ones. This is, of course, what happens when we learn something deeply. We encounter a new piece of knowledge or develop a new skill, rehearse it repeatedly in different contexts, and then that fact or skill takes its place within our existing mental structure. Casual descriptions of this process will often say that our brains have been "rewired," which can be a helpful but also misleading metaphor. It implies that once we have created or reinforced a neural pathway, it remains fixed in place. But, as Carr rightly points out, "our brains are always in flux, adapting to even small shifts in our circumstances and behavior."[20] That flux occurs in response to myriad circumstances: when we learn something deliberately, when we experience strong emotions that are seared into our memories, and when we are first navigating our way through an unfamiliar context.

As Carr argues, such flux also occurs when we engage repeatedly in behaviors that are shaped and conditioned by technological devices. So, the argument goes, if we are repeatedly swiping from one thing to the next on our phone, never pausing to sit and read a long-form article or a book, or never sitting quietly with our thoughts and reflecting on the meaning of life, we are changing our brains into organs that have lost the ability to pay sustained attention. As Carr writes in the conclusion to *The Shallows*, the shallow but endlessly shifting surface of the internet, made concrete and always accessible in the form of our phones, "reroutes our vital paths and diminishes our capacity for contemplation." Worse still, "it is altering the depth of our emotions as well as our thoughts." To be fair to Carr, he does acknowledge, as our history of distraction might suggest, that "the natural state of the human brain . . . is one of distractedness. Our predisposition is to shift our gaze, and hence our attention, from one object to another, to be aware of as much of what's going on around as possible."[21] His point is that our phones intensify and solidify this predisposition of our brains toward distraction, whereas much of the best parts of ourselves as humans—our grand achievements in art and architecture, politics and conversation, religion and community—have sprung from our ability to focus, attend, and contemplate.

The arguments made by Carr and others who tell this story of attention dispossessed by technology look much less convincing when they are placed within the larger historical narrative of concerns about this issue. The history of distraction shows us that we have never lived in some prelapsarian state of attentional grace, in which we focused effortlessly with our calm, linear minds. For one thing, brains cells connect in rich networks rather than in clean lines. But more important, we learn from these historical voices that we have always been distracted. The difference between us and our nineteenth-century cousins is not that our attentional capacities have somehow been permanently diminished, as Carr would have it, but that the people and devices who seek our attention have become better at soliciting it from us. If you feel yourself more distracted than you used to be, or than you would like to be, that feeling may well reflect reality. The pull of our digital distractions is very strong today. You find yourself on social media at times when you could be grading papers or attending to your child. Perhaps you have taken social media fasts, or created digital-free times or zones in your life, and failed to abide by them. You might also perceive significant changes in your students or children, who seem more distracted than they used to be. All of those experiences and observations might still have you wondering about the extent to which our modern distractions might be doing some kind of permanent damage to our brains or fundamentally changing who we are as humans.

I can conclude this chapter with the hopeful note that the current reporting from people who study the brain, and especially attention and the brain, is that we don't yet have any conclusive evidence to support the notion that human attention has suffered some architectural diminishment in today's technological era. Just as we did with television and video games, we can ask people about their smartphone use and then test their attentional capacities. If we see high smartphone use and low attention spans, we can draw the conclusion that smartphones have diminished their attention. But we can just as plausibly draw the conclusion that people with shorter attention spans love to use their smartphones (and watch television and play video games). In 2019, the news and culture site *Vox* posed to multiple scientists the following question: "How is our constant use of digital technologies affecting our brain health?" For the most part, while the scientists all acknowledged the short-term impact that technologies can have on our brains (for example, multitasking can interfere with the effectiveness of studying or learning in the classroom), none of them were willing to assert conclusions about a permanent diminishment of our brains. Stanford psychologist Anthony Wagner explains, with respect to the relationship between multitasking and working memory,

The science tells us that there is a negative relationship between using more media simultaneously and working memory capacity. And we know working memory capacity correlates with language comprehension, academic performance, and a whole host of outcome variables that we care about. The science tells us that the negative relationship exists, but the science doesn't tell us whether the media behavior is *causing* the change. It's too early to really conclude. The answer is we have no idea.

Other respondents to the question argued that we can't draw such conclusions because the impact of digital technologies on the brain might depend on how we use them. University of Wisconsin's Heather Kirkorian points out that we should not be collapsing "video-chatting with a grandparent versus watching an educational TV show versus playing a violent video game versus using a finger-painting app."[22] The implications of Kirkorian's argument are clear: we should not be arguing that digital technologies in general have diminished our brain capacity without acknowledging that we interact with them in hundreds of different ways, each of which may have a differing impact on our brain.

Cognitive scientist Daniel Willingham, who writes frequently to debunk myths about education and to promote research-based perspectives, comes to a similar conclusion in the *New York Times*. "Although mental tasks can change our brains," he writes, "the impact is usually modest. . . . Attention is so central to our ability to think that a significant deterioration would require a retrofitting of other cognitive functions. Mental reorganization at that scale happens over evolutionary time, not because you got a smartphone."[23] Our attention systems, in other words, work in coordination with many other parts of the brain. It would not be possible, Willingham argues, for a system so fundamental to suffer degradation without seeing impacts in many other areas, or without other areas changing dramatically to compensate for the losses. His argument also notes that our attention systems evolved over hundreds of thousands of years; it would be almost miraculous to believe that they could change radically within the space of a generation. A comprehensive view of the state of the research investigating the relationship between technology and attention, published in 2017, stated that "while there is clear evidence that engagement with smart devices can have an acute impact on ongoing cognitive tasks, the evidence on any long-term impacts of smartphone-related habits on attentional functioning is quite thin, and somewhat equivocal."[24] In other words, while your phone use certainly can distract you from the pursuit of your goals (thus having an "acute impact"), the evidence for "long-term impacts" in the form of a permanently degraded attention span, in individuals or in the human species as a whole, just isn't there at this time.[25]

My review of this research has led me to the conclusion that the brains of your students, like the brain inside your own skull, remain capable of the kind of sustained attention that leads to learning. How to invite and support that sustained attention will be the work of much of this book. But before the light at the end of this tunnel can begin to appear, we have to move from the general considerations of attention and distraction to the specific environment about which every reader of this book likely cares, and which seems especially besieged by distractions these days: the classroom.

2

Distracted in the Classroom

In "Frost at Midnight," nineteenth-century British poet Samuel Taylor Coleridge describes sitting in the schoolroom as a young child, his head filled with dreams from the previous night, his attention everywhere but on the task before him:

> And so I brooded all the following morn,
> Awed by the stern preceptor's face, mine eye
> Fixed with mock study on my swimming book:
> Save if the door half opened, and I snatched
> A hasty glance, and still my heart leaped up,
> For still I hoped to see the *stranger's* face,
> Townsman, or aunt, or sister more beloved,
> My play-mate when we both were clothed alike!

We see in this short passage echoes of everything we have learned thus far about our attention, thrown into the particular atmosphere of the classroom. The young Coleridge carries into school the trailing distractions of his dreams, which swim about his mind when he should attend to his textbook. On top of his internal distractions, challenges to his attention come in external forms, as the classroom door opens every now and again, building the expectation that a neighbor or relative will rescue him from the dullness of his study. In the meantime, a "stern preceptor" does what teachers have been doing for as long as we have had schools: he stands at the front of the room and uses his stern looks (and, one assumes, words and perhaps even a paddle) to force the attention of his students on their books—mostly unsuccessfully.

But we don't need to reach back centuries to find unsuccessful attempts to capture the attention of schoolchildren; we can see it everywhere today, including in the kindergarten classroom of my wife, Anne. I spent one morning there in late May observing children on the training grounds of school-based attention. I remember kindergarten as a place filled with play, and you'll still find that in the kindergarten classroom. But early-twenty-first-century kindergartens have taken on responsibilities that used to be reserved for later grades. Although not quite all of them will succeed, every child is expected to graduate from today's kindergarten classroom knowing how to read, which means that the balance between academic work and play time, especially by the end of the year, has tipped significantly toward academics. To achieve the academic learning that prepares students for first grade, and to master the behaviors that will govern students through the rest of their formal education, students need to use their attention—which comes in pretty short supply among thirty five-year-olds.

I arrive as Anne is preparing the children for "center time," which means they move in small groups to different tables, each of which holds a different a task. Instructions for center time are delivered by Anne from a rocking chair, while the children are bunched onto a multicolored rug in a corner of the classroom. She slowly and patiently reviews the tasks at the various centers—most of them involving simple math or letter-oriented activities—as the children listen to her instructions. Or, perhaps more accurately, attempt to listen. But even that's a stretch. As I scan my eyes across the rug, I see twenty-nine bodies in constant motion, like a swaying sea of bobbing heads and flailing limbs. Hands shoot up in the air whether a question has been posed or not. Fingers probe mouths and noses. At least a few children are always looking curiously over at me, no matter what my wife is doing to draw their attention up front. Some are talking, some are whispering, some are staring dreamily off into space. Anne issues a continuous string of brief reminders to individual children: Sit back down. Stop touching your neighbor. Wait your turn.

"What are the three rules for center time?" she asks as they prepare to scatter to the tables. "Work quietly," says one child. "Stay in your seats," says another. They are repeating back rules they have obviously heard many times before. Anne waits for someone to articulate the third rule, but in spite of twenty waving hands and many guesses, nobody can come up with it. At last, a young girl offers, "Work the whole time?" That rounds out the formal rules. As they stand and begin to scatter, a little boy ventures a fourth suggestion: "Concentrate!" Anne nods her head. "Concentrate. I love it." After she dismisses the children to their tables, a heavyset young boy with no front teeth comes up and says to her quietly, "Don't distract other kids." Never mind that he should have been at his center already; he's got the right idea.

At the centers, the chaos continues but is dispersed into smaller groups. No matter the task, the children alternate working on it with looking around, bouncing in their chairs, whispering to one another, and exploring off-task ways of using their materials: coloring parts of the worksheet that weren't meant for coloring, cutting papers in the wrong places. One table of students puts on head-phones and works on a phonics program on iPads. I wander over to them, expecting at last to see children paying attention to their assigned task, absorbed by the shiny technology of the tablets. The kids these days love their screens, after all, and are addicted to them from early ages (or so I have read). But these screen watchers are no better than the rest, alternating brief periods of absorption with jumping up and down in their chairs, fidgeting, staring at me, and bothering one another. Across the whole room, only two children actually pay attention to something for a sustained period of time: the ones who are sitting and reading aloud to Anne or her aide, slowly working their way through simple storybooks—sounding out words and struggling to make sense of sentences and short paragraphs, listening to the feedback and trying again, rewarded by encouragement and praise when they get it right. They—and they alone—seem wholly absorbed by their task, under the watchful eye of a single teacher.

My wife told me later that while of course students can and do learn during center time or whole-class activities, they make the greatest progress in their reading when she or her aide can work with them individually or in small groups. In those contexts, the students are pulled away from the distractions of the full classroom and into a focused encounter with the teacher and the words on the page, with their attention playing the role for which it was born: as a driver of learning.

Attention to Learning

To understand the crucial connection between attention and learn-ing, whether in a kindergarten classroom or a university lecture hall, consider the three phases we must pass through in order to have learned something.[1] First, we must attend to the item, whatever it might be: object, experience, fact, or idea. Our attention might take the form of simple visual perception, or a meeting between any of our senses and an object or experience. It could also take the form of sentences and paragraphs in something we are reading, or a child's simple encounter with a letter of the alphabet. Second, we must process what we have been attending to (sometimes also called encoding) and incorporate it into our existing knowledge frameworks. In some cases, we slot new experiences in neatly (this is an example of X, and I have seen X's before, and I know all about them). In other cases, our experiences change those existing knowledge frameworks (this seems like X, but has some new features, so now my idea of X must change). In educational contexts, we help students process new knowledge by asking them to write or speak about it, to use it to solve problems or answer questions, or to expand their thinking or actions. Finally, for true learning to occur, we have to be able to retrieve the newly learned item from our memory after the initial apprehension and processing. We invite students to engage in retrieval of material when we ask them questions, give them assessments, and provide opportunities for them to apply their learning in experiences outside of the classroom. When a student can retrieve newly learned material in multiple contexts, and transfer it from the classroom to the world beyond, we know she has truly learned it.

In *Powerful Teaching: Unleash the Science of Learning*, Pooja K. Agarwal and Patrice M. Bain argue that educators spend most of their time working on the processing part of learning, the second stage, which represents only one part of what students need. They point educators to the importance of balancing the second and third stages: processing and retrieval. "We tend to think that most learning occurs during the encoding [processing] stage," they write, "but a wealth of research demonstrates that learning is strengthened through retrieval."[2] We do indeed have more than a hundred years of research demonstrating that engaging in retrieval practice—activities that require us to draw newly learned material from our memories—has significant benefits for our long-term learning. (You can read their excellent book for more on how to put retrieval practice into action in the classroom.)

In this book, I am going to recommend, in parallel fashion, that we likewise need to expend more time and energy thinking about the attention stage of learning, or how we initially focus the attention of our students on what we want them to learn. Our attention helps us notice and prepare experiences for processing, and we will not learn what we do not attend to. Neither Agarwal and Bain's argument nor mine is meant to downplay the importance of processing; in both cases we are contending that the traditionally near-exclusive emphasis on helping students process new material—in support of which teachers make beautiful slides, or deliver a terrific lecture, or develop active-learning strategies—gives short shrift to two equally important stages of the learning process, the *before* of attention and the *after* of retrieval.

I would further emphasize the importance of attention by arguing that while all three of these stages—attention, processing, and retrieval—are essential for learning, the latter two won't happen without attention. We won't learn anything that doesn't hold our attention for at least a little bit. In *Consciousness, Attention, and Conscious Attention*, Carlos Montemayor and Harry Haroutioun Haladjian define attention as "a selective processing mechanism (or rather a group of mechanisms) that *enhances and selects perceptual information for executing actions and higher-level cognition*" (italics mine).[3] Attention, in other words, precedes and underpins the kind of cognitive work we expect students to undertake. Attention holds the object, word, or thought up to our minds—puts a spotlight on it, as attention researchers like to say—for some definite period of time, and prepares it for potential processing. Once processing begins, attention still matters, albeit in a different form. We process new experiences, knowledge, and skills in our working memory, which has some significant limitations: we can only hold a small number of items in there at once. We test those few items against one another, consider relationships and hierarchies, see new connections and abandon old ones, slot new knowledge into existing structures or use newly learned knowledge to transform existing structures. Again, one could argue that the items we hold in our working memory at any given time, as we are thinking, are the ones to which we are attending in that moment.

Finally, in order to engage with previously learned material, we have to retrieve it from our long-term memory, draw it back into our working memory, and put it in dialogue with some new context that now occupies our attention. Retrieval thus also depends on attention, as we search in our brains for what we need and apply what we have recalled to a new context. The specific kind of attention required for each of these three stages of learning will differ, but the general concept of attention still seems useful in describing a fundamental and shared component of all stages of learning.

As these crude explanations will indicate, teachers are correct in taking the attention of their students seriously. We need their attention if we wish them to learn. "Without attention," explains cognitive psychologist Michelle Miller, "much of what we want students to accomplish—taking in new information, making new connections, acquiring and practicing new skills—simply doesn't happen. And thus, gaining students' focus is a necessary first step in any well-designed learning activity."[4] Unfortunately, what we too often get from students is divided focus, as they combine the work of learning with other activities that hold their attention, everything from their phones and laptops to their daydreams and their neighbors in the room. Most students today, like many adults, seem to believe that they can manage the trick of learning while attending to other things, otherwise known as multitasking. They *can* do more than one thing effectively, if one of the activities requires little conscious attention and can be performed on automatic pilot: folding laundry while watching TV, for example, or completing simple administrative tasks while listening to music. When a task or activity becomes familiar to us and requires little thought, we can effectively pair it with unrelated tasks.

But doing the hard work of learning while also attempting to answer your e-mail simply does not work. If both tasks require your attention, or if they operate in similar regions of the brain—such as attempting to read while someone speaks to you, which both involve language—then the limited capacity of our attention interferes with our apprehension and processing. As cognitive scientists Yana Weinstein and Megan Sumeracki explain it in their book *Understanding How We Learn*, "When you feel like you're multi-tasking, or paying attention to two things at once, you're actually switching back and forth between the two things you're trying to pay attention to, and . . . going back and forth between two different tasks involves switch costs that decrease efficiency and slow down reaction speeds in *both tasks*."[5]

The notion that we can multitask, and even that we should multitask in today's connected world, has become so pervasive that it can be difficult to convince people of its inefficiency. But I suspect most people will have had the experience of trying to do something with their phone while driving, and looking up from their device after what seemed like just a moment to find themselves drifting from their lane or rapidly approaching a stopped car. The brief burst of panic you feel in those moments is your brain reminding you that you—like your students, and like most other humans on the planet—don't multitask very well.

The stakes in our classroom, and the consequences of multitasking while learning, will never be as dramatic as that panicked application of the brakes—which helps explain why we see so many students attempting to divide their attention, not only in the physical classroom but also while they are studying or learning online.

The Distracted Student

My campus has done an excellent job of providing informal spaces in which students can study individually or in small groups. As I stroll through the primary academic building, or the library that houses the Center for Teaching Excellence that I direct, I observe students doing the work of learning in a variety of ways: writing on their laptops, reading and highlighting textbooks, reviewing and reorganizing paper notes, flipping through flashcards, and taking practice quizzes and tests. With few exceptions, though, I almost always see those studying students doing their work in the presence of multiple distractors. The ones I see are in public places, with plenty of passersby and ambient noise. They of course always have their phones at hand, and pick them up frequently to respond to texts or other social media prompts. When they have their laptops open, they might have a dozen or more browser tabs ready for quick checks of whatever else has captured their interest lately. I see these exact same behaviors in my own children, who range in age from recent college graduate to early high school. All five of my children would be able to report at least one incidence of me discovering them doing homework with the television on and receiving a mini-lecture about why such multitasking was not allowed in the Lang household. Yet, in spite of the obviously cogent and convincing nature of that lecture, some of my children have had to receive it more than once.

These experiences with my own children and the students on my campus reflect what the research has found about the increasing interference of digital distractions on student study behaviors.

A study published in 2013 observed more than 250 students at multiple levels of education, from middle school through college, studying in fifteen-minute time blocks. On average, across all levels, students spent around six minutes focused on the material before they switched tasks, usually turning to social media or texting (and remember what we learned above: such rapid task switching diminishes our effectiveness in completing tasks).[6] Another report used an array of technologies to observe the study and distraction patterns of college students over the course of three hours. With the help of cameras and eye-tracking devices, the researchers found that students engaged with their digital distractions more than thirty-five times during that three-hour period, which meant that they—similar to their counterparts in the first study—were distracting themselves every five or six minutes.[7] Studies like these document only the external distractions of students, of course, and don't take into account the number of times their minds might have wandered without the help of their phones and laptops.

These same distracting devices, as will be no surprise to any teacher today, have infected the classroom. In 2015, Bernard McCoy, a journalism professor at the University of Nebraska, surveyed more than six hundred students at institutions across the United States about their use of digital devices in the classroom for purposes unrelated to the course. On average, students reported straying off-task on their devices more than eleven times during the course of the day's classes. Around a third of the students in the survey reported fairly light usage of only one to three times; another third reported four to ten, and the final group reported either eleven to thirty times or more than thirty times. Only 3.3 percent of students reported never succumbing to the temptations of digital distractions in the classroom. What students were doing in those distracting moments will likely come as no surprise: the most popular activities were "texting" (86.6 percent), "e-mail" (76.2 percent), "checking the time" (75 percent), "social networking" (70.3 percent), and "Web surfing" (42.5 percent). Checking the time seems to me like a pretty benign form of digital distraction, but quite obviously this survey found plenty of other more significant forms. McCoy had conducted an initial survey in 2013, which showed results very similar to these numbers, with only the slightest uptick in the averages from 2013 to 2015.[8]

Because learning depends so heavily on attention, a rash of research studies have demonstrated that frequent interruptions of student attention while they are attempting to learn—whether those distractions are self-created or externally imposed—will reduce the quality of learning. An early experiment tested a group of around sixty business students in a college accounting class. Upon entering the class, the students received written instructions either to turn off their cell phones for the duration of the period or to send three text messages to the professor during class. Not much, three text messages—even in 2010, when this study was published, it would not have required much time or effort from students to send three text messages to a person with whom they were not having an actual conversation. At the end of the class period, all of the students were given a twenty-question multiple-choice quiz on the material from the lecture. The ones who had their phones off averaged around 58 percent on that quiz; the ones who texted averaged around 42 percent. The significance of this difference existed even when student GPAs were taken into consideration; both high-GPA and low-GPA students performed worse if they texted during class.[9]

This study occurred before the widespread adoption of the smartphone. More recent research on device use in the classroom shows similar results. One such study, published in the journal *Educational Psychology*, offers two interesting twists on the usual finding that digital distractions interfere with learning. Students in two sections of a psychology course at a university in the Midwest were given open access to their phones and laptops during half of the class sessions and restricted access during the other half. The classes were taught as interactive lectures, with content presentation alternating with opportunities for students to answer questions on their devices through electronic polling (during the restricted-access days, a proctor monitored the students to ensure that they used their devices only for the polling and put them away afterward). The researchers found that access to devices made a significant difference at the end of the semester: on the final exam, the students scored around half a letter grade better on material from the restricted-access days than they did on the open-access days. A secondary and equally important finding was that this difference persisted even for students who reported in surveys that they had not used their devices on the open-access days. In other words, even when students did not succumb to digital distractions, their learning was still harmed by observing distracted peers around them.[10] I saw this phenomenon repeatedly in classroom observations of my peers. Whenever I could see a student doing off-task work on a laptop, especially when it involved video or social media, I could also see nearby students swiveling their heads regularly toward that screen. The enticement of those flashing pixels a desk or two over proves incredibly difficult to resist, even for the most well-intentioned student.

Students are distracted by their devices (or the devices of their peers) while studying on their own and while sitting in class. When they are taking online courses, they are even more likely to divide their attention. In 2019, a group of researchers published the results of surveys of a few hundred students at Kent State University, asking them about their habits of engaging in off-task behaviors in face-to-face versus fully online courses. The students were asked to report how often they engaged in behaviors like texting or using social media in these two different types of courses. The results revealed that students were 25 percent more likely to multitask in their online courses than they were in face-to-face ones. The problem was worse for students who reported frequent multitasking behaviors or high internet use outside of school. "Students who have positive attitudes about multitasking and prefer to multitask," the authors explain, "appear to better control this academically disadvantageous behavior in face-to-face courses. To the contrary, they do not appear to control this behavior as well in online courses."[11] The results of this survey, and others like it, suggest that we need to think carefully about the problem of distraction and divided attention in our online courses as well, especially as higher education continues to embrace and expand this teaching modality.

Expanding Our View of Attention

Before we begin to consider the practical implications of all of this research for ourselves and our students, I want to note one important limitation in research studies like the ones I have cited above, because that limitation can help us think more expansively about the relationship between attention and learning. Most studies of divided attention in the classroom measure its impact through the use of assessments like multiple-choice tests. While such tests certainly can tell us about some aspects of student learning, they are of course narrow measures that leave little room for the kind of creativity or reflection that might emerge from more comprehensive or challenging assessments, such as essays, presentations, or group projects. And it may well be the case that the occasional sideline from directed attention in the classroom could benefit a student's creative thinking. A professor might throw out a cultural reference that a student doesn't catch, so she does a search for it on her laptop, follows a link in the article to a related site, and suddenly she emerges from her few minutes of distraction with an idea for her paper. Sometimes the enticing and forking paths of the internet can lead us into meaningless distraction, but sometimes they can lead our thinking in creative and productive new directions.

Examples like this one, and some of the classroom activities that we will consider in the coming chapters, offer helpful correctives to our most fearful or reactionary thinking about students and their short attention spans. We limit our thinking about attention's role in teaching and learning if we confine our understanding of it to the kind that we observe in people who are concentrating on a goal-based task for fifty or seventy-five consecutive minutes. Attention *can* look like a student seated in a chair, mesmerized by a great lecturer for an entire class period. But it can also look like a conversation between students working collaboratively on a task, or a student using Google Scholar to skim abstracts and find articles for a research project. It can take the form of someone having a stubborn but meaningful problem in the back of her mind, and taking a walk down the hallway to see if a little movement and change can stimulate new thinking. It can be a series of encounters with some content over an extended period of time, with many gaps and distractions in between that allow for new stimuli to connect to that content and help generate innovative ideas, solutions, and theories. A hundred times during the writing of this book, I got stuck somewhere and decided to leave my desk and complete some household task. While I was doing so, an experience or person or conversation would come up and knock on my brain, announcing its presence, and then rush me back to my laptop to write my way to the solution and into the next problem. Examples like these can expand our understanding of attention and its role in student learning, and help us recognize that we can find student attention in unexpected shapes and places.

But that expansion of our understanding should be precisely that: an expansion, rather than an eclipse. Some writers have posited in recent years that we should abandon entirely the student-concentrating-in-a-chair model of attention, and celebrate instead the new and divided forms of attention created by the internet. N. Katherine Hayles, a literary critic turned education theorist, argues that teachers of my generation and older were trained to prioritize "deep attention," while students today practice "hyper attention." Deep attention involves sustained focus on an object of study; hyper attention features constant shifting between objects of focus.[12] The digital environment in which we all live prioritizes hyper over deep attention, Hayles argues, and the brains of our students are busily adapting to it. We should therefore stop worrying about traditional attention and instead consider how we can help students embrace today's brave new world of distraction, multitasking, and hyper attention.

Such arguments are as limiting as the ones that equate attention exclusively with traditional acts of extended concentration. The most important learning task in the kindergarten classroom of my wife, over the course of the entire year, is learning to read. The children make their greatest progress toward that goal when they are seated by her side, slowly working their way through letters, listening to her patient corrections, and turning each new page with satisfaction and expectation. The children I observed in those moments were paying close and extended attention, and that attention was helping them learn to read. Your students are likewise capable of using this form of attention in support of learning, in acts of extended concentration, when the circumstances are right. They might be studying with multiple screens in view at the same time, but they can still stop and focus when they need to complete a lab or take an exam or give a presentation or sit for a job interview. They harness their attention in tutoring sessions, or when they come to the office for academic advising. They can also shut out their external distractions for hours at a time as they play sports or act in plays or write articles for the student newspaper. A couple of years ago, I was on campus in the early evening hours and saw a student of mine sitting in a classroom with a few others, all circled around a conference table and staring intently at a board game. I popped in to say hello, and asked them how long they would be playing that evening. "Until at least midnight," one of them responded without looking up from his board. It was 7:00 p.m. There were no phones on the table. These were students who were perfectly capable of focusing their attention, sustaining it, and blocking out annoying distractors like me.

In the many models of attention-cultivating strategies I present in the chapters of Part Two, you will find ones that support all of these different forms of attention, from traditional acts of concentration to collaborative and creative activities that will bear a suspicious resemblance to the pursuit of distraction. If the real objective to our thinking about attention in education is the promotion of student learning, we should think as expansively as possible about attention. We need to cultivate it in its traditional forms when students are working to master a difficult concept, or when the development of a new skill will only emerge from sustained repetition and practice. We need to cultivate it in its more expansive forms when we want students to devise creative solutions to challenging problems, working in collaboration with one another, connecting and comparing ideas or resources from multiple sources. We want attention because it supports learning—and just as learning can manifest itself in many different ways in the classroom, so can attention.

But before we turn to the practical strategies that will cultivate student attention in its many forms, I want to make one last pitch for the continued value of attention in its most traditional forms, one that I hope will resonate with your desire to make a positive difference in the lives of your students.

The Joys of Attention

Several decades ago, a psychologist named Mihaly Csikszentmihalyi conducted a very simple experiment he called the "experience sampling method," which consisted of giving pagers to people and asking them, at random periods throughout the day, to pause and describe what they were doing or thinking and their current mood state. Most of us expect that we will be happiest when we have nothing to do, lying in our backyard hammock or sunning ourselves at the beach or just vegging out on the couch. Csikszentmihalyi's experiment revealed that the exact opposite was true: "Optimal experiences" for humans, he discovered, "usually occur when a person's body or mind is stretched to its limits in a voluntary effort to accomplish something difficult and worthwhile."[13] These optimal experiences, which he labeled as "flow" states, are intimately connected with learning: they involve pushing ourselves to the edge of our knowledge or skills, or just beyond, in ways that enable us to bring new order and growth to our minds. They are also, as Csikszentmihalyi describes them, characterized by deep and full attention. When they are in flow states, he explains, "people are so involved in an activity that nothing else seems to matter."[14] They block out time and distractions voluntarily, so captured are they by their absorption in the task.

From many years of conducting this research, Csikszentmihalyi argues, as I have argued above, that the mind caught in the throes of wandering and distraction is the substrate from which periods of optimal experience occasionally arise. "The normal condition of the human mind," he explains in his book *Finding Flow: The Psychology of Engagement with Everyday Life*, "is one of informational disorder: random thoughts chase one another instead of lining up in logical causal sequences. Unless one learns to concentrate, and is able to invest the effort, thoughts will scatter without reaching any conclusion."[15] Yet, in spite of this normal condition of the human mind, we do have these moments of optimal experience, in which our attention has been harnessed and focused. They can happen in many aspects of our lives, often in hobbies or leisure pursuits: reading, playing golf, birding, reenacting battles, painting, and more. Teachers might find themselves regularly experiencing flow in the classroom, as they are deep in the throes of a great presentation of a new concept, orchestrating a complex group activity, or leading a meaningful discussion with their students. These are the classroom experiences in which time seems to fly by, the hour has passed long before you wished it would, and afterward you walk back to your office with that sense of elation and satisfaction that keeps you coming back for each new semester.

Whether they were teachers or welders, the thriving individuals Csikszentmihalyi studied were people who are "open to a variety of experiences, *keep on learning until the day they die*, and have strong ties and commitments to other people and to the environment in which they live" (italics mine).[16] A continually learning person, according to Csikszentmihalyi, lives a flourishing life. Subsequent researchers in positive psychology, who study human happiness and well-being, have elaborated on this argument by suggesting that the more time we engage in flow activities, the greater sense of overall well-being we have in our lives.[17] Your life flourishes in the classroom when your teaching goes well and holds your attention entirely, even if this only happens a few times a week. Teaching brings us joy for many reasons, but one of those reasons is because of the way it sustains our attention in the challenging, ever-changing, and meaningful environment of the classroom. When attention has been achieved and our minds have been raised like an island from the ocean of distraction, even for short periods of time, we are paving the way toward a meaningful, flourishing life.

You should think carefully about how to design experiences in the classroom that will capture and sustain the attention of your students because such experiences will contribute to their learning. But the research of Csikszentmihalyi and others suggests that such experiences also have enormous power to transform the lives of your students, both in school and in their world beyond it. When we create opportunities for students to use their attention to achieve their goals, think creatively, and engage with one another in meaningful ways, we are providing them with experiences that can enhance their learning and improve their lives. I trust that you wish for such happiness and success for your students, and hence I encourage you to consider how you can create a classroom environment that supports and sustains their attention.

3

The Tech Ban Debate

IN THE ERA of mobile devices, our efforts to create a classroom environment in which attention can flourish must inevitably wrestle with the role that these devices should or should not play in the daily work of teaching and learning. No other topic covered in this book captures people's attention like debates about how we should manage electronic devices in the classroom. Laptop and cell phone policies are discussed in baffled tones with our colleagues, through overheated pronouncements on Twitter, and on the pages of learned publications. Consider the following conflicting statements about banning or not banning laptops from the classroom, from opinion pieces in the *Chronicle of Higher Education*, *New York Times*, and *Inside Higher Ed*:

In Favor of a Ban

New York Times: A growing body of evidence shows that over all, college students learn less when they use computers or tablets during lectures. They also tend to earn worse grades. The research is unequivocal: Laptops distract from learning, both for users and for those around them.[1]

Chronicle: In class, people learn less when someone near them is surfing the web; the temptation to follow what's on the screen, rather than what's happening in the class, is simply too great. When I found that out, I banned laptops from my classroom. You can distract yourself, if you so choose, but you have no right to distract somebody else.[2]

Against a Ban

Chronicle: Students should be insulted [by laptop bans]. Telling them they can't use their laptops or smartphones in class is treating adults like infants. Our students are capable of making their own choices, and if they choose to check Snapchat instead of listening to your lecture, then that's their loss.[3]

Inside Higher Ed: Banning laptops or other note-taking devices from the classroom is an extreme stance that isn't right for every student. I once worked with a student with learning differences whose handwritten notes were messy and disorganized. I watched as an accessibility tutor sat with him and helped him to type his words and ideas into a document on his laptop. The result was an exceptionally clear and thoughtful summary of the class. The fact is that some students need laptops or other devices to take effective notes. On that, there should be no debate.[4]

My favorite headline on this subject comes from an essay in the *Chronicle of Higher Education* and reads: "Rethinking Laptop Bans (AGAIN) and Note Taking."[5] Rethinking them for (at least) a second time, and doing so in ALL CAPS, indicates the extent to which this discussion not only has dominated our conversations about student attention and distraction, but has come to seem to many of us like one of those problems that we will never fully resolve.

The collective confusion we are all feeling, faculty and students, about digital devices in the room is reflected in a 2019 article in the *Canadian Journal for the Scholarship of Teaching and Learning* on the subject of technology and distraction in higher education.[6] The authors presented data on attitudes toward technology and its distractions, collected from more than five hundred students and faculty at a Canadian university through electronic surveys, focus groups, and individual interviews. The researchers asked both groups about the extent to which students used technology for off-task purposes in class, how much students were bothered by the distracting behaviors of others, and whether students or faculty should be held responsible for distractions in the classroom. The wildly inconsistent nature of the responses from students and faculty, and between students and faculty, offers a striking picture of the current state of confusion about the place of technology and its distracting powers in the classroom. For example, 49 percent of students reported being distracted by students engaging in off-task behaviors in the classroom, and yet they largely still expressed a desire to continue to use their technologies, even if they strayed off-task themselves—and thereby distracted others. When asked about who was responsible for minimizing distraction in the classroom, the students said they wanted the autonomy to regulate their own behavior—unless someone was really being distracting to others around them, in which case it was the professor's job to intervene. The instructor responses were equally conflicted. Many cited laptops and phones as interfering not only with the learning of their students, but with their own teaching performance; they reported being demoralized and discombobulated by having to teach to rows of laptop covers, or by catching a student off-task. Yet, in spite of this, they resisted the idea that they should be the "technology police," asserting that students needed to learn to regulate their own behaviors.

Our conflicting feelings about classroom technology policies allow assertive voices to rise above the fray. Some writers tell us that if we regulate student technology, we should be ashamed of these infantilizing and unjust policies; others insist that we neglect our responsibility toward students if we allow them to distract one another with devices. Those who make the former argument don't sufficiently take into account the extent to which the technologies in our phones have been carefully designed—and are being continually enhanced by corporate mega-dollars—to exploit the distractible nature of our minds. Those who make the latter argument are putting students into an artificial technology-free bubble that will not last much beyond the walls of their classroom. The research on attention and distraction in the digital age makes very clear that we are easily pulled into the wonders of our electronic devices, even when we have the best of intentions to focus on our learning, our work, and each other. Their enticing powers mean that we need to work with each other and with our students to find strategies to make the classroom a productive environment when distractions are available at every turn.

What follows in this chapter will come as good news if you see legitimate arguments on both sides of the tech ban debate, and bad news if you came here hoping for a one-size-fits-all solution to this complex problem. I'm not going to stake a hard claim on either side of this issue for the same reason that you have to constantly remind students not to gravitate toward black-and-white answers in the messy realm of your discipline: because it's complicated, and there are no easy answers. We can ban laptops, and that produces some benefits for attention while making life more difficult for students who would be helped by a laptop. We can adopt a laissez-faire policy of allowing all devices in the classroom at any time, and that treats students like adults while potentially harming well-intentioned students who might be distracted by the off-task work of their peers. We can also adopt solutions that fall between or outside of these two alternatives. All of these positions have costs and benefits, which we will review. Once we have done so, we'll consider what I believe are the most important imperatives for our laptop policies: how we inform students about the problem, how we present the policies to them, and how we sustain them over the course of the semester.

Creating the Policy

Any tech policy you might adopt in your classroom will likely fall into one of four categories. Here, I present them in order of the policies I find least appealing to the one that, having spent years researching and writing about distraction, has become the norm in my teaching.

The Laissez-Faire Approach

The policy that I find most troublesome is no policy whatsoever, which means students are entirely free to do as they wish in terms of their devices, and the instructor offers little or no guidance about their responsible use in the classroom. This policy prioritizes the notion that students are adults, free to make their own decisions, and we should respect their liberty and trust them to do the right thing.[7] It reflects an admirable conviction that we should not feel the need to police everything students do. Imposing rules in the classroom occurs, according to the laissez-faire argument, because we are assuming that, without those rules, someone will engage in unwanted behaviors. Instead, we should trust students, treat them as adults, and expect the best of them. I love the sentiment behind this argument.

But in the realm of digital distractions, it falls short in two respects. First, it does not take fully into account the ways in which our digital devices have been so effectively engineered to hijack our attention. Adam Alter's book *Irresistible: The Rise of Addictive Technology and the Business of Keeping Us Hooked* reminds us of the challenges that both teachers and students face in our efforts to keep the distractions within our digital devices at bay, even when we have the best intentions to turn our attention elsewhere:

> The people who create and refine tech, games, and interactive experiences are very good at what they do. They run thousands of tests with millions of users to learn which tweaks work and which ones don't—which background colors, fonts, and audio tones maximize engagement and minimize frustration. As an experience [such as an app or game] evolves, it become an irresistible, weaponized version of the experience it once was.[8]

Both our devices and the apps that populate them give us endless short bursts of satisfaction, while the satisfaction we take from learning is usually hard-won and spaced out over time. Learning is difficult work, even when the teacher is doing everything right, and our devices offer us easy alternatives. We shouldn't blame our students for defaulting to them during moments when they feel challenged or bored in the classroom; that impulse runs through us all.

Second, a laissez-faire approach seems arbitrarily selective. Even if we trust our students, we still have rules and guidelines that govern behavior in our classrooms. We can think about such rules as tyrannical impositions from on high, or we can think about them as conventions that help us treat one another with respect and create conditions for learning. We don't allow students to play music on their phone speakers in class, for example, even though technically I could teach with a student's weekend mix playing quietly in the background. We don't allow students to engage in audible conversations while another group of students is giving a presentation. We don't allow students to interrupt one another in discussions, or make insulting comments about each other's arguments. In all of these cases, the conventions prevent students from diverting the attention of the other students in the room (music, conversations) or interfering with the community we are trying to form (interruptions, insults). We adhere to such rules for behavior because they help us understand how to treat one another respectfully and support the attention and learning of all. The reason we don't view distracting devices in the same light as audible music or conversation is because distraction seems like a private, single-student issue. The student playing music distracts the whole room; the one watching a silent YouTube video seems to be distracting only herself.

Of course this is not true, as we saw in Chapter Two. I cited there studies that have demonstrated that learning can suffer when students are in view of other students who are engaging in distracted behaviors. This negative impact on learning does not appear immediately to either the distracted student or the learner, which again might make us take it less seriously than students playing loud music or insulting one another. But the evidence is clear that any students engaged in off-task behaviors on their devices can negatively impact others in the room, derailing their attention even when they have the best of intentions. I experienced a version of this myself once on a long flight, when I was trying to get some work done on my laptop. I was seated in the aisle, and in the aisle seat across from me and one row ahead a man was watching an action movie. In spite of my best efforts to focus my attention on responding to a backlog of e-mails, I could not keep my eyes from straying to that screen, over and over again, significantly reducing the amount of work I completed. Students are experiencing this same phenomenon in class; no matter how hard they might wish to focus on a lecture, discussion, or activity, they can be drawn away from it by a distracted peer.

The laissez-faire policy thus represents, in my view, an abdication of our responsibility toward the community we are trying to create in the classroom, in which we do the hard work of giving our attention to each other as well as to the course material. We will take this notion up in much greater detail in the next chapter, but for now I will conclude by saying that teachers have a role to play in helping students with the task of learning in a community setting and in supporting the attention they give to difficult cognitive work.

The Total Ban

Next on the docket we have the complete ban of digital devices in the room, or a total ban with exceptions for students who have accommodations for their devices. The impetus behind a complete ban on digital devices takes seriously all of the research on distraction and attention that we have considered thus far, which demonstrates how easily distractible we are. It recognizes that our digital devices are especially good at playing on our distractible natures, drawing us away from the people and places around us and into electronic worlds, or electronic representations of the physical world. Those who argue for bans on laptops do so with good intentions, as they cite research or teaching experience that demonstrates that students hurt their own learning, and the learning of their peers, when they distract themselves in class. Some faculty who have instituted such bans report positive results. Trevon Logan, an economics professor at Ohio State University, was inspired to institute a laptop ban in his classes after reading Susan Dynarski's *New York Times* editorial. At the conclusion of his first semester with a no-laptop policy, he described the benefits he observed for his students in several areas: "The policy had helped them to maintain focus and to take better notes, kept them engaged, and increased their enjoyment of the course."[9] In addition to these general benefits, he also documented improved grades on course exams.

But technology bans pose two very challenging problems. A total ban on technology in the room, with no exceptions, doesn't take into account the increasing number of students who need digital devices in order to learn. As I write these words, a new semester is about to begin, and in my introductory class of twenty-two students I have accommodation letters for four of them that specify that the student should be allowed to take notes with a laptop. We are all seeing an increasing number of these students in our classes, and we have both an ethical and a legal obligation to make learning in our courses fully accessible to them. We can always ban laptops and make exceptions for students with accommodation letters, but this presents its own ethical problem: any student who has a laptop in the room has been outed to her peers as having an accommodation, something she might have preferred to keep private. In the journal *Hybrid Pedagogy*, Rick Godden and Anne-Marie Womack raise this argument against device bans with exceptions. Godden identifies himself as a disabled scholar who requires assistive technologies in a learning environment. A device-ban-with-exceptions policy forces individuals like Godden to out themselves as disabled in some way. A student with an invisible disability like a processing disorder might not want everyone in the classroom to know about that condition. Deciding whether to identify themselves as disabled seems like it should be left to students, rather than to a college faculty member.[10]

I will confess that this argument especially struck home for me because of the invisible disability with which I have lived for my entire adult life. I have Crohn's disease, and the primary symptom for me has been a sudden and urgent need to use the bathroom. Fortunately, my disease has been mostly in remission for close to a dozen years now. But when it was not in remission, I sat through every meeting worried that I might suddenly have to make a break for the nearest restroom. If a meeting organizer had announced to the group that people were allowed to leave the room but only in the case of impending and urgent diarrhea, my needs would have been accommodated— but I would have been mortified if I had needed to take advantage of that accommodation. It should be my choice to reveal my Crohn's disease—just as it should be a student's choice to reveal their accommodations to their fellow students.

The second major argument against a technology ban is that it obviously closes off opportunities for learning that might be more robust with digital devices than with paper and pen. If you have students working in groups to create a concept map, you can certainly have them do it on paper, posters, or whiteboards. But you could also have them use a free online concept-mapping program, and then they could save their maps for future study, upload them to the learning management system for all to see and review, and engage in commentary and critique of one another's work. You could do all of those things without computers, but it would take much greater effort to produce less storeable and shareable results. And while some students might distract themselves during a lecture, others might be working very productively on a laptop: taking and revising their notes, googling terms or ideas they find confusing, bookmarking articles related to the course content. International students could be using their devices to look up vocabulary words and keep pace with a lecture or discussion. "When you open up the classroom with technology," argues educational psychologist Christine Greenhow, "you are giving students the ability to connect to translation services, with databases to do research in real time, with other people they can connect with to get questions answered."[11] Finally, cost-strapped students can often save money on textbooks by buying electronic versions, and those textbooks might contain links or other resources that are not as easily available to students with non-digital copies.

Banning technology might well increase the attention of your students in the classroom, especially if you pair that policy with the other attention-focusing practices presented in this book. I do know of good-willed faculty who institute technology bans, and who do their best to meet student accommodation needs in smart and compassionate ways. Some of those faculty teach very large classes of several hundred students or more, where they are not able to implement some of the teaching strategies to support attention that we'll consider in subsequent chapters. But ultimately, technology bans close off many opportunities for learning, and so the costs might well override the benefits. Godden and Womack argue, from the theoretical framework of disability studies, that one-size-fits-all solutions like device bans don't take into account the increasing diversity of learners in our classrooms: "There is no *one* answer," they write, "even within one classroom. In contrast to singular best practices such as a universal ban on screens in classrooms, disability studies promotes multi-modal options and flexible design."[12] The following two policies move much closer to these ideals of multimodality and flexible design to address this problem.

Student-Generated Policies

When I first began writing this book, I intended to build this chapter around advocacy for a single strategy: inviting students to help you decide what your technology policy should be. This approach has many benefits. First, it enables you to spend a little time at the beginning of the semester educating students about attention and distraction. Before offering them the opportunity to make their decisions, for example, you could provide them with information about how students can be distracted by other distracted students. Second, this approach treats students like adults, in that it involves them in the process of establishing rules for the community in which they will learn. It thus fulfills the directive of trusting students: having first educated them on the issues, we trust them to make a good decision. Finally, it provides the opportunity for students to present creative solutions that might not have occurred to you. Their collective wisdom will be informed by the technology policies they have experienced in other classrooms, and you might learn a new approach from them.

At a more theoretical level, this approach to technology policies takes advantage of the power of autonomy as a motivational tool. You have likely heard of Daniel Pink, whose TED Talk on motivation has been viewed by about a billion people across the galaxy. Pink provides a deeper look into motivation in his book *Drive: The Surprising Truth About What Motivates Us*, in which he makes the case that the three fundamental drivers of intrinsic motivation—or motivation that comes from within, rather than being imposed and controlled by punishments or rewards—are autonomy, mastery, and purpose. Pink begins his analysis with autonomy, signaling that it serves as a fundamental condition for motivated and engaged work in any context. Although his book speaks primarily to readers in work environments, both the research and its implications speak just as clearly to education. The conclusions are clear, according to Pink: "A sense of autonomy has a powerful effect on individual performance and attitude. According to a cluster of recent behavioral science studies, autonomous motivation promotes greater conceptual understanding, better grades, enhanced persistence at school, and in sporting activities, higher productivity, less burnout, and greater levels of psychological well-being."[13]

People value the opportunity to determine what shape their working conditions will take, whether they work in an office cubicle, on a practice field, or in a classroom. This shouldn't be a difficult argument to accept for college faculty, whose working conditions feature as much autonomy as almost any other profession. Most of us work on schedules that provide us with generous opportunities to determine the precise shape of our days, even though we of course have plenty of obligations to fulfill. Beyond our schedules, we select our research projects and may have choices in the specific classes we teach and the committees on which we serve.

The value of autonomy, and the practical benefits that might result from giving it to my students, remains a convincing reason to me, and I believe inviting students to help craft the technology policy can work for faculty in many contexts. But I am stepping away from advocating for it as the single best solution, as I originally intended, in part because of the obstacles I encountered when I attempted to put it into practice while I was writing this book. I tried this approach in a senior seminar, which I thought would be the right place to experiment. A first-year college student might have difficulty formulating a policy that would govern the behavior of her peers, but seniors have several additional years of maturity and experience and should be able to respond meaningfully to a policy invitation. I presented the idea to students in the first class of the semester, showed them some of the research outlined in Part One, and then created a discussion thread in the learning management system and asked them to post their ideas about what our tech policy should look like.

The initial response was almost complete silence. The class met one night per week, so a few days before the second meeting I sent a message reminding the students about my invitation to help formulate our tech policy. Eventually some responses began to dribble in; in the end, perhaps two-thirds of the students offered an opinion. Some of those opinions were informative to me. One student explained that he preferred to get his books electronically, so he wouldn't want to see devices banned from the room; another suggested that any PowerPoint presentations be posted to the learning management system, which would reduce the desire for students to take notes frantically on their laptops. These were good and important points for me to hear. But there were only a few such comments, and none of them offered a very firm opinion. For the most part, I think I can best summarize the tenor of their responses like this: "I don't need to use technology in class, but I don't mind if others do, even though I do find it distracting when other people use laptops." It became very clear to me, from both the posted responses and the brief discussion we had in the second class, that the students didn't want the freedom to create the policy for the course, and they felt especially uncomfortable with the responsibility of devising rules that would be imposed on their peers.

A few months after this experience, I came across Barry Schwartz's book *The Paradox of Choice: Why More Is Less*, which helped me better understand what happened. Schwartz argues that we love the idea of having complete freedom to choose our destinies, but in reality we often find ourselves paralyzed in the face of that freedom. "As a culture," he writes, "we are enamored of freedom, self-determination, and variety, and we are reluctant to give up any of our options. But clinging tenaciously to all the choices available to us contributes to bad decisions, to anxiety, stress, and dissatisfaction."[14] We have a restaurant near my house that serves reliably good food, but the menu is massive, stretching for a half-dozen pages or more. I dread the prospect of having to review all of those choices, and so I pretty much order the same thing every time. I'd be happier still if the chef just came out and told me what I was getting. Schwartz, a professor of social theory at Swarthmore, argues that "we are better off if we embraced certain voluntary constraints on our freedom of choice."[15] Looking back on that semester, I realized that my students were floundering without constraints. I decided in the end that setting the policy was ultimately my responsibility, in the same way that it's my responsibility to select the texts, organize the learning activities, and work to build community and foster attention in the classroom.

I will say, however, that I enjoyed having the conversation with students about attention, distraction, and technology at the beginning of the semester, that I learned some interesting things from them, and that I had very few problems with distraction during that course (although this might also have been related to the fact that it was a small class, they were all seniors, and most of them were future teachers). You might find a way to make this strategy work more effectively than I did. My experience, in dialogue with the work of Schwartz, suggests that you might be better off presenting the students with some options, rather than just leaving it open for them to formulate the policy for you. Cathy Davidson, for example, explains that when she wanted to create a "class constitution" with her students to allow them to cocreate the course's "terms of engagement," she started by posting to a shared space an example of such a document from another organization, which students could then comment on and revise.[16] I suspect something similar might work for a technology policy cocreated with your students. Begin with a draft policy, one created by you or someone else, and then invite them to comment on and revise it. That approach should provide the students with some of the constraints they might need in order to engage more easily with the exercise.

The Context-Specific Policy

The policy that now guides my teaching is a simple one: whether technology is allowed in the room depends on what we are doing. Sometimes we should all be using it; sometimes the students can choose whether or not to use it; sometimes nobody should be using it. When I'm lecturing or presenting new content, the students are welcome to take notes by hand or via their laptops or other devices. When we are doing in-class writing (as we do in almost every class), we default to handwriting, but I am happy to allow students to use their devices for writing if they prefer to do so—either because they have an accommodation or just because they find handwriting too slow and difficult, as I sometimes do. But when we are having a whole-class discussion about a work of literature and what it means to them personally, I don't want to see people staring into their screens. In those moments, I want students attentive to one another and to the conversation. They don't need to take notes in those parts of the class, so we don't need screens—or notebooks, for that matter. We just need the poem, story, play, or passage in front of us and our thinking and feeling brains. Likewise for the times when I invite them to do something creative, like work in groups to create a character map on the whiteboards, or recite poems aloud to one another, or watch a video of a famous poet reading her work. In those moments, what matters is what comes out of them, not what they hear from me, and they don't need screens for that.

This policy ultimately springs from my deepest convictions about teaching. Our classrooms should be a space where students have the opportunity to engage in multiple forms of learning. Sometimes they are receiving first exposure to new information and ideas (through lectures); sometimes they are generating examples of how those ideas connect to the world beyond the classroom (through discussions or group work); sometimes they are practicing the skills we want them to demonstrate in their papers, projects, or exams (such as writing, presenting to their peers, or solving problems). The classroom should serve as an active laboratory of learning, a place where students engage with the course material through multiple cognitive streams. Some of those streams will flow more easily with technology; some of them will be diverted by it. The technology policy should thus be adaptable to what is happening at any given moment in the course, just as our use of technology in our personal lives depends on context. I don't need my phone to talk to the fifteen-year-old twins who live in my house, so at dinnertime we put our phones away and talk; if I want to talk to my three older daughters, who are in college or living in other cities, I pick up my phone.

A context-specific device policy has had two major side benefits for my teaching. First, it has helped me think more strategically about what students are doing in my classroom and why. Do they really need first exposure to course material from me? Or can they get that from the textbook or a video? How much time have I allowed for active learning, and how much time am I lecturing? How deliberately am I thinking about the shape of the class period—the opening and closing minutes, or the middle section when students need a change of format to renew their attention? (We will consider all of these questions in greater detail in subsequent chapters.) Second, it has led to greater transparency in my teaching. I am convinced that many problems with students arise because they misunderstand the purpose of so much of what happens in the classroom. My technology policy has helped me become more transparent about the nature and purposes of our daily classroom activities, as in:

- "Today I am lecturing because this material is incredibly complex and I'd like to boil it down to a few essentials for you. You're very welcome to follow along or take notes on your laptop; you'll find the slides in the course web pages."
- "We're going to spend the last fifteen minutes of class thinking and talking about why we should still read poems like this one: Why do they still matter to us today, two hundred years after they were composed? You don't need to take notes for the next part of class, so I want devices closed, so we can give our full attention to one another."
- "We use groups in this context because I want to help you connect with the peers you'll be working with on your final projects. You don't need your devices here; I want you to focus on working with each other, and you will only need one person to record your work on the whiteboards around the room. Afterward you can take pictures of the board if you want to preserve the ideas for yourself."

Such transparent talk articulates whether they will need their devices, but that's really a side issue. More importantly, it clarifies the purposes of all of our work. It makes the classroom more like a communal learning experience than like a magician performing for his mystified audience. The device policy connects to the rationale for everything we do, which means we have such a rationale—and students deserve to know about it.

I have attached the document that presents this policy to my students as an appendix to this book. As you will see, it does include an invitation for them to comment on it and recommend changes. I thus do allow for the prospect of a policy cocreated with my students, which means my approach really combines the third and fourth options we have just considered. Practically speaking, I have not yet seen much willingness on the part of my students to play a very active role in the policy-creation process. Your students might well be different from mine, and might jump at the opportunity to shape the technology policy of the classroom. If that's the case, I still would urge you to give them some initial ideas or a draft policy to work with, followed by an invitation to comment and revise, rather than just leaving it open for them to craft from scratch.

Presenting the Policy

I favor the student-generated and context-specific policies, but I also believe that good-willed people can disagree and may choose one of the other policies, some variation or combination of them, or some alternative I have not articulated. More important to me than the details of the policy is that whatever you choose provides you with an opportunity to engage in a conversation with students about their technology use. That conversation can educate them in ways that will make them better students and better citizens of the classroom and campus community. You reading this book means that you are becoming more informed about the complexities of attention and distraction in the classroom and the way that our devices intensify those complexities. How much of what you are learning here, or in other resources, can become part of the conversations you have with students? How would you translate the arguments of this book into the technology policies you craft? How would you critique or respond to these ideas? How would they affect the way you present those policies to your students?

One excellent example of a faculty member informing students about the role of technology in their lives and in her classroom comes from Ashley Waggoner Denton, a professor of psychology at the University of Toronto, who has made available through her website a set of slides that she shows to students in her psychology classes, and which others are free to use or adapt. The slideshow is entitled "Making Informed Decisions: Laptops, Smartphones, and Your Studies," and it includes in the notes Waggoner Denton's explanations of each slide, as well as links to references and related sources.[17] The slides themselves provide summaries and graphs from experiments or observational studies—all of which have been replicated—demonstrating first how the use of distracting technologies can harm the learning of the distracted student, and second how it harms the learning of those around him. She also reviews some of the studies that have been conducted on the advantages of taking notes by hand over taking notes on a laptop. Finally, she reminds students that technology use can also interfere with their studying outside of class, and provides some resources from which they can learn how to manage their device use while studying.

What she does not provide are clear answers about what all of this means for a technology policy. She explains to students that there are no easy answers when it comes to device use and learning, but that understanding the research can help them make better choices:

The key message that I try to get across to students is that our electronic devices are not the enemy—they are wonderfully useful tools that have enhanced our lives in myriad ways. But like *any* tool, they are not ubiquitously helpful. Research can help us figure out when these tools are useful and when they are not, and my goal is to present them with some of the key findings in this area so that they (as individuals) and we (as a class) can make informed decisions about how best to deal with electronic devices in the classroom.

In support of facilitating her students' decisions and the classroom policy, her presentation includes two slides where students are invited to share their thoughts about what policy recommendations they would make based on the research. Waggoner Denton has built even more flexibility into the presentation by giving instructors permission to use and adapt it to their own needs, which means that you can use her research to educate students about the issue, and then provide the reasoning behind whatever policy you have developed. The open-source nature of the presentation seems like it would be especially helpful to faculty who are teaching large classes, for whom a collective effort to set a technology policy might prove especially complex.

Whether or not you use the excellent work developed by Waggoner Denton, and whatever policy you choose to implement, your rules should be presented to students in ways that provide a clear rationale for them—and that, better still, acknowledge the complexity of the issue and demonstrate your empathy for the challenges your students face in keeping their attention in the classroom rather than on their devices. The first time I addressed devices in the classroom was in the spring of 2008, when I put the following warning on my syllabus: "Put away and turn off your cell

PHONES! If your phone rings or vibrates in class, or I see you check-ing it or texting, you will be absent for that day."

The all caps and exclamation point certainly let students know that they were NOT (!) allowed to use their phones in class. But this was the entire statement. I made no effort to explain why those de-vices represented such a problem in my courses, which run largely through discussion and in-class activities of various kinds. After a few years of yelling at my students on the syllabus, I learned to ex-plain my (evolving) policy more clearly: Since so much of the work we do in this class depends on your participation, it's important to me that you are here and present for one another. In our classroom, we listen to each other as much as we listen to the texts, and that listening is supported by respectful attention.

As it turns out, research on syllabi suggests that providing this kind of rationale to students makes a significant difference in terms of how they perceive the course and the instructor. In a 2011 study, two researchers presented students with a sample syllabus from a candidate for a potential faculty job that was written in ei-ther "warm" or "cold" language. A cold-language syllabus offered facts, information, and policies. The warm-language syllabus pro-vided a text that was more empathetic and personable and—most important—offered a rationale for the course's policies and assign-ments. The students rated the warm-language instructor as more approachable and more motivated to teach the course. Although their questions did not specially address the technology policy in the syllabus, the researchers drew conclusions that seem eminently transferable to this issue:

> Presenting students with an effective syllabus written in a
> friendly, approachable tone can influence perceptions of the
> instructor and the course. Consequently, creating a syllabus

for a course should not be an afterthought for instructors. Indeed, care should be taken in developing the syllabus with particular attention to its tone, because impressions are made that may facilitate faculty engagement with students.[18]

As you work on the policies on your syllabus that talk about the way digital devices can detract from the sense of community in the room, take another look at that language and evaluate its temperature. What does it convey about the kind of experience the students are going to have with you? One in which Samuel Taylor Coleridge's "stern preceptor" keeps an eye out for offenders, or one in which teacher and students work together to help one another be present? A warm-language introduction to a technology policy (or even separate from such a policy) might begin along these lines: "The time we have together each week is short, and so I really want us to remain present for one another during that time. I hope you will learn from me, and from your fellow students, and I know from past experience that I always learn from you. We will thus make being *present* a core value of this class, and there are a few ways in which I will try to support that value . . ."

Sustaining the Policy

I'm pretty sure I've seen at least a dozen variations of the split-screen meme in which someone is yelling something about the course on the left panel, and the right panel features a smug and/or angry cat responding, "It's on the syllabus." No joke about college teaching might be more popular than ones that riff on the notion that students frequently ask questions that are answered on the syllabus. Of course, the reason students frequently ask questions about the syllabus is because we present it to them on the first day and then never revisit its contents. We use the syllabus to provide a sales pitch for the course, information about our office hours, an overview of the assessments, an academic integrity policy, the schedule of readings, and more. But it's the first day of the semester, and students are getting five or more of these documents, decorating or restocking their rooms, reconnecting with their friends, and doing all of the other things that students have to do. We should not be the slightest bit surprised to find that they don't commit to memory every policy on every one of their syllabi.

However warmly and convincingly we present our technology policies to students on the syllabus and on the first day, these policies will need revisiting and reaffirming throughout the semester. That can take many forms, depending on your class context. Let's assume that you have created (or cocreated with your students) a thoughtful policy, that you presented it in warm language on your syllabus, and that you devoted time on the first day of the semester to discussing it. Having done that, you could follow up in three easy ways:

- **Midterm evaluations.** Almost every teacher I know receives end-of-term evaluations from their students, which are helpful for our ongoing development but useless for the class we just finished teaching. Many teachers, including me, thus have students complete evaluations halfway through the semester, and use those evaluations to modify our teaching and remind students about policies or procedures of which they might have lost sight. A midterm evaluation can easily include a question designed to remind students about the device policy and reorient them toward its purpose. Variations could include: "To what extent are you noticing distracted behaviors in yourself or your peers in class?" "What can I do to help ensure that we are bringing our attention to one another in class?" "How well are you adhering to the technology policy we created together?"

- **Notebook or discussion-board responses.** One check-in midway through the semester will be far more effective than no check-ins at all. But if you have some regular way that students engage informally with the material from your course, you could fold your follow-ups into that process. For example, once or twice per week, students in my course write one-paragraph exercises in response to our readings or discussions. If I am noticing distraction as a problem in my class, I can pose one of the questions above at any point in the semester, and then use their responses to host another discussion about the issue.

- **Individual reminders.** Occasionally it happens that a class is generally doing really well in terms of their management of potential distractions, but one or two students are consistently off-task in class. In those cases I prefer to reach out to those students individually, either by e-mail or as a quick note added to a returned writing exercise. I keep these notes as neutral as possible: "I have noticed you using your phone frequently in class, and wanted to remind you about our technology policy. If you are having a problem that I can help you with, let me know." One of the things I have learned from sending such notes is how surprised students are to find that their off-task device use is visible to me. Once they realize this, the behavior usually (but not always) stops.

The warm language that you used on your syllabus should persist through all of these class conversations or individual comments.

Students might be using their devices to manage difficult problems at home, to communicate with a sick relative, or to deal with childcare. If you begin these conversations compassionately, you are more likely to find solutions that work for both you and the students—and you will be less likely to assume the role of the technology police.

You can also always ask the students themselves to help you determine how to hold them accountable to the class's polices on technology and distraction. In November 2019, I attended a workshop on digital distraction and attention at the annual conference for faculty and administrators who focus on teaching development in higher education.[19] The facilitator for this section walked us through an exercise we could conduct with students in the first week of the semester, in order to educate them about the way multitasking interferes with their learning and the learning of their peers. The final step in the process she modeled for us was to have students "plan new behaviors" that would help them use their technology responsibly in the course. She suggested having students write a paragraph that responded to each of the following three prompts:

- Write out the one change they plan to make
- Share their ideas with you and peers and get feedback
- Develop and implement an easy way to monitor their plan and its effects over time

Following a process like this one hits many of the best ideas we have considered in this chapter. It allows you to create a policy that fits with your teaching context; it provides an opportunity for you to educate your students about the challenges of distraction and attention, whether you use a resource like Ashley Waggoner Denton's or some other material; it encourages the students to assume some agency in relation to the potential distractions in the room; and it includes explicit thinking about how the decision that both you and your students make at the beginning of the semester will be monitored and reaffirmed throughout the term.

Flower Darby, an instructional designer at Northern Arizona University and the author of *Small Teaching Online: Applying Learning Science in Online Classes,* has written about the way many online teachers mistakenly take a slow-cooker approach toward their courses. They create the content and assume the course will just slowly simmer away without intervention until the learning has been cooked all the way through.[20] We have to be careful that we don't take a similar approach to our technology policies and the ways in which they support or interfere with attention in the classroom. If we value attention, as we should, we need to develop thoughtful policies, engage students in conversation about them, and continue those conversations throughout the semester.

Model Device-Free Attention

The year I graduated from high school, a commercial appeared on television in which a young man is lying around in his room listening to music, rocking out to his headphones. His father comes in, switches off the music, and then confronts him with a box of drug paraphernalia, asking him repeatedly where he got it and who taught him to use drugs. After initial denials, the boy finally responds angrily, "I learned it by watching you!" The camera shifts to the shocked face of the father, and the voice-over arrives to pound us over the head with the moral: "Parents who use drugs have children who use drugs." Even if you were not hanging around in a living room in the Cleveland suburbs watching MTV in the summer of 1987, you've likely heard someone utter this phrase, in jest, as a description of the ways in which we sometimes say one thing to children or students and then do another.

You see where I'm going with this, right?

On more than one occasion, strolling through the hallways and observing people teaching in their classrooms, I have seen faculty members staring intently at their phones while students were engaged in some task. I have seen this most frequently while students are taking an exam or engaged in group work, or perhaps when the class has not quite started yet. Of course, these moments in which you are not actively teaching would allow for this kind of behavior, and you are an adult who should be able to make responsible use of your phone during the workday. But it's hard for me to reconcile these behaviors with teachers' concerns about the distraction of their students. After all, some of these moments provide you with opportunities to engage in activities that would support students' learning and attention. Before class, you could be engaging them in casual conversation or trying to learn their names; while they are completing a group-work task, you could be circulating among them and checking their understanding. Faculty phone use seems least troublesome when students are taking an exam, but even here you might consider whether you should feel obliged by the conditions under which you have asked them to abide. What message does it send when you request or demand a phone-free or device-free classroom, and then occasionally say "Except me" or "Except now"?

If you are the parent of young children, or a caregiver of any kind, you might well want or need to have your phone available in class and have the numbers of your key contacts set to ring in case of emergency. Otherwise, you could make your reading of this book the moment that marks a new habit in your teaching life. From now on, you can engage in a very simple behavior designed to remove one key distractor from the classroom: your own phone. Leave it in the office, and keep your mind free to focus on the students in front of you. I carry my phone with me everywhere I go, as most of us do these days, with one exception: I don't bring it to the classroom. Initially this was a little unsettling, as I was so accustomed to the feel of it in my pocket or the sight of it on my desk. But after a couple years of this behavior, I have come to embrace the freedom it seems to bring to my attention in these moments when I most need it and want to model it for my students. And you can bet I give myself a little time to unwind on Twitter when I get back to the office after a couple of hours away from my social media accounts and e-mail.

Unlike a 1980s public-service announcement, I won't beat you over the head with this message. Occasionally checking your phone in class probably won't make the difference between attentive and inattentive students. But of course that's true for everything I am arguing in this book. Not one of the strategies I have recommended here or will recommend in Part Two will turn your classroom into a distraction-free environment. They all represent small opportunities to build a culture of attention, rather than single solutions. But I am a firm believer that small decisions we make in the design of our courses, classroom practice, and communication with students have the power to accumulate into significant achievements, and the absence of your phone in the classroom—and the presence of your attention—represents one of those small decisions.

Students did not learn to distract themselves with their phones from watching us, but they may yet learn from us the value of becoming present to one another, and to fascinating ideas, in the communities of our classrooms.

Quick Take

In this chapter and all of the ones that follow, I make practical recommendations for building and supporting an attentive classroom. Each chapter from here out thus includes a quick recap of those recommendations. You will find them repeated and compiled at the conclusion of the book as well. I highlight the recommendations in this way so that you can return to the book briefly at the beginning of each semester—or when attention flags in the fourth, ninth, or twelfth week of the course and you need a quick reminder of some of the ways you can stir it back up again.

- Use your technology policy, whether you impose it or co-create it with students, to have a conversation with your students about attention, distraction, and technology in your classroom. Provide the rationale for your decision, and ensure that you are being fair to students with accommodations.
- Present these explanations, and your technology policy, in warm language. Be empathetic. Attention is hard for us all, and you have designed your policy to support your students' learning and the continuous development of the classroom community.
- Sustain the conversation about responsible use of digital devices throughout the semester. Use journals, discussion boards, or midterm evaluations to provide opportunities for students to report their experiences with distraction and for you to remind and reinforce the policies you have established.
- If you wish your students to engage in device-free attention at least sometimes throughout the class period, model that behavior yourself. When students are working in groups, or arriving in the classroom, or leaving the classroom, use those moments to get to know them a little better, either as persons or as learners.

Conclusion

When it comes to the policies we create for digital devices in the classroom, the only mistake we make is not to address the question at all. A thoughtfully crafted technology policy—one that you discuss with your students—helps us avoid that mistake. Technology policies can be imposed like fiats from on high, or they can be evolving guidelines that educate students about the impact of technology use on their peers and their learning (and the professor). More important than the details of the policy, in my view, is the education that you can provide to students about their technology use and its intersections with their studies and their futures. Matt Reed, the author of a regular column for *Inside Higher Ed*, argues that "device etiquette," or how we manage our devices in the presence of each other, "is becoming a new workplace skill."[21] The graduates who are most successful in their careers may well be the ones who understand how to work productively with their devices and how to step away from them to manage their personal and professional relationships. They know how to work productively in the office, at home, or at a coffee shop, but they also know how to listen respectfully in a meeting, attend to a client over dinner, or brainstorm creative new ideas at the corporate retreat.

Each of us has an opportunity, however small, to shape for the better the way our students manage their relationship with technology. Our cumulative work can create students who feel no compunction at slinking behind their screens at any time or place, or who understand how and why they should carefully manage their relationship with their devices in class and beyond. Collectively, we need as many humans as possible to get to that latter place. Teachers can play a role in getting young people there, and the technology policy provides the stage upon which we can fulfill that role.

I have included as an appendix to this book the technology policy from a recent literature class I taught. This document was presented to the students on the first day of the semester. They were given the opportunity to read it on their own after class and e-mail me with questions and comments, and then they were asked to sign it at the beginning of the second class. Before spring break, I issued a midterm evaluation in which—among other things—I reminded them about the policy and asked them to describe whether it was still helping them stay on task in the classroom. Readers are welcome to steal, borrow, and adapt any part of this policy or its implementation as they see fit.

part two

PRACTICES OF ATTENTION

4

Communities of Attention

ON A SUNNY day in early June, I stepped into the classroom of
Stephanie Yuhl, a professor of history at the College of the Holy
Cross. Yuhl was the inaugural recipient of the Burns Career Teaching Medal at Holy Cross, an award for which she was nominated
by both colleagues and her current and former students. She teaches
high school teachers through the US Department of Education's
Teaching American History program, and she is a sought-after public speaker for adult education programs like One Day University.
On the day I observed her, she was teaching a summer course on
the American civil rights movement, an upper-level history seminar that took place in two-hour sessions, four days a week, for
six weeks. These kinds of time-intensive seminars strike me as one
of the most challenging types of environments in which to hold
students' attention, both because of the extended time period and
because of the heavy cognitive demands these seminars place on
student brains. I feel pretty confident that I can shepherd students
(and their attention) through a fifty-minute class session, but I

always feel challenged when I am pushing through the second half of a longer seminar period.

I had expected to see Yuhl, a decided extrovert, hold the attention of her students by sheer force of personality, and to a small extent that was true. She worked the room like a professional actor, maintaining eye contact with students and regaling them with fascinating stories, humor, and passionate invocations of the relevance of the history they were studying and their ability to make a positive difference to the world. But after observing her teach, and speaking with her about her philosophy, I realized that her personality was far less important to her success in holding students' attention than the continued, deliberate efforts she made to build community in the classroom. This process began from the moment she walked into the room, five minutes before class began, when she immediately initiated conversations with students waiting for class to start. "How was your mom's birthday party?" she asked a woman in the front row, who laughed in response and then briefly described the festivities. "Did you get the internship?" she asked another. As she held these conversations with students, she spoke to each of them by name. Although she was doing some quick preparations at the front of the room during these conversations, her students were the primary focus; getting her handouts in order seemed more like an afterthought.

Even though it was the beginning of the third week, two new students were joining that day, which gave me the opportunity to observe how Yuhl welcomed them into the room and the course. When the class period officially launched, she greeted the two new students, and said this: "My theory about teaching is that it all comes out of community. It's really important that we all know each other's name. When you refer to a point made by another student, you refer to that student by name." This was all to prepare the new students for their baptism by fire. First, she asked them to introduce themselves. "Tell us something interesting," she said. "What do we need to know about you that will help us remember you?" When they had finished, she asked one of the current students to stand and recite the names of the dozen or so other students in the room. Then, to much laughter and appreciation, she had the new students try repeating the names themselves. Surprisingly, and with just a little help, they both managed it. After they sat down, Yuhl explained to them that knowing and speaking one another's names in class was a core value in her teaching, and that she would ask them to recite the names of their peers over the next few days until they had it down pat.

The other important thing Yuhl wanted the new students to know was that they would be regular contributors to the conversation. "Everyone speaks in here every day," she said with a smile. As the class unfolded, she accomplished this—with the new students and with the rest of the class—by continuing to invite people into the conversation by name. She worked the room very deliberately, making sure everyone's voice was heard. When two students near the front made several points in a row, she pointed this out: "You guys are talking a lot, which is fabulous. But I'm going to hold off on calling on you for a little bit so we can hear from some others." This strategy of regular invitations to the conversation kept everyone attentive; students were actively engaged in the discussion, or writing in their notebooks, throughout the period. When the class took a break—"Go get some water and some sun," she told them— and I had a chance to speak with her about what I had observed, she told me that her continued emphasis on students' learning and speaking one another's names, and the careful solicitation of commentary from every student, was not limited to the first day of the semester or the arrival of newcomers. "Community is not something you establish on the first day and then forget about," she said. "It has to be continually reinscribed." This value mattered to her more than anything else in her teaching, she said. Community came first; content followed.

With community comes attention, which is why Part Two of this book, which focuses on practical pedagogies, begins with a consideration of how we pay attention to one another in the classroom: students to teacher, teacher to students, and students to students. The least distracted classroom I observed, in the dozens of observations I made during the writing of this book, was Stephanie Yuhl's. That had much less to do with any specific teaching practice and much more to do with the way her classroom was a place where her students learned in community, attentive to her and to one another, as she was to each of them. No matter how many students you have, all the teaching strategies I will recommend in the chapters that follow will be more successful if they are used in a room in which you have built a sense of community—one founded on a shared commitment of attention to one another.

Community and Attention

We are built to pay attention to other human beings, whether we are using the cerebral machinery dedicated to recognizing individual faces or managing the complex web of relationships that we form through our social media accounts. The Centers for Disease Control and Prevention notes one of the developmental milestones for infants at the end of the second month of life is "pays attention to faces."[1] Research on the development of attention in infants has documented a bias toward human faces almost from birth; that bias intensifies over the course of the first year of life.[2] From the simple focus on faces in infancy, we continue to grow and develop in terms of the extraordinary value we place on our relationships with other human beings. This truth has been recognized by our earliest philosophers and our most contemporary social scientists.

In the *Ethics*, Aristotle notes that "a human being is meant for a city and is of such a nature as to live with others. . . . It is necessary for the happy person to have friends."[3] In her book *Hivemind: The New Science of Tribalism in Our Divided World*, psychologist Sarah Cavanagh argues that we are so fundamentally tied to one another that we unconsciously synchronize thoughts and behaviors with the people around us, which helps explain mysterious social phenomena like mass hysteria or the sudden explosion of trending topics in the news and social media. Our attention orients itself automatically toward other humans, and toward what those other humans are paying attention to.

This is one of the reasons both you and your students find social media accounts so appealing: because they are *social* media accounts. They help us keep tabs on our many levels of social connections: from siblings or parents in other cities to classmates from ancient school days. Facebook connects us with people we might otherwise lose touch with, or friends we perhaps don't see as regularly as we might like. For many of us on academic Twitter, that platform reveals the people and personalities behind the bland research profiles we might read in a bio statement. Instagram shows us pretty pictures, but we link those pictures to the humans who take them, and we feel more connected to them through the images they choose to share with us. The fact that your students scroll obsessively through their social media accounts before class, and sometimes during class, testifies to the extraordinary power that other human beings have over our attention.

Our social media accounts amplify that power, as they give us unfettered access to the social networks of friends and strangers alike, at every moment of the day. The pull of digital social connection is so strong that it can draw us away from our immediate surroundings, including the physical social connections around us. In *A Deadly Wandering: A Mystery, a Landmark Investigation, and the Astonishing Science of Attention in the Digital Age*, author Matt Richtel describes his observation of an experiment in which a subject in a driving simulator has been asked to follow and respond to two streams of texts: one that offers driving directions to a party, and one that provides updates on the (imaginary) people at the party. The subject's driving suffers from having to respond to the texts, just as we might expect. But a second fascinating finding emerges, as Richtel describes it: "At the end of the simulation, [the subject] takes a quiz. What does she remember about the drive? What she recalls are the names and details of all the fictional characters from the party: Michelle and Gendry and Michael. What she misses in the quiz: everything else. The driving directions, the number of interchanges she passed, the buildings she passed."

The pull of social interaction, coupled with the attention-grabbing power of our devices, is so strong that even imaginary people have the power to draw our attention away from our surroundings, including our (simulated) driving. The problem for educators arises when the prospect of interacting with other humans through our phones and laptops tempts us away from our immediate environment, away from the people in the room we are there to learn with.

In recent years, we have seen welcome attention paid to the idea that the classroom represents a community in which learners should feel connected to one another and to the instructor. We ask people to take risks in the classroom; to try at things, fail, and try again; to do hard cognitive work with little immediate reward. For most people, our willingness to engage in those kinds of activities, and the quality of our efforts, will improve when we are attempting them in the company of a supportive community. Community with classmates and instructors not only empowers students to take the risks that learning requires, but it also enhances the experience by expanding the source of ideas and insights to the full range of diverse minds in the room. In *Connected Teaching: Relationship, Power, and Mattering in Higher Education*, Harriet Schwartz argues that "through connection with others we become our most authentic, creative, and productive selves," and that holds as true in the classroom as in other aspects of our lives.[4] We thus should be concerned that getting lost in their devices can prevent students from becoming their better selves in the classroom, as they choose their social media networks over the physical social network around them. We have likely all noticed that distracted students don't participate as much in class discussions. They don't give the comments of their peers the kind of attention that would enable them to respond thoughtfully. When their fellow students are giving presentations, they might tune out completely. If we don't want these things to happen, we have to cultivate community in our classrooms.

To create learning environments that are supported and enhanced by a sense of community, we need to pay attention to one another, students and teacher alike. A group of people sitting together in a room does not constitute a community. A group that has completed an icebreaker on the first day of the semester is also not a community. To create a community, people in the room need to be present to one another, week after week. Communities need continuous tending, in the same way that marriages and friendships do. They need to be, in the words of Stephanie Yuhl, "continuously reinscribed." In the three practical pathways that follow, I will make recommendations for how we can help build community in ways that make us attentive to one another and lay the foundation for attention to the course material.

From Individuals to Community

We tend to make quick and easy assumptions about distracted students in the classroom: they are not taking our courses seriously;

they are texting their friends about the coming weekend; they are watching nonsense on YouTube. But now is the time to acknowledge that students might be distracted from our teaching for very good and understandable reasons. During the semester in which I was finishing this book, I had a student who let me know in the first weeks that her mother was dying of cancer. There was no chance for a cure; they were simply hoping that she would survive through Christmas. You can rest assured that this student was occasionally distracted, and you can be just as assured that she had every right to be. Any attention she paid in my classroom was, as far I was concerned, a pretty miraculous achievement. In every class you teach, every single semester, you will have students who are distracted because of family tragedies, health problems, mental-health challenges such as anxiety or depression, fights with their boyfriends and girlfriends and roommates, a few nights of terrible sleep, an upcoming series of job interviews, the prospect of a failing grade in another course, and much more. The distracting behaviors of these students might have much more to do with trying to manage their lives during your class than with trying to view funny memes on Reddit.[5] That doesn't mean we shouldn't still try to cultivate and sustain their attention; it means that we should not jump so quickly to the assumption that a distracted student is a poor or inconsiderate one.

We should especially take this more empathetic approach toward distracted students who might be questioning their place in your classroom, or in higher education more generally. The increasingly diverse student bodies we have seen in recent decades—diverse in almost every demographic we can imagine—mean that more and more students are coming to our courses with questions about whether they belong in college, whether they fit in with their peers, and whether they have the preparation and skills to succeed. We might think here of first-generation students or traditionally underrepresented students, but really any student can feel overwhelmed and underprepared in certain contexts. These students might be sitting in a classroom in which they have lost the thread of the lecture or activity, and they are looking around and (mistakenly) assuming everyone else gets it. They are wondering what they are doing here, why they are so stupid when everyone else is so smart, and how long it will be before they flunk out in shame. When those feelings become overwhelming, they might do what all of us are inclined to do in moments of anxiety or frustration: turn to the easy comforts of digital devices.

To help these students, we can take an initial step to build community in the classroom, help them feel secure in their seats, and lay the foundation for their attention by beginning the semester with a simple first-week exercise: the values affirmation. The core element of this activity is to ask individuals to identify or articulate values that are most meaningful or important to them. Multiple research studies have shown that this simple exercise has the power to make a positive difference to students, especially those who might feel concerned about their prospects of success in a particular course: women in STEM classes, for example, or first-generation students in introductory college courses. In one study conducted in introductory physics courses with close to four hundred students, researchers used a values-affirmation exercise to try to address a previously documented achievement gap between males and females in the course. Students in the experimental condition viewed a list of potential values (such as family or friends), identified the ones that mattered most to them, and wrote explanations for their choices. They did this twice during the beginning of the semester, once at the beginning of the course and once a few weeks later. Students in a control condition wrote about those values in relation to other people (that is, why the values on the list would be important to other groups of people). Female students in the experimental condition significantly outperformed those in the control condition in the course, raising their modal grades by a full letter.[6] Different versions of this experiment have shown similar results. One study of close to eight hundred students in gateway biology courses showed that first-generation students who completed a values affirmation twice during the semester (early and midway through) not only raised their course grades, but were more likely to continue into the next course in the biology sequence.[7]

Various theories have been proposed about the mechanisms by which values-affirmation exercises produce such significant results in terms of student learning and success. The authors of a third study argue that when students feel isolated or threatened in the classroom community, part of their mental resources—including their attention—is being siphoned away by negative emotions. The values-affirmation exercise reduces the impact of those negative emotions and helps the students recover space in their brains for learning. "By reflecting on their core values in a brief writing assignment," the authors argue, "students can bolster their self-integrity, making identity threats less salient and enabling students to dedicate more cognitive resources to the relevant academic task."[8] Remember that attention is a limited-capacity resource. When some of that capacity is being used up by worry about whether the student belongs or has the ability to succeed in the course, it diminishes what is available for attention to the material. The values affirmation tips the scale of attention away from negative emotions and back toward learning.

More philosophically, a values affirmation establishes that students are individuals in a meaningful community, rather than faceless numbers in a crowd of seats. Students carry their own unique perspectives, ideas, backgrounds, and strengths into the classroom. Each of them thus brings something special to the community, something that might help shape what happens in that space. In this sense, values-affirmation activities are part of a more general shift we can make in education, from a deficit perspective to an asset perspective. In other words, we can view students primarily through a deficit lens: they lack the knowledge and skills we have to offer. But students also come into our rooms with assets: they have prior knowledge that they can bring to our courses, skills in communication or leadership that they can apply to assessments and classroom activities, and life experiences and diverse backgrounds that can help inform discussions and expand the teacher's and students' perspectives. Similarly, students have values that they can express in our courses, and those values might inform the way we teach, the connections they make with their peers, and how they choose to learn and respond to the course material.

The first step you can take toward building a community of attention in your classroom, then, is to invite students to share their values or assets with you. You can do this through exercises on the first days of the semester or through your learning management system. You can do it in ways that are private, so that they are seen only by you, or more public, so that students can see each other's contributions. The possibilities here are multiple, but to get you started, here are two simple sets of questions you could ask students at the start of the semester, in whatever form you choose:

- What are your most important values? Why do they matter to you? How might those values intersect with the subject matter of this course?
- What specific strengths do you bring to our classroom community? How could those strengths help support our work here?

With both of these sets of questions, you might need to provide examples. Most values-affirmation exercises in the research invite students to choose from a list of a dozen or more possibilities. Likewise, if you are asking about strengths, you might need to offer descriptions of possible academic strengths: I am a great team leader; I write very well; I participate frequently in class; I am an excellent notetaker. Have them choose, have them write, have them share, according to what fits best with your classroom context.

Questions like these provide a confidence boost to students who might need it, reduce the demands that negative emotions make on student attention, and support attention through the social connections they help create. They provide you with an opening view of your students as real humans who bring into your classroom their values, histories, and struggles, many of which might resonate personally with you. If students have the opportunity to share their affirmations with one another, they are also likely to experience connections with their peers that might otherwise emerge only from a random discussion comment—or never emerge at all. Those connections can make everyone more present to one another and help build a level of community that supports attention. It's easy to disengage from a room full of anonymous strangers, as you can see from walking into any waiting room in the world, where people are all lost in their phones while they wait for the doctor or car mechanic. Disengaging from a room full of people who have become real to you through a values affirmation doesn't come as easily (which is not to say it can't and won't happen). The ultimate point of a values affirmation, at least in terms of its potential benefits for attention, is to give everyone in the room the opportunity to make themselves known to both you and their peers as a fully-fledged person, and in so doing invite all of us to see and attend to one another more fully.

Attending to Names

Stephanie Yuhl's classroom modeled another effective strategy we can use to sustain community, and the attention of our students, beyond the opening values affirmations: learning and using student names. Our names have tremendous power to capture our attention. This begins as early as a few months into our lives. In 2010, an international research team published the results of a series of experiments that demonstrated the power of names to five-month-old infants. The researchers measured brain waves in the infants while they were exposed to different variations of word strings, including their names. Not only did the infants show increased activity at the sound of their name, but they showed that increased activity even when they heard approximations of their name (such as a name that began with the same syllable). What was even more striking was what happened after the infants heard their own name. Following either their name or random sound patterns, the infants were exposed to pictures of different objects. Their brains showed more activity as they studied these new objects after they heard their name. The researchers explicitly connect the infants' attention to names to subsequent learning: "Hearing her own name prepares the infant to receive new relevant information." Just as curiosity arouses our brains and opens it to new learning (as we shall see in the next chapter), so hearing their name seemed to brighten up these infants' brains and caused them to pay closer attention to what they were observing.[9]

Our tendency to hear and respond to our names receives both affirmation and reinforcement in our earliest schooling. Returning once again to the kindergarten classroom of my wife, I learned there the extensive use that she and other kindergarten teachers make of names in order to help children learn to read. Anne creates cards that contain large-print versions of each child's name and displays them on a grid in her classroom. As they are learning their letters and words, the kindergarteners are encouraged first to recognize their own name and then to compare the letters and syllables they see with those of the other names on the grid. James notices that his name and Jack's begin in similar ways; Maria notes how her name concludes like Sophia's. The children's early lessons in reading are built around attention to names, and of course one of the first things that they learn to write is their own name. Our names are intimately tied not only to our earliest awareness of language, but also to our earliest efforts to read and write.

Studies have demonstrated the connection between names and attention in adults as well.[10] Our names solicit our attention no matter how many distractions are whirring around us, a fact that has been famously dubbed the "cocktail party effect." Envision yourself at a cocktail party, with all of its ambient noise, participating in a conversation. Even though your attention might be fully focused on that conversation, if someone within earshot speaks your name, you will hear it and tune your attention to that direction. I have witnessed the classroom version of this more times than I can count, when I have spoken the name of a student and watched him snap from a reverie, suddenly awake and attentive. Now we come to the happy crossroads at which we will find ourselves in every chapter of this book, where we recognize that a teaching practice that supports attention also supports other important pedagogical values. Speaking the name of a student will perk up her attention in the ways that laboratory experiments have demonstrated. But it also communicates that we are teaching individuals, and each one of them forms an essential part of the classroom community. We want students to feel recognized as people—with their distinctive histories and values and desires and names—and of course students want that as well. In the first days and weeks of the semester, we can invite students to share their values with us; in the days and weeks that follow, we can continuously reaffirm their individuality by learning and using their names.

That's the essence of this section's recommendations: learn and use student names. Some readers will have this as a standard practice in their teaching; others might not. Some of those who do not will attribute it to the fact that they are "not good at remembering names." I have heard this from more faculty members than I care to count. While of course there are variations in people's ability to remember names—just like some of us are better at doing math or throwing a football—the truth is that remembering names is difficult for everyone, and if we want to remember a name we have to make an effort to do so. With the exception of people who might have special cognitive challenges, the likeliest reason that you are not good at remembering names is that you are not putting in enough effort to learn them. Perhaps past experiences in which you have had difficulty remembering a name have convinced you that you aren't good with names, and so you have decided to focus your attention elsewhere. But most people can learn names, even though it may require more effort from some of us than others. If we are expecting students to do the hard work of paying attention in class (which, likewise, will be more difficult for some than others), then we have to be willing to do some hard work ourselves, and mastering their names represents one of those areas in which our efforts will produce benefits for attention.

You can google plenty of strategies to help you better remember the names of your students, but I'll just mention two. First, the reason that we have difficulty remembering names is because the connection between individual human beings and their names typically comes without the kind of context that helps us remember almost everything else we learn. Whenever we learn something new, we are usually building on or modifying our existing knowledge frameworks. You tell me a fact about China, and I will take that fact and try to fit it within my existing knowledge about China. If you tell me about an author I should read, your description of her work might remind me of an author I already know, and that will help me remember the new author.[11] Names, though, are unique identifiers of unique individuals, outside of any meaningful knowledge framework. When I meet a student for the first time, I have no context for her name other than her unique face. So to remember somebody's name, we either have to just memorize it like an isolated fact ("Tirana is the capital of Albania") or we have to associate it with meaning. We can do the latter by putting the student's name within the context of knowledge about him as a person—precisely the kind we might obtain from the values affirmations (or other icebreakers) we conduct at the beginning of the semester. Thus any invitation for students to share information about themselves—through the learning management system, index cards or information sheets, or icebreakers on the first day of class—will give us some context with which we can associate their names. You'll remember how Stephanie Yuhl invited her new students to tell the class something about themselves that would help everyone remember their names. I usually ask students to tell me their hometown and one thing they like to do outside of class. Consider how you can gather such contextual information from students, and use it to help you learn their names in the first week or two of the semester.

Second, we can look to a very large body of research in cognitive psychology to provide us with another tool for memorizing names. As we will discuss more fully in Chapter Seven, that research tells us that if we want to remember something, we have to practice remembering it. The more times we retrieve a fact or idea—or a name—from our memory, the better we are able to retrieve it in the future.[12] It might seem like a great idea to call roll every day, or have students tell you their names every time they walk into the room, but research on the power of memory practice suggests that it will be more effective for you to hear their names a time or two, and then try to remember without their help. I stumbled my way into this technique years ago, without knowing the science behind it, just by name-learning trial and error. I found that after my initial class or two with students, the best way for me to memorize names was to walk around the room at the beginning of each class and try to speak each person's name. Each time I stand awkwardly in front of someone's desk and try to draw a name from my memory, even when I'm unsuccessful, is paving the way for a long-term memory of that person's name. This has now become one of the lighthearted ways in which I bond with students early in the semester. As I walk around the room at the beginning of each class, trying to remember names, they laugh as I stumble and fail, or try to give me small hints and see if they can help me succeed. It's not an easy process, but it works: I know the name of every student in my class by the end of the second or third week of the semester. And it works for reasons that are easily explained by research on how our memories function.

A few years ago, however, I learned that I could still improve my work with student names. I was paired with another faculty member on campus in an observation exercise; she watched me teach and I watched her, and then we met afterward to discuss what we had seen. She pointed out something that I would never have noticed: while I obviously knew the names of all of my students—I was able to hand back writing exercises without asking for names, for example—I almost never used them in class. When someone raised a hand, I pointed to them or just said things like "Yes, go ahead." I was stunned. Had I really memorized all of those names just so I could return their quizzes more efficiently? After my colleague noticed this, and I observed Stephanie Yuhl's persistent use of her students' names throughout the class period, I made a much more deliberate effort to use students' names whenever possible. This quickened the pace of my learning; the more I invited students into our conversations by name, the more rapidly I was able to master their names early in the semester. But using their names also reinforced something I had experienced more sporadically in the past—whenever I called a student's name, I had that student's attention. This occurred not only when I was speaking to that student, but when I subsequently referred to student comments or questions: "That reminds me of something Lucie pointed out to us yesterday . . ." A comment like that not only brings Lucie's attention fully into the room, wherever it may have been, but affirms that she has made a valuable contribution to our community.

To further support a classroom community in which names matter, you should also help students learn each other's names. You don't have to have students stand up at the front of the room and recite everyone's name, as Yuhl does, a strategy that will only work in smaller classes. Learning one another's names can and should be an ongoing value throughout the semester. We do a lot of small group work in my courses, and for the first half of the semester I mix up those groups in different configurations and begin each activity with this simple instruction: "First, introduce yourselves to one another." When they refer to each other in class, I remind them to use their names. I always pause students when they say, "I agree with what she said" and ask them to specify the person they mean. If they don't know the name, I help them and we move on. In doing so, I am continually sending the signal that it's important for us to know and call one another by name—for the formation of our classroom community first, but also for the way that it keeps us all attentive to one another.

If you have classes of fifty or a hundred or more students, and several of those classes in a semester, you won't be able to learn everyone's name. One immediate response to the challenge of learning names in such an environment would be to ask students to place table tents on their desk with their names, so you can call them by name when they ask questions or when you are soliciting responses during an activity or discussion. Such placards won't necessarily help you remember the names of those students when you are outside of the classroom, but they will allow both you and the students to refer to one another by name when someone asks a question or makes a comment to the classroom as a whole.

According to one study, just using student names in a large course, even if you don't have them memorized, might be enough to make students feel recognized as individuals. Instructors in a co-taught, large-enrollment biology course had students use name tents throughout the semester. At the end of the semester, students were asked to identify whether the instructor knew their name, and close to 80 percent of them reported that at least one of the instructors knew their name. When the instructors were actually asked to identify students by name through photographs, they could only correctly identify around 50 percent of them. The researchers also asked students whether it mattered to them that the instructors knew their name, and more than 85 percent of them responded in the affirmative. "I feel like I'm just a face in the crowd most of the time," one student reported, "even in classes where the teacher is really excited about teaching and helping students understand. Knowing my name makes me feel more noticed and welcome."[13] This student comment reinforces a point I made above: the pedagogical strategies that support attention will be even more effective when they are conducted in an environment in which we know and attend to one another as individuals in a community.

The teaching centers of many large universities have web pages devoted specifically to this issue, if you teach large classes and are looking for more concrete strategies to learn student names.[14] What struck me over and over as I read through these tip sheets, and even watched some video tutorials on learning names in large classes, was how many faculty members still made it a priority to try to learn student names, even when they were dealing with a hundred or more students in a class, and even when names were difficult for them to remember. In the end, I suspect that's what matters in those contexts—not whether you have memorized every student's name, but if you are trying to. Carol Holstead, writing for the *Chronicle of Higher Education*, conducted surveys with her large classes in which she asked students "what made them feel that a professor was invested in them and in their academic success." The top response she received: "When the professor learned their names." But one student clarified in the survey that the knowing was less important than the trying; what she really valued was seeing professors "making an effort" to learn her name.[15] Make the effort to learn as many names as you can, use table tents or other strategies that enable you to call names in class when you can't remember, and let students see that you are trying.

Bodies in the Room

The final practical way you can support both community and attention comes through the use you make of the physical space of the classroom. The arrangements of bodies and furniture can orient students toward the course content and the classroom community, or it can leave them vulnerable to distraction. Some of us will have the freedom to shape the interior of the classroom; others will not. But even if we can't design our own rooms or move the furnishings, we can still consider the choices we make in terms of how bodies are positioned and how that changes—or doesn't change—over the course of a class period. All of these choices can affirm the work you have done to create a community of learners, or they can work against that value and isolate you at the front of the room with your students arrayed in their neat rows, all of them with their eyes trained on a screen.

Before I make practical recommendations for classroom practice, I'll begin with two paragraphs that you can photocopy and show to the administration at your institution. The most valuable gift we can give to any instructor who wishes to support the attention of her students is a classroom that is open to multiple configurations, no matter how large the space or the number of students. Derek Bruff, the director of the Vanderbilt Center for Teaching and the author of *Intentional Tech: Principles to Guide the Use of Educational Technology in College Teaching*, argues that his favorite technology in the college classroom is "chairs on wheels."[16] What he means by this is that the most essential component of any classroom is its flexibility, which should be considered far more important than stuffing the room with new technologies, most of which are unlikely to be used by the typical professor. What faculty need are opportunities to configure the classroom in ways that will help support the attention and learning of their students—and that means that they should be using a variety of teaching strategies over the course of the semester, each of which might benefit from a different layout.

Flexibility should take primacy over technology. One study of a classroom redesign at Iowa State involved the transformation of a traditional classroom into a flexible space with movable tables and chairs, portable whiteboards, and shiny new technologies. The researchers conducted focus groups with faculty and students who had used the redesigned space, and they discovered that the new technologies played a secondary role. "The lower cost features," the authors explain, "such as portable whiteboards and movable chairs, appeared to provide the greatest affordances for learning and student engagement." Faculty and students cited the value of being able to solve problems or create work on the portable whiteboards that were visible to the instructor, who could easily check progress and provide feedback.[17] When I served on a committee that helped design classrooms in a new building on my campus, this was the most common request we heard from faculty, much more common than any technology requests: they wanted more whiteboard space. The addition of sophisticated technologies to a classroom will benefit certain professors and make sense for certain disciplines, but this study, like others before and after it, demonstrates that creating an effective classroom space does not require blowing your budget on the latest tech trends. What matters more than the buttons and screens are the opportunities for teachers to design the classroom as they see fit. Because there is not one correct way to build or arrange a classroom that supports attention, administrators and faculty members who help make decisions about classrooms should favor chairs-on-wheels flexibility whenever possible, which will give instructors the freedom they need to think creatively about how the spaces they teach in can support student attention.

We'll consider first the happy prospect that you have been given this gift of flexibility—assigned to teach in a room that has chairs and tables on wheels, generous whiteboard space (or portable whiteboards), the technology you need, and room for you all to wriggle around a little bit. In that case, I would argue that the decisions you make about the arrangement of furniture should depend primarily on how it will help support the attention of your students (and perhaps yourself). When you are lecturing, it seems obvious that faces should be oriented toward the front of the room. If you want students engaged in a whole-class discussion with one another, and yet you still want to preserve the role of moderator, or you want to write down insights from the discussion on the whiteboard, then a double horseshoe seems like the right strategy. But instead of tying every possible teaching strategy to a room configuration, keep in mind the following two principles of attention, some details of which we have discussed already and some of which will appear in later sections of the book.

First, as I have been arguing in this chapter, community matters to attention. At least some of the time, you should opt for layouts in which students can easily see, hear, and work with one another. Equally important, consider whether it will help build community if you ask students occasionally to leave their normal spaces and sit in a different part of the room or engage in paired or group work with new partners. Second, as we saw in Part One, novelty sparks attention. This means that you should not default to the same configuration every time, just as you should not default to the same teaching strategy every day. Every once in a while, begin class by having them help you rearrange the space to create a new room for the students, one that will reinvigorate their attention. Rearranging the room might also occur midway through the class period, especially in longer classes. While it might seem like a waste of a few minutes to pause mid-class to shift the chairs and desks from lecture rows to a discussion horseshoe, this brief physical activity might be precisely what your students need in order to renew their attention for the second part of class. Don't fear a few minutes of messy reorganization; embrace the power of novelty and change.

Some reflection on the ways in which you can configure and reconfigure the space of the classroom might also be precisely what you need in order to kick-start creative thinking about your teaching. If you are walking into the default setting of the classroom for the tenth class period in a row, a little reflection on shaking up the physical space might encourage you to think about an activity that will get the students up and moving, collaborating with one another, or trying something new.

We now consider the less-happy prospect that you are teaching in a space of fixed furniture, with no opportunity to reconfigure. Perhaps you are in a large lecture room with tiered rows of tables or chairs and a single screen on the front wall, and the obvious place for you to stand is behind the podium that someone has set up next to the technology station. Even if you step out from behind the podium, you still are likely to confine yourself to the empty space at the front of the room. Doug Lemov, the author of *Teach Like a Champion*, describes this space as separated from the students by an invisible plane, an "imaginary line that runs the length of the room, parallel to and about five feet in front of the board, usually about where the first student desks start."[18] Remaining behind that imaginary line has the advantage of directing all eyes on you, just as the seats in a theatrical performance train all eyes on what's happening on the stage. It has the disadvantage of separating you from the students behind an imaginary barrier, enabling them to pursue their distractions out of your sight while you lecture to a half-attentive audience.

The first and most obvious solution to this problem is a simple one: break that plane. From the first day of the semester, you should make it a habit to move throughout the space in which your students are sitting. We have discussed already the prospect of you walking into the seats to have informal conversations with your students, which will launch you into this practice. Continue it throughout the class period. Walk up and down the aisles of those tiered rows, stand occasionally and talk about your slides from the sides or middle or back of the room, and as students ask questions or make comments, approach them so you can make eye contact as they speak. Your physical presence invites attention. When my wife gets a student in her kindergarten class who has been diagnosed with attention problems, one of the strategies that always accompanies that student's individual education plan is "close proximity." In other words, that student needs to sit near the teacher. The teacher's presence helps keep the student on task. Our adult learners are no different. You might not want to force students to sit next to you, but you can bring that presence to them in the seats.

For several years early in my career, I attended an annual series of workshops on teaching that included lessons on communication and performance from Ann Woodworth, an acting teacher at

Northwestern University. Drawing from her work coaching students to perform effectively in front of audiences, she provided us with numerous strategies to engage the attention of our students, two of which have stuck with me to this day.

First, make your movements around the room deliberate; stand near different groups of students throughout the class period. Nothing will make a student snap to attention like finding the professor standing nearby. This might sound a little creepy, but think of it instead as working deliberately to make sure you are giving your attention to the students in every corner of the space, just as actors move around the stage and speak lines toward different segments of the theater. Especially in large classes, students can feel like anonymous faces in the room. Join them in their space, and make eye contact with the students around you as you speak or listen to their contributions.

Second, we want students to listen not only to us, but also to each other. A simple tip to support this involves occasionally moving in the other direction from a speaking student, thereby requiring them to address not only you but others in the room. If a student on the right side of the room raises a hand to speak, I might migrate my way over to the left side, putting rows of students between us, which means that the student's comment must be addressed to all of us, not just me. Obviously you should practice this one with care, as an introverted student might find it disconcerting. But too many student questions and comments unfold as a serial dialogue between teacher and student, rather than as a whole-class conversation. This practice invites everyone to attend to the speaking student.[19]

If you are not used to moving around the room, ease your way into these practices. When I first began teaching, I learned a tip from an experienced lecturer of large classes: Before the semester begins, visit the room where you will be teaching and walk around it, speaking from different parts and noticing where students might feel especially disconnected from you and their peers. This initial movement around the empty room will make it easier for you to remember and practice those same movements when students are present. Once the semester begins, in every class period make a concerted effort to stand somewhere else for a while, and direct your attention to the students around you. The more you can give your attention to each one of them, the more they are likely to return that attention to you.

If you are looking for the simplest possible strategy to reduce off-task digital use in your classroom, this might be your lowest-hanging fruit. I have been observing classes of other faculty for many years, and in most of those classes I park myself somewhere in the back of the room, which means I have a very clear view of all of the screens, the students with phones on their laps, and even those students who have their laptop open *and* their phone sitting on the keyboard, so that they are facing the prospect of dual distraction. It's almost always the case that students in the back of the room are more likely to be doing something else on their laptop than the students in the front of the room. The teacher who stands at the front, and has students in the back on their laptops, might be losing the entire back third of the room to distractions over the course of the class period. She will gain many of those students back simply by standing more regularly in their presence, supplementing her efforts toward community with a conscious use of the classroom space in support of attention.

Quick Take

- Begin the semester by providing an opportunity for students to articulate their values and strengths to you and one another. Use this research-supported strategy to help students feel greater confidence in their academic abilities, make a stronger commitment to their learning, and build community in the classroom.

- Learn and use student names; in larger classes, have students bring name placards to class every day. We jump to attention at the sound of our names. Learning and using the names of your students will not only help spark attention but also build community among your students.
- Whenever possible, choose to teach in spaces that have flexible furnishings, and advocate for such rooms. As you plan each class period, spend a moment considering what arrangements of furnishings will best support the kind of attention you want from students that day. Enlist the help of your students to create that room.
- Break the symbolic plane between the front of the room and the students in the seats. Move deliberately to different parts of the room as you lecture, engage in discussion, or monitor individual or group tasks. Give your attention to students in every part of the room.

Conclusion

We began this chapter in a small classroom in New England, and we finish it in a massive lecture hall in Texas. That's where Asha Rao plies her trade in biology, teaching introductory classes of up to three hundred students at Texas A&M. And yet, in spite of the enormous number of students who pass in and out of her classroom every day, Rao makes community a fundamental value of her teaching, beginning with her efforts to learn as many student names as possible. "I want each of the 300 students in my class," she told me, "to know that he/she is not just another body, but is an individual whose presence and learning I deeply care about." She communicates this dedication to her students with a very simple statement at the beginning of the semester: "Your job is to learn amazing things about biology . . . and my job is to get to know you." That sentence, which Rao said to me during a workshop I was conducting at Texas A&M, might be the most perfectly concise statement I have heard about the commitment we should make to the community of students in the room.

The most prominent way Rao manifests this commitment to her students is through her industrious efforts to learn their names. "I will give you everything possible to help you learn important concepts in biology and earn an A in this class," she says to them on the first day of the semester, "and you will provide me with name tents and anything else you can, to help me learn your names." In response to my post-visit interview questions, Rao listed for me the numerous ways in which she challenges herself to learn names throughout the semester:

- "When students are busy working in groups or discussing, I walk the classroom, stop by groups, look at their name tents and try to associate their names and faces."
- "Outside of class, when students visit me during my office hours, I ask them to sign their names on a signup sheet. I then use the names to interact with them in my office. When the same students return to my office hours the next time, I try to recall their names before they sign in."
- "I frequently log in to [the Texas A&M portal], which has the image roster of my class, and put names and faces together."

In 2020, Texas A&M completed an innovative new classroom building, specifically designed to create a "culture of excellence in teaching and learning." The building includes a large lecture hall with seats circled around the lecturer at the center, which means that there are only eight rows, reducing the distance between the teacher and the students in the "back" of the room. Rao was one of the university instructors selected to teach in this new room, in part because of her deep commitment to building community even in the largest of classes.

The core lesson I have learned from the research on community and attention in teaching, as well as from teachers like Stephanie Yuhl and Asha Rao, is that attention has a very strong social component. Attention from the teacher invites attention from the student. Perhaps more accurately, attention *to* the student—the individual student, named and valued—invites attention *from* the student. The reverse is equally true: distraction invites distraction. When we don't give our full attention to our students, they return the favor. When we don't provide opportunities for them to develop meaningful relationships with one another, they are more likely to disengage from the room full of strangers around them. If we want our students less distracted in class, the first thing we must do is pay attention to the extent to which we create a strong sense of community in the classroom, and work deliberately to develop structures and strategies that support our students' attention to us and to one another.

5

Curious Attention

IN THE PREVIOUS two chapters, we considered the strategies that will lay the foundation for attention in your classroom, first through the policies you create and then through the community you establish. Assume your students have been convinced that attention matters, and that they feel welcomed and connected in your classroom. Even in such a supportive room of peers, people can be bored and distracted, if nothing in that room seems worthy of their attention. What we teachers ultimately hope will capture and sustain the attention of our students is the fascinating subject matter of our courses. In this chapter, we thus shift our focus toward a more challenging question: What strategies can you use to cultivate the attention of your students toward political theory, or British literature, or mammalian anatomy?

Most teachers have their first opportunity to cultivate the attention of students toward their course content through the syllabus and the opening days of the semester—and, in my view, too many of us drop the ball in these key moments. I did myself for a very long time. I want you to envision yourself as a nineteen-year-old student, plopped down in a seat in Professor Lang's section of British Literature Survey II, a course that is required for English majors and that also counts as a general-education requirement for all students. In other words, it's a mix of students who are almost exclusively taking the course to fulfill some degree requirement or another. Professor Lang walks into the classroom, introduces himself, and then hands you a packet of papers that begins with this description of the course:

> Following upon British Literature Survey I, this course will introduce you to the major works of British literature, and their cultural and historical contexts, from approximately 1800 to the present day. These two centuries are generally divided into four broad literary periods: Romantic, Victorian, Modernist, and Contemporary. Because of the large amount of ground the course covers, we will focus upon reading the major canonical authors from this period who represent the most significant trends in the development of modern literature.

Have I captured your attention? Have I convinced you that reading British literature will improve your life, or enrich your understanding of the world, or even provide you with any enjoyment? Have I whipped you up to a fevered pitch of excitement, eager to dive right into the semester? If those opening words weren't enough to send students reaching for their phones, I would have followed reading this paragraph aloud with a long explanation of all the rules of the classroom, intimidating descriptions of the work I would be assigning, and warnings about what would happen if they plagiarized. Some variation of these words and procedures were all vintage Jim Lang, circa 2002, in pretty much every course I taught.

This reflects the way too many of us open learning experiences that we hope will capture student attention. We show our courses to students as boxes of content, packaged in bloodless syllabus descriptions like the one presented above. The issue here is not so much the actual opening paragraph of the syllabus, which often has been written for (or lifted from) a course catalog and is required to appear in some form. But describing our courses with content-box language, even just on the syllabus, can affect everything we do. It might condition our first-day activity and lead us to hand out the syllabus and then provide an introductory lecture on the course, instead of seeking to capture the attention of our students with an intriguing question or a fascinating problem. It might lead us to focus more on what we need to cover, rather than what students need to learn. It might lead us to blame students for their lack of attention, rather than considering the possibility that we could be doing more to bring the material to life and make it deserving of their attention.

In Chapter Four, we considered how to make students present in support of their learning. In this chapter, we shift our focus to considering how we can use curiosity, one of the great drivers of human attention, to shape the encounters that our students have with course material. Curiosity makes us sit up and take notice, makes us wonder and reflect, and spurs our desire to know more. It captures our attention and can hold it well beyond the confines of the classroom. But not all curiosities are equal. To understand the role that curiosity can play in harnessing attention and directing it toward learning, we will explore some variations in this very complex human emotion, and then consider the choicest ways to place curiosity at the forefront of your courses and how to use it as a core strategy for the support of student attention.

Curiosity and Attention

"*Homo sapiens,*" writes Josh Eyler in his book *How Humans Learn: The Science and Stories Behind Effective College Teaching,* "is the species of curiosity."[1] Eyler, the director of faculty development at the University of Mississippi, draws this conclusion after an extensive review of the literature about curiosity, tracing its origins back along both evolutionary and developmental lines. Curiosity first helped drive our evolution as a species; Eyler describes it as an "evolutionary adaptation that has allowed us to discover, to invent, and to learn. Our species has been shaped by nature to be wide-eyed children . . . always striving to know more."[2] Curiosity drove our early ancestors to nibble at new food sources, explore strange territories, and communicate with other social groups. Curiosity pushed us to experiment, explore, and discover. The curiosity-driven evolution of humans plays itself out in a parallel way within individual human lives. Curiosity helps each one of us grow and learn from the earliest stages of our life. Children are driven by their curiosity to build an understanding of the world around them, to resolve discrepancies or obstacles they encounter, and to communicate with others. Of course, we are not the only species that demonstrates curiosity; primates in general are curious animals, as are other species to varying degrees. But our curiosity combines with other aspects of the human brain to make us animals that have achieved remarkable feats of both learning and application of that learning to the world around us.

In spite of its importance to human development, curiosity proves extremely difficult to define. Mario Livio is an astrophysicist whose account of the origins and effects of curiosity in humans was driven by his own wide-ranging curiosity. In his book *Why?: What Makes Us Curious*, he argues that "what we refer to as curiosity may actually encompass a family of intertwined states or mechanisms that are powered by distinct circuits in the brain."[3] In other words, we can't locate just one part of the brain in which curiosity resides; like attention, it seems to draw from and connect to different aspects of our emotions and cognitive processes. However we define it, the research is clear that we learn more effectively and deeply when we bring curiosity to a task. Livio writes that curiosity is "a drive state for information. . . . [It] is the desire to know why, how, or who."[4] That drive state can be directed toward a specific end, such as seeking particular information, or it can be more open-ended, simply wondering and thinking about bigger questions. In either case, the state of curiosity opens our minds for exploration and more firmly fixes into our brains whatever we learn.

One group of researchers conducted a fascinating experiment that demonstrated the powerful link between curiosity and learning. The researchers showed subjects a long series of questions and had them rate their curiosity about each one. Then the researchers put the subjects in a brain scanner, and showed them the questions again; after the subjects saw the questions this time around, they experienced a short delay, saw an image of a face, and then saw the answer to the question. When they returned a day later, the subjects had a better memory of the answers to the questions they were curious about—and also a better memory of the random faces that popped up before they saw those answers. Curiosity opened their minds to new learning, and they became like sponges that soaked up whatever they encountered in that aroused, curious state.[5]

One of the reasons that curiosity spurs learning is that it directs our attention to the subject we are pursuing. Cognitive scientists Yana Weinstein and Megan Sumeracki devote a chapter to the connection between attention and learning in their book *Understanding How We Learn*, and they review a theoretical model that explains two types of interest that students can take in our course material: individual and situational. Individual interest refers to the prior interest that you bring into a novel context, which will drive you to explore and learn in order to satisfy it. Situational interest arises as the result of you arriving on the scene and finding something there that intrigues you, which spurs you to want to know more. Using their own book to explain the difference between the two types of interest, the authors explain that "individual interest is the extent to which you yourself are already interested in applying cognitive psychology to education, whereas situational interest is how absorbing our text is or how enjoyable you find the illustrations."[6] Swapping in the word curiosity for interest gives us *individual curiosity* and *situational curiosity*, and the connection to education is easy to make. Students with individual curiosity would come into a course wanting to know more about the subject matter (for example, students in a psychology course who always wondered about how their minds work), whereas students with situational curiosity might find themselves unexpectedly intrigued by the subject matter (for example, a student who was required to take psychology and discovered there how fascinating brains were).

Weinstein and Sumeracki make the case that "as teachers, we are in control of situational interest, but not of individual interest."[7] At one level, this is obviously true. We can't control the interests or curiosity that students bring into our courses. Our first responsibility, then, is to see how we can make the material as fascinating as possible in order to stimulate their situational curiosity. Most of the recommendations in this chapter will focus on the support of attention through the development of situational curiosity in your courses. But we shouldn't give up entirely on the prospect that individual curiosity can play a role in our teaching work. A student who arrives to a psychology course without any understanding of psychology or particular interest in it will most certainly have other types of interests and curiosities. The student might, for example, be a budding entrepreneur, whose primary goal has always been to learn how to succeed effectively in the market. It will most certainly turn out, though, that things she learns about the human mind and human behavior can help her become a more successful entrepreneur, if the instructor gives her the opportunity and encouragement to see the connection between the course content and her own interests. The individual curiosity that students bring into their courses, then, can always be solicited and connected to the material. These two different types of curiosity strike me as intertwined, able to influence and strengthen one another in an educational environment.

The recommendations that follow cover four ways you can induce better attention in your courses through curiosity, the first three of which connect more with situational curiosity, in that they seek to pique the curiosity of students in relation to the course material you present to them. The final recommendation invites students to bring their own questions to bear on the course material, and hence leans more toward individual curiosity.

The Course Question(s)

I began this chapter with the opening paragraph of a syllabus because our course descriptions provide us with a handy testing ground for our ability to cultivate curiosity in our courses. If the goal is to begin the semester by invoking the situational curiosity of our students, then the first thing we have to do is shift away from content-box course descriptions, and instead set those descriptions on the launchpad of human curiosity by asking questions. In his book *Why Don't Students Like School?: A Cognitive Scientist Answers Questions About How the Mind Works and What It Means for the Classroom*, cognitive psychologist Daniel Willingham argues that most of the courses we teach are designed to help students answer deep and fascinating questions: Why do some people get sick and others don't? What is the best form of government? Why do humans speak so many different languages? Unfortunately, too many of us skip these big questions and go right to the answers. "The material I want students to learn," Willingham writes, "is actually the answer to a question. *On its own, the answer is almost never interesting.* But if you know the question, the answer may be quite interesting."[8] The implication here is that we should begin the process of framing and presenting our courses by identifying the questions that underpin them, and enfold the course content within those questions.

But not all questions are equal or alike. Some of our course questions might be small and specific, and some might be large and mysterious. Ideally, a course will include both kinds of questions. Ian Leslie's provocative book *Curious: The Desire to Know and Why Your Future Depends on It* gives us more precise language for distinguishing between questions large and small, specific and open-ended. Leslie points out that we can be curious about both puzzles and mysteries. Puzzles intrigue us, but they do so because we know they have a solution that just happens to evade us at the moment. We expect to solve them or have them solved for us. Your favorite mystery novelist excels in the creation of puzzles, which she generally resolves for you by the end of the story. Mysteries are those big, open-ended questions that fascinate us, and yet have no easy answers, or no answers at all. Mysteries are capable of long, sustained study or exploration without resolution. Your favorite poet, whose body of work leads you continually to wonder about the meaning of human existence, deals in mysteries.[9]

To begin the process of evoking curious attention to your course material, take a look at that first passage of prose that your students will see when they encounter the course, and ask yourself whether you have written it to present a box of content, or to stir curiosity for the intellectual journey they are preparing to undertake. What is the mystery that lies at the heart of your discipline? How can you evoke it for students in the opening of your syllabus? Identifying a mystery at the heart of your course can be challenging initially, especially if you have not thought in these terms before. But consider the fact that almost every academic discipline arose as the result of something that humans wanted to know, and that eluded us. We might study psychology because we wonder why people act in sometimes baffling ways; we might study physics because we wonder about how the material world operates; we might study literature because we want to know how stories and language can have such a powerful impact on us. Whatever reason you study what you study, something about it caught your attention and provoked your curiosity at a very basic level. Can you find your way back to that original moment, and then evoke it for your students?

This notion was captured well in an interview that education writer Jessica Lahey conducted with Teller, of Penn & Teller fame. Before becoming a magician, Teller taught Latin for six years, and Lahey asked him about how he got students interested in that subject matter. One of the first things he mentions is that teachers have to retain their initial wonder at the subject: "If you don't have both astonishment and content," he says, "you have either a technical exercise or you have a lecture." To get beyond technical presentations of material and into the kind of learning experience that grabs the attention of students, you have to keep that astonishment alive in yourself. The interview concludes with a beautiful statement of how that sense of wonder connects to learning: "When I go outside at night and look up at the stars, the feeling that I get is not comfort. The feeling that I get is a kind of delicious discomfort at knowing that there is so much out there that I do not understand and the joy in recognizing that there is enormous mystery, which is not a comfortable thing. This, I think, is the principal gift of education."[10]

Note the appearance of the word "mystery" here, evoking once again the notion that we are driven to attention and learning by the questions that puzzle us, that keep us wondering. These are the questions we need to surface in ourselves and present to our students.

Rebecca Zambrano, a director of online faculty development, suggests a number of pathways toward helping instructors develop course-level conceptualizations that will capture the attention and pique the curiosity of students (the following are excerpted quotes from her essay):

1. What fills you with a sense of wonder? What aspects of the content you teach lead you to a sense of awe at the deeper mysteries beneath the skill sets you teach?
2. What large questions remain unanswered by the great minds of your field?
3. What are some of the most "magical" paradoxes or mysteries in your field of knowledge? Perhaps there are case studies that seem to contradict each other or data discrepancies that seem impossible to reconcile given current knowledge.
4. What stories of wonder and passion led foundational thinkers in your field to give so much of their lives to unraveling important mysteries?[11]

I love the notion embedded here: that we need to reconnect with our own questions about our discipline before we can cultivate the questions of our students—and their attention. To begin the process of using curiosity to capture the attention of your students, use questions like the ones above in order to rewrite the course overview that appears at the beginning of your syllabus. Write it like you are inviting students into the most fascinating learning journey of their lives. Don't worry if they skim right over it when you first hand them the syllabus; the process of rewriting that opening paragraph will help remind you of what makes your discipline so fascinating, and your curiosity about its deepest questions can then spill over into all other aspects of the course—including and especially the first class period.

The First Day of Class

The first day of the course provides our first opportunity to capture attention—an objective that will be made more difficult if you begin by handing out and reviewing the syllabus, which was my modus operandi for many years. But nothing says "check your phone" more than the teacher walking into the first class of the semester and providing an overview of the course, all of the work students will have to do, and all of the policies that will govern their behavior. Begin instead with the goal of evoking curiosity.

One strategy for doing this is to create an opening-day activity that gets students engaged in thinking about or trying to solve the mystery that you have identified in your syllabus. Cate Denial, a historian at Knox College in Illinois, provides an excellent example of what this might look like.[12] In her history courses, Denial wants students to find fascination in the way history changes, how the way we think about an issue like slavery today differs from how historians thought about it fifty years ago. New sources are discovered, new perspectives are developed, and the story we tell about the past changes. That raises some pretty profound, epistemic mysteries: Can we ever really know the truth about the past? Does such truth even exist? What does that say about our understanding of our own pasts, both individual and collective?

Denial wants her students to begin asking these questions about the past on the very first day of the semester, and has developed an intriguing method for getting them to do so. After welcomes and introductions, she hands out a "document packet" of sources related to a single historical event. The contents of each packet vary from student to student; some items are in every packet, others are not. For this exercise, Denial chooses a historical event that she will not cover in the course, in order to ensure that all students—including those who might have signed up for the course because of prior interest or expertise—will have to struggle with unfamiliar sources. Students are put in random groups, which she has selected in advance, and asked "to put the sources in the order that makes the most sense to them, and tell the story the sources supply." This activity, according to Denial, takes fifteen to twenty minutes of class time. Afterward, each group is asked to share their story with the class. Of course, no two stories end up alike, and Denial then leads a discussion about that, which allows her to introduce a core theme of the class: "History changes as more sources are found, old ones are re-examined, and new theories suggest new interpretive frameworks. For the duration of the term, every student in the class will be a working historian, putting sources together to understand one part of our collective past." The puzzle of this first-day activity—How can I put together these sources in a way that tells a coherent story?—leads Denial and her students to the mystery at the heart of her courses, and at the heart of her discipline.

Denial's technique works especially well because it engages students with the puzzle of the day and the mystery of the course by having them work with course materials. Talented lecturers might be able to draw students into a mystery with a great presentation of a story, case, or problem that points to the deep questions of the discipline. But if you want students to participate actively in your course throughout the semester, it is best to foster that engagement on the first day and set the tone for the semester. Build the puzzle, and let them take a crack at solving it. Consider classic or contemporary cases or problems in your discipline, present them to students, and see what they come up with: Here's an example of a business that did everything right according to accepted management theory, and yet failed spectacularly in the first year. What happened? A woman came into the doctor's office presenting with the very familiar symptoms of the flu, and a week later died with the following complications. What could explain this? A skeleton with the following characteristics was discovered in a remote corner of Europe that didn't fit with then-contemporary theories about how humans evolved. What other theories could explain its strange features? When students have had the opportunity to learn about and wrestle with these puzzles, finish by letting them know that the course will provide them many opportunities to engage with such fascinating problems, and with the deeper questions that underpin them.

The Daily Questions

Questions designed to evoke the situational curiosity of students should continue beyond the first days of the semester. The first time I observed a question-based lesson plan was a decade ago, when I visited the classroom of Greg Weiner, then a professor of political science and now the provost of Assumption University. At the beginning of class, he showed students four questions on a slide. He then proceeded through a standard mix of lecture and discussion. At the end of the period, he returned to the questions in order to remind students that the class material for that day had been intended to supply them with potential answers. This strategy had the positive side effect of demonstrating to students that they had acquired some concrete knowledge over the course of the class period: their ability to answer the questions on the slide at the end of class meant that they knew more than they had before. Weiner had also made those questions available to the students in advance of class, to help guide their reading and homework. But having the questions visible at the start was designed to draw out their curiosity in those crucial opening moments of the period.[13]

Another colleague of mine, Aisling Dugan, takes a different approach: the question is the same every day, but it is applied to different content. Dugan teaches a course in microbiology on my campus, and she begins each class period by putting up a slide with the "microbe of the day." Next to the name and image of the microbe, she lists some categories that scientists would use to understand and classify it. The question she poses is a simple one: "What can you discover about this microbe in each of these categories?" Class formally opens with students spending five minutes looking up everything they can find about that microbe, using their phones and laptops. Dugan allowed me to observe this opening ritual in her class one afternoon, and it was striking to see how quickly the pre-class student conversations quieted down, and how intently the students became absorbed in this five-minute task. My informal survey of the room, from my vantage point in the back row, showed me that every student was on task during those five minutes, seeing what they could discover about the microbe of the day—which was the one that causes the plague, chosen playfully by Dugan to mark Halloween that day. After five minutes were up, she asked students to report what they had learned. Together the room filled out the picture of this scary microbe, and throughout Dugan was able to connect their findings to other questions: "Do you remember which previous microbe had that shape? And where do anaerobic microbes live in the body?" Dugan's classroom demonstrates that we don't have to scramble to find completely different questions every day. The basic form of the question might remain the same, but we can apply it anew to each day's course material.

My favorite method for posing daily questions to students takes the form of the peer instruction pedagogy developed by Harvard physicist Eric Mazur. I have seen him model this technique, and discuss its origins, on more than one occasion.[14] In his physics courses, Mazur explains, he found that his students were able to use memorized formulas to solve problems without really understanding the concepts that underpinned them. So he began posing conceptual questions and asking students to respond with handheld clickers, the results of which were instantly visible to him. He could then see how well the students understood whatever concept was at play in that class period and adjust his teaching accordingly. If few students got the answer correct, he would return to the material; if many were right, he knew he could move on. The handheld clickers that Mazur used now have been mostly abandoned for free online programs like Poll Everywhere or Socrative, which allow faculty to write questions into a presentation slide and students to respond with their phones, tablets, or laptops, the results again immediately visible to all. (Mazur always points out, however, that low-tech versions of this process work equally well, with colored index cards or even just raised hands or fingers accomplishing the same result, if a little more messily.)

But what's most striking to me about the process that Mazur developed was the extent to which it seems designed to first raise and then intensify the curiosity of students. The core process of peer instruction as Mazur practiced it followed this pattern:

1. The instructor poses the question.
2. The students submit their responses.
3. The students have to turn to a peer, explain their response, and listen to the explanation of their peers.
4. The students have the opportunity to change their mind, and can resubmit their answer.
5. The instructor invites some students to explain their answers.
6. The instructor reveals the answer.

Throughout this process—which could take just a few minutes or last as long as a half hour, depending on the time you allot to steps three through five—both curiosity and attention are slowly building. Mazur argues, and I would concur, that having students make an initial commitment to an answer is a crucial part of the process. Once they have committed, they are curious to know whether they are right. In other words, the process wouldn't be as effective if you simply posed a question and asked a few students for their responses. In the peer instruction model, everyone commits, everyone speaks to a peer, and everyone thus has a stake in learning the answer.

I have seen the power of this approach in my own classes, but my favorite places to use it are in the faculty workshops that I conduct on other campuses or in conference keynotes. I am often asked to speak to these groups about how research on learning and attention can inform our teaching. After I present some basic principles of learning theory, I tell the audience about a 2013 publication in which a team of psychologists analyzed ten common learning strategies that students use.[15] The psychologists' purpose was to determine what research indicated about the effectiveness of each of those strategies; they rated all ten of them as high, moderate, or low utility. In my talks, I describe all of this, provide some background on the study, and then show the faculty five of those ten strategies on a Poll Everywhere slide. Only one of the five was rated high utility, I explain; keeping in mind the learning principles I just described for you, see if you can identify that high utility strategy and use your device to respond. I then walk them through the peer instruction process, asking them to explain their answer to a peer, letting them change their mind if they wish, and having some participants explain their responses. After the group has heard those responses, the atmosphere in the room is always the same, whether I am doing this activity with a dozen people or five hundred: everyone is on the edge of their seat, wondering whether they got it right. I never have the attention of the room more fully than in the moments before I reveal the answer to the question I have posed. Every time I conduct this exercise I see how effectively peer instruction gradually builds and intensifies curiosity—and, with curiosity, attention.

Your discipline or course—or even just your teaching personality—might not lend itself to asking factual questions that have a correct answer. Your questions might be more designed to get the flavor of the room on a particular topic, or to invite students to express their understanding of a text, or begin to form their convictions about a problem. You know best what kinds of questions emerge from the heart of your discipline and your course, and even what questions fascinate you. If you can identify one great question per day, or even one great question per week, and make it a centerpiece of your teaching, you can turn the classroom into a place where answers come in response to questions, instead of a place where answers are provided whether anyone has questions or not.

"What Question Do *You* Have?"

I've spent much of my career working with faculty to advocate for small changes that can make a positive difference to our teaching, and one of the best changes I've ever heard recommended was the simplest one you could possibly imagine. So many of us finish or pause in our presentation of material and say, "Any questions?"—a prompt that is usually met either with silence or with a question or two from your most vocal students, and that might be viewed by some as a quick opportunity to check their phones or hop online. This is unfortunate, because the formulation of questions has multiple learning benefits for students. In a review of the role that student questions play in the learning process, Christine Chin and Jonathan Osborne argue in the journal *Studies in Science Education* that "the act of 'composing questions' *focuses the attention of students* on content, main ideas, and checking if content is understood" (italics mine).[16] The small change here, designed to elicit those benefits, involves a very simple rephrasing of this question into a slightly modified one: "What questions do you have?" The logic behind this question is that you have just been hearing about complex material and ideas, so *of course* I know you have questions, and I am very willing right now to pause here and learn all about them. The question has to be accompanied by actions that reinforce its intention, which include waiting for at least ten or fifteen or even thirty seconds, and maybe even doing a little bit of browbeating when no one responds immediately: "C'mon, I know you have questions. I want to hear them, and I'm willing to wait." You won't have to do this more than a time or two before your students get the idea and start asking their questions.

You can solicit their questions in this informal way, but I like a bit of creative thinking along the lines of this strategy from Meriah Crawford, a professor at Virginia Commonwealth University. Crawford found, as many of us have, that students often don't ask questions in response to open solicitations, and that these "unasked questions represent anxieties and uncertainties that negatively affect students' performance in class and inhibit their learning." She thus developed a concrete method for soliciting student questions at critical points during the semester: on the first day, as well as on days surrounding key assignments, she hands out index cards and asks students to write down a question they have. She collects them, shuffles them in order to maintain anonymity, and then takes the time to respond. On her course evaluations, one student responded to this activity by saying that the index cards were "a good way to get unresolved questions answered as well as possibly obtain crucial information I hadn't thought about based on the answers to other students' questions."[17] Thus, not only does this technique allow students to voice and hear responses to their questions, but it allows them to open up to the questions of others and wonder about those as well.

A final way to elicit questions from students, and surface whatever individual curiosity they bring into your classroom, could come through a simple variation on a popular teaching technique in higher education called "the minute paper," in which an instructor ends class by asking students to write short responses to the following questions: "What was the most important thing you learned today?" and "What are you still confused or uncertain about?" I frequently mention this strategy to faculty when I am giving workshops on teaching, and on one occasion a participant raised her hand and suggested we consider a third question: "What do you want to know more about?" Put in terms of this chapter, we might rephrase that questions as, "When it comes to this course material, what are you curious about?" I love that question as a way to evoke the individual curiosity of students, which should provide you with information on what might be most likely to capture their attention in an upcoming class period. Once they have told you what they are curious about, find ways to acknowledge their questions or provide opportunities for them to search for answers. You might offer them the chance to pursue their questions in an assessment, such as an upcoming paper or project. More simply, you can keep their interests in mind as you plan each class period and find ways to point to their questions. Nothing will make students sit up and pay attention like speaking or writing their name and mentioning a question they asked previously, noting that the lecture, reading, or discussion for that day will help to address it.

Quick Take

- Foreground questions at the opening of your course. Remind yourself about the deep questions from which your course material emerges, and then rewrite the opening paragraph of your syllabus, as much for your benefit as for the benefit of your students.

- Begin the course with a first-day activity designed to invite student curiosity through some engagement activity; ask them to solve a puzzle at the heart of your mystery. Hold off on presenting your syllabus until you have piqued their curiosity.
- Use questions, problems, and stories along the way of your course. Identify the moments of transition, or the openings of new units, as times when you can inject life and attention into your course with questions.
- Develop methods for actively soliciting student questions. Formulating questions can help students improve their learning, and hearing their questions can help you identify future topics and strategies that will get their attention.

Conclusion

In *The Distracted Mind*, Adam Gazzaley and Larry Rosen provide one final conceptual framework for understanding how questions and curiosity can support attention and reduce distraction. They argue that distraction occurs as a result of a conflict between two fundamental features of the brain: our ability to create and plan high-level goals and our ability to control our mind and our environment as we take steps to complete those goals. The challenging and complex nature of the goals we set for ourselves means that they require an extraordinary amount of work from our attention system. We have to decide, plan, attend to individual tasks, monitor progress, and more. As they explain: "Our ability to establish high-level goals is arguably the pinnacle of human brain evolution. Complex, interwoven, time-delayed, and often shared goals are what allow us humans to exert an unprecedented influence over how we interact with the world around us, navigating its multifaceted environments based on our decisions rather than reflexive responses to our surroundings."[18]

Not all of our goals take the form Gazzaley and Rosen articulate, but almost all of the tasks that we ask students to complete in our courses could rightfully be described as "complex, interwoven, and time-delayed." Everything from preparing for a test to writing an essay to completing homework problems will entail multiple cognitive processes, spread out over time, working together to achieve that goal. The best way to understand the origins and nature of distraction, according to Gazzaley and Rosen, is to envision it as a "mighty clash" between our impressive ability to set and pursue such complex goals and the features of our brain that welcome easy distraction.

The real purpose behind cultivating curiosity in the classroom is to help students develop learning goals that matter to them. When I am curious, I have an immediate goal: I want to learn more. The stronger my curiosity, the more I focus my attention—and the less I feel tempted by distraction. If we can create genuine curiosity in our students, we are boosting their ability to resist distractions by helping them establish meaningful goals. Moreover, a little distraction won't hurt a truly curious student. I have been distracted a thousand times during the writing of this book, but I came back to it every time and pursued it to the end, because I never stopped being fascinated by a simple question: What helps students pay attention? Likewise, we need to help students discover the questions that will become their academic goals, and that will give them the boost they need to put away their distractions and focus on learning. If we envision distraction as arising from a conflict between the pursuit of a goal and the obstacles that interfere with that pursuit, we can then see that one way to reduce the power of distraction is to maximize the power of our goals. The cultivation of curiosity gives the brains of our students a helping hand in the mighty clash between goals and distraction.

6

Structured Attention

FOR CHRISTMAS ONE YEAR my wife bought us tickets to the Boston symphony, which meant we could have one of those sophisticated adult evenings that we always long for but almost never seem to actually experience. On a cold January evening, we settled into our seats at the symphony hall after a nice dinner at a nearby restaurant and perused the printed program. A very short modern work would be followed by a work from a lesser-known classical composer, or at least a composer that was lesser-known to me. The evening would conclude with the famous *New World Symphony* by Antonín Dvořák, a work with which Anne and I were both familiar.

At 8:00 p.m., the conductor walked out to the front of the stage, gave us all a bow, and waved his baton to launch the evening. The first of the three works was quick and had some nice moments; I never felt like I found my footing with it, but it was short and dynamic enough that it held my attention. It was followed by a brief break in which the musicians reset themselves and the rest of us shifted around in our seats for a minute or two. The second piece of music, according to the liner notes, consisted of five separate movements, but—unlike a typical symphony—did not contain clear breaks between them. It played continuously for twenty-plus minutes. Those twenty minutes, I will confess, were long ones. The music was completely unfamiliar to me, so I had to listen carefully to see if I could hear melodies or musical themes that I could latch on to as the piece progressed. I enjoy classical music, and often listen to it while I am reading or writing, but I was apparently not sophisticated enough to identify whatever melodies or themes held that piece together. As a result, it didn't take long for my mind to start drifting. I wasn't the only one, either. I could see many of my fellow patrons were in a similar boat, as quite a few heads around me were swiveling to view their fellow concertgoers or the decorative features of the concert hall. Although I did not pull out my phone, the unfamiliarity of the music and the lack of a clear structure in the piece left me yearning to.

A longer intermission followed the conclusion to this piece, during which time we could get drinks or use the restroom, and then the orchestra launched into Dvořák's symphony. One of the most striking features of the *New World Symphony* is the fact that Dvořák builds it up from some very simple, catchy melodies, ones that would not be out of place in an Irish folk tune or even a contemporary pop song. But the symphony does something quite brilliant with these simple melodies. Rather than just repeating them over and over again—in contrast to, say, Maurice Ravel's *Boléro* or, for parents of younger children, the "Baby Shark" song—the melodies are subject to several types of variation. They are passed around from instrument to instrument, thus giving them a different flavor with each repetition. You begin to notice, as the work progresses, that you are hearing shorter pieces of the melody—just the opening few notes, for example—and then some new twist on the remaining part of it. It seems to grow and evolve, taking different forms as the work unfolds. Finally, Dvořák (and the conductor) varies both the volume and the speed of the piece throughout. At times we are walking with it very slowly, and at times it gallops. There are moments when one lone instrument calls out the melody, and other moments when a host of instruments are playing the tune. In short, the symphony does not hesitate to draw its listeners in with a catchy melody, but then it keeps us on our toes as we listen for the ways it returns to us in many different variations. Because the core melodies are repeated so frequently, change and variety play an essential role in sustaining the listener's attention.

In this chapter, we will consider how to sustain student attention throughout the entire class period by drawing inspiration from creative artists who have long counted as one of their tasks to keep listeners and viewers' attention to works that stretch over extended periods of time, especially composers and playwrights. Creators of live, prolonged performances of any kind demonstrate a clear awareness of the limited attention of their audiences, which helps explain the structure of many of these experiences. Plays unfold in acts and scenes, with short transitions between segments, and usually at least one longer intermission when patrons can hit the restroom or have a drink. Classical music concerts are likewise parceled into three or four different performances, with an intermission, and symphonies are divided into movements. The changes and transitions are even more regular at modern rock or jazz concerts, where new songs are launched every four or five or ten minutes. Today's modern TED Talks likewise recognize the limits of our attention spans, and speakers are asked to keep the length of most talks between ten and twenty minutes.

The classroom is one of the only places where we expect humans in seats to maintain their attention through an extended, uninterrupted performance of an hour or more. I suspect this happens because we (the teachers) are able to keep ourselves fully engaged during the class period, and we expect that the students should be likewise attentive. I once had the opportunity to observe a talented lecturer teach a seventy-five-minute class. He paced the room energetically, summarized the ideas of great thinkers in his field, made funny comments, and told entertaining stories. I was impressed with how thoroughly he was engaged in his own performance; he was truly in the zone, and I'm sure the hour-plus class period flew by for him. The story was not the same for his students, whom I also observed throughout the period. They cycled among rapt attention, struggling to pay attention, and just checked out. It struck me forcefully how different it was to attend to complex ideas when you were the speaker instead of the listener.

I expect that many readers of this book are teachers who use a variety of active-learning strategies in their classroom already, and it may seem to those readers that maintaining attention over an hour of discussion or group work would be less of a concern than it is for a committed lecturer. Perhaps students in your classroom sit around a seminar table and talk. Or perhaps you run an active-learning classroom, and students are working on problems all throughout the semester. Maybe you teach with simulations, or game-based activities, or case studies, or some other highly engaging pedagogical approach. You might thereby assume that these kinds of active classroom formats foster student attention throughout, as the students are engaged and working, rather than sitting and listening to a lecturer. I would have made this same argument myself at the beginning of my teaching career, when I taught largely by discussion. But anyone who has spent seventy-five minutes trying to host a discussion knows better than this. It doesn't matter what teaching technique we are using—at some point throughout the class period, attention will flag. This doesn't happen because of any particular teaching method; I am an agnostic when it comes to the choice of method, believing that all of them can be done both well and badly. The flagging of attention happens because that's how attention works. It happens not only within the space of a single class period, but within the rhythm of the semester. Attention peaks and troughs over fifteen weeks, just as it does over the course of fifty minutes.

Learning is hard, and so is attention, especially for students. Yet we have only a short amount of time to spend with them each week and each semester, and we have much work to do. If we want to help students maintain their attention throughout the class period, we have to begin by thinking like playwrights and composers, recognizing that students need changes of scene, shifts in format, and opportunities to pause and catch their cognitive breath. Absent that kind of planning, we are in conflict with what the research tells us about the limits of student attention in the classroom.

The Limits of Student Attention

One of the most frequently cited maxims in education is that students can pay attention for ten or fifteen minutes before their attention starts to wane. If this is true, as I have heard many teachers say, it means that we should limit our lectures to ten or fifteen minutes in length, and put them at the beginning of class, while student attention is high. Then, as their attention starts to wane, we should shift into engagement activities. I was actually talking about this piece of pedagogical folk wisdom in the kitchen one afternoon with my wife, while one of my high-school-aged daughters was doing her homework nearby. "Seventeen minutes," my daughter said, looking up from her book. "That's how long students can pay attention in class."

"Where did you get that from?" I asked.

She shrugged and returned to her homework. "That's what my teacher told us."

There are written sources for this theory, but a review of them published in 2007 by two psychologists at Saint Louis University concluded that the evidence for this claim was thin and sometimes based on shoddy research methods. No doubt student attention waxes and wanes throughout a class period, the researchers agree, but trying to map it onto an upside-down bell-shaped curve doesn't do justice to the complexities of attention or the humans who wield it.[1] Their conclusions match well with the findings of another group of researchers, who gave clickers to students in chemistry classes and asked them to report their lapses of attention throughout fifty-minute periods, in which teachers used three different teaching formats: lectures, demonstrations, and poll questions. The authors found no evidence of the fifteen-minute period of student attention. Attention, the authors explain, instead "alternates between being engaged and non-engaged in ever-shortening cycles throughout a lecture segment. . . . Students report attention lapses as early as the first 30 [seconds] of a lecture, with the next lapse occurring approximately 4.5 min into a lecture and again at shorter and shorter cycles throughout the lecture segment." The paper contains a number of graphs in which students' self-reported lapses of attention are mapped across the minutes of the class period, and they look like the beeping heart-rate monitors you see in hospitals, with pulses of inattention occurring with depressing consistency throughout the period.[2]

However long attention lasts or doesn't last in the classroom, the important point is that it degrades over time and thus needs regular opportunities for renewal. This idea informs a theoretical model called attention restoration theory. According to this theory, any activity that requires our attention, including attempting to learn in a college classroom, makes significant demands on what some psychologists term "directed attention." Environmental psychologist Stephen Kaplan argues that directed attention (a concept that he traces back to philosopher William James) has several key features: it "requires effort, plays a central role in achieving focus, is under voluntary control (at least some of the time), is susceptible to fatigue, and controls distraction through the use of inhibition."[3] The element that I want to highlight here is that our directed attention is "susceptible to fatigue." Kaplan claims that "any prolonged mental effort leads to directed attention fatigue." Like many researchers in this area, Kaplan adduces potential evolutionary reasons for this feature of our attention: "To be able to pay attention by choice to one particular thing for a long period of time would make one vulnerable to surprises. Being vigilant, being alert to one's surroundings may have been far more important [to early humans] than the capacity for long and intense concentration."[4] According to this line of argument, our brains have good reason to nudge us away from directed attention on a regular basis and force us to disperse our attention back into the broader environment.

Because our directed attention fatigues over time, longer periods that demand our attention must feature regular change and variety. In plays and symphonies, the artist provides an opportunity for attention renewal through breaks and intermissions. Although I had been lulled into distraction by the twenty-minute piece during my night out at the symphony, I was returned and ready for Dvořák thanks to a trip to the restroom and some chatting with my wife. In the classroom, especially if you are teaching in two- or three-hour blocks, you might well provide breaks for students to get up and stretch, use the restroom, or check their phones. But for the typical class period, just under or over an hour, I would argue instead for the more familiar teaching strategies of change and variety. Short of intermissions, plays still have transitional moments in which the scene changes, the lights darken and return, the background scenery changes, and the actors come off and on the stage. In a symphony, the musicians pause between movements (often for just ten or fifteen seconds), the themes change from one movement to the next, and a movement that ends quietly might be followed by one that begins with a roar. In these transitions from one scene or movement to the next, attention can pause and catch its breath; in our anticipation of change, attention is renewed.

Research on student attention suggests that these attention dynamics operate in the classroom as well. The researchers who used clickers to study student attention in the chemistry classroom also analyzed the lapses of student attention preceding and following the use of one of the two major active-learning strategies in the course: demonstrations and polls. What they found was not only that student attention perked up during these changes in format from lecture to active learning, but that the reverse was also true: student attention was heightened during the lecture segments following an active-learning experience. The authors finish the essay with a section entitled "Implications for Teaching":

> Teachers should be aware of student attention cycles within a lecture and strive to improve student attention by using student-centered pedagogies at different times throughout a lecture, not only to decrease student attention lapses but also to increase student attention during the lectures that follow the use of such pedagogies. This research demonstrates that the positive effect of student-centered pedagogies does more than decrease student inattention during their duration but also has the added benefit of a carryover effect to a subsequent lecture segment. This supports the idea that *changing pedagogies within a class period can not only be seen as a way to present concepts in an alternate format but may also help engage students in subsequent lecture teaching formats.* [Italics mine.][5]

This study helps affirm three essential points about the importance of changing our teaching strategies over the course of a class session. First, attention and distraction cycle off and on with very regular frequency. Second, deliberate efforts to renew attention with moments of active engagement have a positive effect not only in the moment of engagement, but in the period immediately following it. Third and finally, those moments of engagement do not require an extraordinary amount of time or creativity. In some cases in this study, the polls or demonstrations lasted just five minutes.

Another affirmation of these points comes from a 2019 study published in the journal *Studies in Higher Education*. The author invited more than seven hundred first-year students in the United Kingdom to fill out surveys indicating the times when their interest was especially piqued during a lecture. The author notes that she had various hypotheses about what would capture the students' attention, including when the lecturer was using humor or multimedia. But the surveys revealed something different. The students reported interest when they were invited to participate in activities that provoked what the author called "cognitive activation." She describes examples of this as the teacher "posing a question" or "introducing a problem or puzzle to be solved."[6] In other words, there was nothing too radical here—just a pause in the usual routine and a shift to something different. Cognitive activation would be one way to explain why attention perked up in those moments, but I would argue that there is an equally likely culprit in the room: the pause and the change. Indeed, because these cognitive activation techniques were all different, there was only one consistent element among them: they represented a transition from one teaching strategy to another.

Both of the studies above affirm the larger body of research that supports the use of active-learning techniques in the classroom. Student attention was piqued when the lecturer stopped talking and asked the students to do something. My suspicion is, however, that if you spent the entire class period doing polls, demonstrations, or some other active-learning technique, you'd see the same cycles of attention turning on and off as you'd see with lectures. What helped stir up the attention of students was the shift from passive to active—and, as the first study demonstrated, attention remained high after the shift back to passive. What mattered was the change. Studies like that one, paired with the accumulated wisdom of our artistic traditions and our everyday experience, support the idea that variety and change help maintain and renew attention.[7] Conversely, lack of variety dulls attention and pushes us toward distractions. If we want to maintain student attention throughout the class period, we need to plan classes that feature changes, and that include plenty of opportunities for students to sit up and engage actively in the classroom, even if there is also lecture time. We don't have to shift formats manically; a fifty-minute class period might need only a couple of changes to keep students moving along. In this respect, I think teachers need to think more like composers or playwrights, envisioning the classroom experience as an unfolding one, featuring change and variety.

The first three recommendations of this chapter provide a plan for developing a variable course-period plan, showing that plan to your students, and being prepared to improvise creatively when attention flags. The final recommendation narrows our focus onto those presentation slides that many of us use to structure our lectures, and considers what the research tells us about how those slides can support—or undermine—student attention.

Make It Modular

Sustaining student attention throughout the structure of the class period means providing regular opportunities for change, whatever teaching methods you use. A lecture or a seminar discussion will create the need for attention renewal; in both cases, pausing mid-way through and asking students to have a quick conversation with a peer might achieve that effect. But it might work equally well to have them stop and complete a five-minute writing activity, or have them do a quick bit of research on their laptops, or something else devised by your creative pedagogical mind. Likewise, if students are solving problems in groups in your flipped classroom, the best thing you can do to renew their attention might be to pause at the midpoint and give them a ten-minute lecture, or ask them to write down the solutions they have devised on the whiteboards, or have them stop and write in their notebooks for a few sentences about what they are struggling with. In all of these cases, the specific techniques you use (although of course we want to use effective ones that fit with our teaching knowledge and personalities) matter less than the commitment to break from longer tasks of directed attention with opportunities for cognitive activation and renewal.

All of this can be done deliberately, without as much work as you might imagine. You can accomplish it by thinking about your teaching as modular, by which I mean that what you do in the classroom consists of a series of different cognitive activities, each of which could be considered its own module, and any given class period is constructed by combining modules in ways designed to support both attention and learning. A modular approach helps you become more aware of your teaching strategies and routines, and that awareness can help you become a more effective steward of the attention of your students.

Although I had basically been using a modular approach to teaching for most of my career, its value became most apparent to me in a workshop I attended on our campus, hosted by Michele Lemons, a biologist who had recently returned from a faculty development session at her professional conference.[8] Lemons had us write on index cards the different activities (or modules) that we usually did in class, one per card. That was the first time I had written out a list of my teaching modules—an activity that was eye-opening enough on its own. Then she asked us to consider an upcoming class, and to think about what we wanted students to accomplish during it. Finally, she had us take the cards and use them to build that class period. It was a fascinating visual activity to put the cards in different orders, seeing how each of them would lead to a new approach to both learning and attention in that class period. I highly recommend trying this on your own or with peers on your campus, doing so specifically with attention in mind. What are the modules that prove most difficult for your students to attend to? How can you enfold those modules within more active approaches—thus taking advantage of the research findings described earlier, which demonstrate that cognitive engagement persists beyond moments of student activity and into subsequent lecture periods? To answer these questions for yourself or with your peers, there are three steps you should follow.

Articulate the teaching modules you normally use. Begin by identifying the different kinds of activities that you use in class. Be creative and comprehensive. Write them down on a whiteboard in your office, on index cards, anywhere you can see them and move them. My list would include:

- opening writing exercises
- closing connection notebook-writing exercises (see next chapter)
- discussions of writing exercises
- group worksheets on literary texts
- lectures on historical biographical context of authors
- review of key passages in literary texts (teacher directed)
- creating story or poem "maps" on the board (student directed)

- open discussions of meaning and theme
- poll questions with peer instruction
- opportunities for student questions
- short videos connected to course content
- analysis of images connected to course content
- slides on effective writing techniques
- overview of assessments or assignment sheets

After you have created that list, you can check to see whether you feel like it's comprehensive enough, whether it involves mostly content presentation or mostly student-centered activities, and whether you feel like you need to add some new strategies to your repertoire.

Use the modules to build the class period. Once all of my strategies are laid out, I can see much more easily and quickly how to put together a class period that has regular shifts in format and that never pushes the limits of my students' attention too far. In a fifty-minute class period, I might have room for three or four modules, with almost none of them lasting longer than twenty minutes, and most of them less than that. A typical class period in Introduction to Literature might look like this:

- opening writing exercise (five minutes)
- discussion of responses (ten minutes)
- lecture on key passages from text (fifteen minutes)
- class creation of character map (twenty minutes)

As I build up my modules, I work very deliberately to make sure that active and passive formats are mixed. I almost always put mini-lectures or passage reviews (where I march the students through a text we are reading, highlighting key passages for them to notice) in between two modules in which they are active—as in the above example, where I have crammed it in between an open discussion and a group activity at the board. I also try to take a week-level view to ensure that modules are not neglected for too long or overused throughout the week.

Vary the pattern. Routines and patterns are helpful to students, especially in the beginning of the semester, when they are struggling to master both the initial material and your teaching style. In those opening weeks, I tend to start with a handful of modules that I use regularly, to make sure that students become familiar and comfortable with them. But of course familiarity can dull attention, so over the course of the semester I begin gradually and deliberately adding in new strategies and changing the order of things. Although we usually do a writing exercise at the beginning of class early in the semester, by week ten I might save it for the middle of the class, or finish with it.

I'll note finally that taking this modular approach can have tremendously positive effects on the labor you put into teaching and the time you spend on course preparation. Early in my career, I would agonize about how we would spend the seventy-five minutes of class and overprepare massively in order to ensure that I always had something to say. These days, class preparation takes me a fraction of the time it used to, as some of the modules require nothing more than for me to come up with a great question. Christine Tulley, a professor at the University of Findlay, writes in *Inside Higher Ed* about the ways modular teaching, which she calls "pattern teaching," can help new faculty members avoid the trap of overpreparation. She cites the example of a new faculty member who could never figure out when to stop preparing for class and who, as a result, was not making any progress on her research. After Tulley introduced her to modular teaching, the faculty member began sitting down each Friday to lay out her pattern for the following week, which finally gave her the freedom to make progress on her writing. Taking a modular approach to teaching will not only benefit the attention of your students—it may also give you the ability to return your attention to the parts of your professional life that don't revolve around the classroom.

Signposts and Structures

Using change and variety within the structure of your class period will help sustain attention over the hour. But you can enhance the effectiveness of that structure when you make it visible to students. A trip to the theater or symphony always begins with receiving a program, and that program outlines the structure of the event for you. Many programs will not only show the number of acts, scenes, or movements; they often will also tell you how long the experience will last. Throughout the performance, you have a sense of where you are and what remains. If you are in a slow passage and feel your attention fading, you can always remind yourself that a break or change should be coming soon.

Likewise, when you observe effective speakers give longer lectures, you'll hear them give sequencing clues all the time. They might show you an outline at the beginning of the talk and then include subheads along the way to remind you where you are within that structure. Along with the sequencing clues, speakers often will emphasize or remind you about key points. They might use oral signposts pointing you to the big ideas: "This is the main point I want to make this evening," or "I've said this before, and I want to repeat it because it's important." Sequencing clues and emphasis on main ideas support your attention through a clear awareness of the organization of the experience and of your core takeaways. That awareness helps keep your attention on track. In the classroom, such awareness will especially help students who struggle with attention disorders, an increasingly common experience among our students. One difficulty faced by individuals with attention challenges can be an inability to discern between the salient features of an experience and the less important ones. A medical doctor's overview of the challenges faced by students with Asperger's syndrome, for example, memorably describes them as being "tyrannized by details; they accumulate them, and cannot prioritize them."[9] Everything seems equally worthy of attention, and so attention disperses more thoroughly and frequently than when the listener has a clear understanding of what matters. Providing visible pointers toward structure and key ideas from a class period will help students maintain their attention, but it's also sound educational practice that will help all students learn. In their book *Dynamic Lecturing: Research-Based Strategies to Enhance Lecture Effectiveness*, Christine Harrington and Todd Zakrajsek argue that experts tend to have an immediate and clear view of the difference between important points and supporting details in the material, but students have trouble making those distinctions: "Because new or novice learners don't have the necessary background knowledge to differentiate between the important and not-so important content, they often spend more time and energy focused on details rather than the big ideas or major points. This can result in students failing to learn the essential information."[10]

You can catch a glimpse of this problem yourself if you ever have the opportunity (and fortitude) to look at student notes from your courses. They can provide a startling view of the challenges that students face as they are trying to see the orders, structures, and hierarchies of course material. Their inability to see the bigger picture obviously hurts their learning; it can also result in the kind of problems with attention and distraction that we frequently see in the classroom. When too much information is coming at students from the lecturer or her slides, students can get lost attempting to identify the key points—and just scribble away everything they see or hear—or they can become overwhelmed and check out.

You can help reduce those distractions by making visible to your students the structure of the class period, and the most essential ideas they should take from it. Four common methods of keeping those elements in view include:

- **Old school.** Segment off a section of the whiteboard and write down the outline or key ideas for the day, leaving it up and visible throughout the class period.
- **Tech-y.** If your class is driven by slide presentations, include, somewhere at the beginning (perhaps after the slide designed to provoke curiosity), a brief outline of the presentation and its key ideas. Use the subhead features throughout to remind students where they are in the presentation.
- **Verbal.** If you don't use whiteboards or slide presentations, or even if you do, you can still use verbal signposting to let students know where things stand throughout the class period: "First I want to describe a case for you, and then we'll consider three major theories that we could use to understand that case. . . . Now as a reminder, we're on our last theory. After that we'll do a quick writing activity and that should lead us to the end of the hour."
- **Guided Notes.** You can provide students with outlines of your lecture, giving the main ideas but then leaving spaces for them to fill in details. Harrington and Zakrajsek point out that such notes especially help new learners in a subject; as people become more familiar with the material, they can get by with less guidance and scaffolding.

Those four prospects should provide you with enough impetus to consider what strategy fits in your classroom—it might be one of the above or something completely different. All that matters is that you make some effort to reduce the need for students to use up mental energy wondering about the sequencing and main ideas of the class period.

The bonus of this recommendation is that if you have clarified the plan for your students, and are providing verbal signposts of where you are within that plan, some or all of those signposts can be invitations to attention. For example, let's say you have three major ideas you want to cover in a lecture, and as you are shifting to the third one, you see students have been slumping in their chairs and angling toward their distractions. You have a moment there to call them back into the room: "OK, I know that last point was complicated, and I appreciate you sticking with me for a few minutes there. We are now going to tackle the final and most important point here, so let's focus on this last part for ten more minutes and then we'll stop and give you a chance to practice some problems." I am sure you can attest to the power of a simple statement like this from your own experiences at academic conferences. I have sat through many talks during which I found my mind drifting, and then was suddenly called back into the room by the speaker making a verbal signpost or some sort: "Now we shift to the second half of my talk, in which I will argue . . ." And there we all are again, newly attentive to the coming material. When speakers make such comments, they keep me aware of the structure of the talk (which helps me identify the main ideas) and return my attention when I have drifted.

Can you do the same for your students?

Pentecostal Pedagogy

Taking a modular approach to your teaching, varying the patterns you use throughout the semester, and making those patterns visible to students—all of these actions will give your classroom an attentional boost. But even excellent planning and execution of these strategies won't change the fact that brains get tired. The directed attention of students in the room will always experience some ebb and flow. It will be subject to fatigue, in need of restoration and renewal, capable of being both lost and found throughout the class period.

But accepting flagging attention as normal does not mean we can't or shouldn't respond to it. To the contrary, becoming more aware of the dance of attention and distraction in your classroom should help make you more alert to the imperative to intervene and help your students restore their focus. The good news that we learn from attention restoration theory is that such interventions do not require an excessive amount of time—just a few minutes can be enough to do the trick. On those days when you have planned everything well, and yet you still find that student attention is flagging, consider what you can learn from the work of Christopher Emdin, the author of *For White Folks Who Teach in the Hood . . . and the Rest of Y'all Too: Reality Pedagogy and Urban Education*. In his book, Emdin advocates for something he calls "pentecostal pedagogy," which draws lessons on teaching from the wisdom of black churches. The experience of worshipping (or even observing) in a black church is fully engaging, Emdin explains, with continuous interaction between the pastor and the congregation, rich and varied music, and a decided orientation toward sustaining the attention of the audience. Pastors in black churches seem to recognize the limitations of human attention and craft the rhythm of their services around its continuous restoration. One of the core strategies that Emdin points to is the use of "call and response." When a pastor is giving a sermon, and feels that the attention of his audience might be flagging or just needs a quick jolt of energy, he issues a call: "Can I get an amen?" The congregation responds: "Amen!" The pastor has that "amen" in his pocket throughout the sermon, and is always ready to break it out when he needs it for attention renewal.[11]

Teachers need a similar attentiveness to the ebb and flow of attention, and need to be ready to use such quick renewal devices. We have been considering how you can structure opportunities for change and attention renewal into your course planning; pentecostal pedagogy entails a more fluid, in-the-moment mindfulness of the tenor of the room, and a recognition of when students might need a quick injection of attention renewal. I will give your creative brain just a few avenues for thinking about how to accomplish this in your own classroom, as potential strategies will vary according to discipline, class size, and your teaching persona. But consider some or all of the following.

Reading. In my literature classes, my favorite quick renewal strategy is to pause when I feel the discussion is lagging and read something aloud—or have a student read aloud. If I'm teaching poetry, I might shift us to a new poem and ask everyone to put their pens and books down and listen while I read it. Or I might ask them to put their pens in hand and highlight key words as I read the passage. In both cases, this strategy puts everyone's eyes and ears back on the text, and gives me an opportunity to do a little dramatic performance of a great work of literature. It works almost as well when I ask a student to read something aloud, which shifts attention away from me and to some other point in the room (I recommend this only in smaller classes, where you will know your students better and are less likely to make the mistake of calling on a student who might have trouble reading to the class for whatever reason).[12]

Writing. You can always stop and ask students who are drifting away to write something down—something other than the notes they have been taking (or not taking). When the discussion is lagging, or the lecture seems to be fading, pose a question and ask everyone to write down one or two sentences in their notebook in response to it; let them know that you'll be asking three or five or ten of them to read their sentences aloud afterward. These questions could be related to the content, or you could always jump to the meta level: What are you confused about right now? What do you see as the most important part of what we have discussed thus far? What aspect of the material could you use in your essay? To make this work, you will have to be willing to circulate around the room and encourage their participation, since some students may prefer to just sit and "think" about the question instead of writing. This strategy will be even more effective if you explain at the beginning of the semester, and even on your syllabus, that these quick writing prompts are an important part of their participation in the course and will happen as frequently as once or twice per class.

Moving. I try not to recommend teaching practices that I wouldn't undertake myself, so I'm not going to advocate for one-minute stretch breaks, or having students do jumping jacks, or anything else that probably would be quite effective but that I would never do in a million years. Instead, consider the following example of a content-related way to get students up and moving. At a conference on education sponsored by the United Nations, I attended a session in which the workshop leader wanted to model a way of getting students actively engaged in a discussion. He posted a principle on the board, and then had everyone in the room get up and stand in relation to our position on that principle: if you agree with it, stand close to it; if you disagree, stand far away. After we had positioned ourselves in clumps around the room, he walked among us, asking us to explain our positions, posing questions, and getting us all thinking. This session contrasted profoundly with what happened during the rest of the conference, which consisted largely of panel discussions where speakers from different countries explained why education was important and 75 percent of the audience worked on their laptops on unrelated matters. What would it look like to use movement, instead of just words, to spark a great discussion in your classroom?

Seeing. So much of what students experience in the classroom comes in the form of words, whether they appear on a PowerPoint slide or are spoken by the people around them. Images can help break up our normal routines. Whenever an image might be appropriate to explore in the classroom, I will keep a tab with it open on the computer in the room and have it available to analyze when we need it. For example, when we read the poetry of William Blake in the British Literature Survey, I will have available some of the images that he drew to accompany his poems. In a lagging moment, I can throw one of those up onto the screen and ask students to tell me what they see. Sometimes I will ask everyone to get up from their seats, come to the front of the room, and look closely at the image so they can notice details. When the students are back in their seats, I have them describe for me whatever they noticed, and I write down their observations on the board. Once we have a few of those, we can start to analyze. How do the details connect to the work we are reading? What ideas from the class could they connect with? This is an easy and low-stakes discussion that gets students thinking in new and different ways.

Reading, writing, moving, seeing—any of these, and combinations of them, can be quick renewal devices in your pocket for when you feel attention sagging. A confident teacher with lots of experience might be able to insert these with just a moment's consideration, but a better approach, especially if you have not thought in these terms before, would be to identify a small number of strategies that you will use on a regular basis and be very deliberate about deploying them for a while, until you get comfortable knowing how and where to use them—at which point you can add new ones and expand your repertoire of interventions in support of attention renewal in your classroom.

(Less Text, More) Images

Finally, many teachers use slideshow presentation as their default mode of structuring and directing the attention of students throughout the class period. In the dozens of class sessions I observed while writing this book, at least 75 percent of them included a segment where the teacher was presenting content to students with the use of slides. I thus feel compelled to conclude this chapter with a recommendation about this teaching strategy, which has become such a staple in today's classrooms.

Most of the slides I saw in my observations, or have seen while in the audience at conferences, are joyless affairs. They are pumped full of text, sometimes so small that it's impossible to read from the back of the room, and contain zero design elements and no images. That's unfortunate, because it turns out that visual elements like images and graphic design have extraordinary power to grab our attention. John Medina's book *Brain Rules: 12 Principles for Surviving and Thriving at Work, Home, and School* argues that "visual processing takes up about half of everything your brain does."[13] He points out sensibly that for most of human evolution, we were not reading text; we were looking at our environment, which means that an acutely developed visual sense was what we needed for all aspects of our survival: hunting, gathering, hiding, reproducing. Michelle Miller, in her book *Minds Online: Teaching Effectively with Technology*, explains that "information with rich sensory associations tends to be better remembered. Visual imagery is particularly powerful; we're more likely to recall a word if it's accompanied with a picture, or if we just see the picture and no text at all."[14] Too many of us neglect the power of images in our slides, and use them instead as repositories for really important words.

That has unfortunate consequences for the attention of our students—and not just students. My wife has to attend professional development events pretty regularly, with presentations from administrators, guest speakers, and fellow teachers. As I was working on this chapter, I asked her about how often she encounters presentation slides that are devoid of images and overstuffed with text. All the time, she told me. But they don't bother her that much because she follows a simple rule when it comes to slides with lots of text: "If I can't read it in five seconds, I don't read it at all."

When she sees a wall of text, in other words, she just ignores it and assumes the speaker will tell her whatever she needs to know. She does this for the same reason that your students do: when they see a barrage of words on an otherwise blank slide, they give up hope that they'll be able to make heads or tails of it within the space of a minute or two, and they either stop taking notes and listen or they check out and sneak a peek at their phones.

The power of pictures, images, and even graphic design elements on slides to support student learning and attention has been much discussed in the research. The initial results, drawn largely from studies documented by Richard Mayer in *Multimedia Learning*, suggested caution. This was warranted by the fact that some images may actually detract from learning. Michelle Miller explains that Mayer's research identified three kinds of images that can be used in the presentation of course content. "Seductive" images "are those that are interesting but unrelated to the material in any meaningful way." These can actually distract the learner from the important content. "Decorative" images also "have no conceptual link to the material" but aren't as interesting to the viewer and have a neutral impact on learning. What we ultimately want are "instructive" images, which directly relate to the course content and provide another way for the learner to understand what is on the slide.[15] When I am teaching the nature poetry of William Wordsworth and providing students with background information about his life, an instructive image would show the Lake District where he grew up, scenes from which occur throughout the poems we will read. I try to support the instructive nature of that image by explaining this to students. Your use of images can always be supported in this way. If the images really are instructive, take a moment and explain what they are doing on the slide. If you can't offer such an explanation, you should consider whether you might have a seductive or decorative image, instead of an instructive one.

Chris Drew, writing for the Learning Scientists website—an excellent and ongoing collection of essays and resources for teachers—argues that Mayer's cautious approach to the use of images in teaching did not fully take into account the potentially positive impact that images and graphics can have on attention and motivation, which can more than compensate for potentially distracting effects. Drew points to research that shows the positive impact of "warm" colors and graphics in slides, and even of cartoonish images that evoke baby faces—because who doesn't pay attention to babies, right? But more seriously, Drew argues that newer research on images in slides and other learning resources suggests that

> a mix of words and images can have the effect of sustaining attention. Large amounts of uninterrupted text appear to be demotivating for learners, leading to decreased learner interest. By contrast, visually appealing texts may sustain intrinsic motivation. In other words, learners appear more likely to be interested in and more engaged with learning materials if the content is presented with visuals and texts rather than visuals alone.[16]

When you read that "large amounts of uninterrupted text appear to be demotivating for learners," you realize that we are back at the Anne Lang five-second rule, and you note again with both irritation and gratitude that Anne Lang is always right.

From his survey of the most recent research in this area, Chris Drew draws two conclusions, both of which help underpin the very simple principle I am advancing here: you should reduce the amount of overall text on your slides and enhance that text with images or other strategically chosen graphic elements. As Drew explains it:

- Mayer showed us that visually appealing but excessively irrelevant graphical features on multimedia texts seem to harm learning by causing cognitive overload. Images may be a distraction from learning; but
- Subsequent cognitive psychologists have shown that visually appealing graphical features that direct our attention to the content could have benefits such as sustained motivation and attention to tasks.[17]

I am sure you have seen presenters show slides that were crammed with text, or just crammed with too much stuff overall, and have shaken your head in frustration. And yet in spite of the fact that most of us seem to know we should reduce text and enhance our slides with images, very few of us do it. I have sat through multiple presentations in which speakers have said something like, "Sorry, I know there's too much text on this slide . . ." and then soldier right on, either trying to explain it all or suggesting that we ignore it and move on.

Take the reading of this summary of the research as the impetus to declutter your slides of text and add visual design elements or one great image at least every other slide. Becoming thoughtful about the role that slides can play in supporting the attention of your students might be the easiest way for you to sustain attention throughout a lecture, especially if you are combining those well-designed slides with some of the other methods recommended in this book.

Quick Take

- Build your teaching around modular activities that you articulate, sequence, and vary with attention in mind. Begin the process by writing down your regular teaching activities on index cards or a whiteboard, and then experiment with planning a class by shifting them around and thinking about the sequence that will best hold the attention of your students and lead to the most effective learning experiences for them. Vary the sequencing you use over the course of the semester.
- A visible structure to the class period can help keep learners on track when attention becomes a challenge. Without such structure, students might also have trouble distinguishing the supporting points from the key ideas, or identifying the purpose of engagement activities. Use your slides, the whiteboard, or oral signposts to provide continual reminders for students about the structure of the class period and its most important ideas.
- Stay mindful of the rhythms of attention and distraction throughout the class period, and have a small number of attention-renewal activities prepared that you can deploy when you observe student attention flagging. Consider reading, writing, moving, or seeing—whatever works with your teaching persona, can be normalized into your

teaching routines, and can be dropped into the room whenever you need it.

- Research in cognitive psychology attests to the power of images to capture the attention of humans and promote their learning. When you are presenting content with the use of slides, reduce text and enhance them with images and graphics that will invite the attention of our sight-loving brains.

Conclusion

I mentioned in Part One that one of the ways I enhanced my own thinking about attention was by considering how it waxed and waned in both myself and others in noneducational environments. Those considerations were especially helpful in thinking about attention in relation to structure. Attention was on my mind while I was listening to the symphony, attending plays, watching movies and television shows, listening to guest lecturers on my campus, attending social events like parties or receptions, and even playing sports or pursuing hobbies. During some of those experiences, I saw examples of structural strategies that I had already encountered in the literature on attention in education; in other cases, I observed something that I had not yet encountered, and it led me to the literature to see what support for it I might find there.

To give just one example, I have a terrible habit of staying up late and flipping around cable television in search of something mindless to watch before bed. Occasionally I will pass over a televangelist working the crowd in some megachurch, and in the past I have sometimes stopped on those shows just to get a sense of how people who are very different from me think. But while I was working on this book, I stopped on those shows much more frequently, because I realized how masterful the preachers were at holding the attention of their audiences. When I encountered Christopher Emdin's arguments about pentecostal pedagogy, they were more convincing to me because I had seen many examples of televangelists using similar techniques. Certainly they called out for those amens, but they used other methods as well. Occasionally they asked everyone in the audience to recite a familiar prayer with them, in a communal act of refocusing attention. At other times, they asked everyone to open their Bibles and follow along as they read a passage aloud, just as I do in my literature courses. They also regularly inserted jokes and self-deprecating stories into their more prosy expositions of the day's Scripture reading, providing the opportunity for people to turn to one another and laugh.

If you want to get new ideas for yourself about how to sustain student attention through the structure of your class periods, make yourself into an amateur attention researcher over the next few months. When you are an audience member or a participant in an extended, structured experience of some kind—whether that means symphonies, sermons, or department meetings—pay attention to your own reasons for tuning in and tuning out. Check the faces (and devices) of those around you. See what draws you in and what checks you out. And then ask yourself this very simple question: What can I learn from this for my own classroom?

7

Signature Attention
Activities

WHEN THE PULITZER PRIZE–WINNING poet Mary Oliver died
in 2019, she left behind an extraordinary body of work, a recurrent
theme of which was the value of attention to a good life. In her
poem "Mindful," she describes herself as having been put on this
earth in order to help renew our sense of attention at the wonders
of the world:

> It is what I was born for—
> to look, to listen
> to lose myself inside this soft world
> to instruct myself
> over and over
> in joy
> and acclamation.

But she doesn't need to visit the grand places of the world to lose herself and feel that joy, she explains; she finds it in the most humble and everyday experiences around her:

> Nor am I talking
> about the exceptional,
> the fearful, the dreadful,
> the very extravagant—
> but of the ordinary,
> the common, the very drab,
> the daily presentations.[1]

Take a tour through Oliver's collected works, gathered in the pages of her book *Devotions*, and you'll see what she means. Poems testify to the astonishing sights of a dead black snake on the road, a freshly sliced melon, or stones on the beach. These poems model for us how to pay closer attention to the world, and in "Sometimes," she makes her wishes for her readers most explicit: "Instructions for living a life: / *Pay attention. / Be astonished. / Tell about it.*"[2] The italics and the periods at the end of each line make her instructions emphatic: the quality of our lives hinges on the attention we pay to the everyday world around us.

Oliver's work focuses explicitly on the power of attention to enhance our lives, but of course one could argue that much of our literary and artistic heritage does the same. Poetry, in particular, often trains a lens on the everyday experiences that we share with one another, and asks us to look at them in new and unusual ways. From Robert Burns, we learn to look with empathy at the devasted home of a mouse, overturned by our plow in the fields; with William Carlos Williams, we taste with fresh wonder the plums that were being saved in the icebox; Elizabeth Bishop helps us see the multicolored beauty of a grunting fish wrenched from the ocean. Other arts likewise shine light on our everyday experiences, provide us with food for contemplation and renewed wonder at our daily rounds of experiences. Impressionist paintings ask us to see the world through a different lens, focusing more on the essences than the details. Still-life paintings hold the simplest things up to our gaze, and we see the everyday objects from our homes—a bowl of fruit or a single flower—as startling new visions of beauty. One could argue that all of these works are meant to make us see the world anew, to be astonished by it as we once were as children. They make the familiar strange again, and in so doing they reawaken our attention to it.

We can become overly familiar with the everyday world around us, and students can likewise become overly familiar with the classroom experience. We should not be surprised to find some dulling of attention throughout the semester if students come into our classes and find themselves engaging in the same activities in the same order every day. The index-card exercise I described in the last chapter has the power to help combat that kind of familiarity, as long as we are deliberate in thinking about how the classroom experience is varied over the course of the semester, and how routines are both established and disrupted. In this chapter, I will introduce another way of thinking about how to disrupt the normal classroom routine in the service of awakening attention, this time by thinking less like a playwright and more like a poet.

Reseeing Attention

When I was a child, we drove the same route to church every Sunday. My father would pile all seven of us into the station wagon ('70s) or minivan ('80s) and navigate the well-trodden two miles from our home in suburban Cleveland to our local parish church.

Part of this route involved passing a gas station that had been there as long as I could remember. At some point in my early teens, the gas station was torn down and an empty dirt lot took its place. We had been driving by this new dirt lot for at least a month or two when, one sleepy Sunday morning, my father stared at it and exclaimed in surprise, "Hey, the gas station's gone!" This was met with laughter and incredulity from the rest of us, who had seen the gas station disappear many weeks ago. But the attention of my father had been so deadened by the repetitive patterns of our weekly route to church, and perhaps the weekly routine of attending church, that he had tuned out his surroundings completely while he drove. The overly familiar route that he drove each week meant that he didn't need to pay attention to the world outside of that car, and he could distract himself with whatever happened to be on his mind that Sunday morning.

Attention researchers have identified at least two different ways that things right in front of our face fail to capture our attention as they should. The first of those is called attention blindness (or inattention blindness). Christopher Chabris and Daniel Simons have been the most famous expositors of this concept, which refers to the way our focus on *this* makes us blind to all of the *thats* around us. Attention puts a spotlight on whatever we are seeing, hearing, or sensing, and that spotlight darkens the world around us. Chabris and Simons famously demonstrated this effect by showing subjects a video of people passing a basketball back and forth, and asking them to count the number of times the ball changed hands. In the meantime, someone in a gorilla suit walked across the back of the set, thumped his chest, and then walked off. Most people who watched the video and counted the passes, as they were instructed, did not see the gorilla pass by. "For the human brain," explain Chabris and Simon in their book *The Invisible Gorilla: How Our Intuitions Deceive Us*, "attention is essentially a zero-sum game: If we pay more attention to one place, object, or event, we necessarily pay less attention to others." If you're focusing hard on counting passes, you won't see the gorillas in the room. At times, this inability to focus on more than one thing can be frustrating or dangerous (for example, texting and driving), but it also means that we have the capacity to tune out distractions and focus when we really want to. Attention blindness, Chabris and Simon explain, "is the cost of our exceptional—and exceptionally useful—ability to focus our minds."[3] Our ability to survive, work, love, thrive—all of these depend on our capacity to zone in and tune out distractions when we need to. But that capacity can hurt as well. Attention blindness besets the classroom when students are zoned into their devices and failing to give their attention to their peers, the teacher, and the course material. Most teachers concerned about inattentive students are talking about the attention blindness caused by devices.

But there is another way attention can become dulled, and that's what explains my father's ability to completely miss the razing of that gas station. Researchers call this change blindness. We can become blind to new features of our daily experiences—people, places, routines, and more—when they become overly familiar to us, either because of our long experience with them or because of our long-held expectations. "Change blindness occurs," write Chabris and Simons, "when we fail to compare what's there now with what was there before."[4] The expectations we have about a familiar experience, one that we have encountered many times, are so strong that they can keep us from truly experiencing the present version of that encounter. Change blindness can have an insidious effect on teachers, who might come into the same classroom each year, teaching the same content, and lose sight of the fact that our approaches must take into account the unique characteristics of each group of students we meet and the changing context of the new academic year. I have been guilty many times of returning to teaching techniques that worked for me in the past long after they have stopped working for me in the present, simply because I was unwilling to step back and see the novel context of that year's distinctive group of students.

Likewise, our students can become easily caught in a form of change blindness that comes from repeated exposure to the school experience as they trudge from one classroom to the next, experiencing the same basic rotation of activities: lecture, discussion, group work, polling, and so forth. Change blindness interferes with their learning when they put themselves on automatic pilot throughout their classes, each of which has the potential to offer them new, different, and exciting forms of knowledge and skills. We help our students overcome the lack of attention induced by change blindness when we structure experiences that reawaken their awareness of novelty, of difference, of experiences that conflict with their expectations. "Attention is about difference," writes Cathy Davidson in *Now You See It*. "We pay attention to things that are *not* part of our automatic repertoire of responses, reflexes, concepts, preconceptions, behaviors, knowledge, and categories."[5] We want our students to set aside that automatic repertoire in our classrooms and come face-to-face with the wonders on offer in our classrooms, our courses, our disciplines.

To snap students awake again, we need to create at least some learning activities that will nudge them out of those familiar routines and back into meaningful and transformative encounters with one another, with us, and with the content of our courses. Such experiences need to occur consistently throughout the semester—perhaps not every day, but certainly on some regular basis. "The most effective way to increase our ability to pay attention," writes Ellen Langer in *The Power of Mindful Learning*, "is to look for the novelty within the stimulus situation."[6] When we invite our students to look at something with a new perspective, seeing it as if for the first time, we can awaken and hold their attention. The core recommendation of this chapter for sustaining student attention is thus to seed throughout our teaching what I call signature attention activities, which are specifically designed to jolt students out of their familiar routines and expectations for the classroom, the course material, and even your teaching. Signature attention activities are your opportunity to think as creatively as possible about your teaching; they should be the highlight of your course. I suspect many teachers already have teaching strategies that would qualify as signature attention activities, in which case all I am really arguing for here is that you deploy them strategically, with an eye toward attention renewal throughout the class period and the semester. Don't expect students to sit and listen for thirteen weeks and then reward them with one great creative activity in the final weeks. Consider instead how you can take your most engaging teaching strategies, the ones that you know make them sit up and see everything anew, and use them in more bite-size chunks for attention renewal throughout the class period, the unit, and the semester.

Signature attention activities don't have to be long, as you will see from some of the examples below. They do need to be moderately varied, however. If you come up with a great teaching strategy, and then use it every day at the same time in class, it will lose its power as an attention-renewal activity. But you don't want to tip too far in the other direction, and come in every day with some surprising new activity, which students might find disconcerting. The three types of signature attention activities outlined below are designed for you to deploy and vary over the course of the entire semester. But they all have the same purpose: to reawaken students in your classroom, and to help them see your course material with the new and wondering eyes of attention.

Focusing

The first pathway toward a signature attention activity comes through the act of focusing, in which you invite students to pause and look carefully at some aspect of your course material in the service of awakening or reawakening their wonder at it. Such activities might take only five or ten minutes, but they require the students to step back from their normal classroom activities, their devices and distractions, and look closely. In the final section of the Introduction, I gave an example of a focusing activity that art historian Joanna E. Ziegler used with her students, asking them to view the same painting every week for the entire semester, continually searching for new insights into it. A signature focus activity brings that idea into the classroom, and invites students to pay close, sustained attention to something and then report on their experiences in some way.

My favorite example of a signature focus activity comes from Kathleen Fisher, a theologian on my campus, whose technique awakens student attention to the familiar texts that form the heart of her course on the Bible. In this in-class exercise, she draws from the ancient tradition of Torah study, in which practitioners slowly read the sacred scriptures of Judaism aloud to one another, pausing, discussing, and questioning at every turn.[7] The assignment sheet she gives to her students on the handful of days when they complete this activity invites them to get a taste of this experience. Students sit across from one another in pairs and are given these instructions: "Take turns reading the selected text aloud with your partner(s). The Bible is meant to be read out loud. *Go slowly!* I mean REALLY

slowly!! Don't worry about getting through the whole text. It's better to ask many questions about one verse than to read fifty with
little thought." Fisher directs her students to attune themselves especially to passages that contain ambiguities and multiple meanings.
"Jewish and Christian texts," she explains, "are written in a very
concise style that allows a lot of room for interpretation." She does
not want students to settle into familiar understandings or theories,
so she speaks clearly about what it means to read mindfully, and she
guides them through an activity that helps them do so.

Fisher was kind enough to allow me to visit her class and observe her students engaging in these slow readings of sacred texts.
The class was preparing to read a twentieth-century play, *Inherit
the Wind*, that centers on a famous trial in which advocates of
creationism and evolution are pitted against one another. Understanding the play thus depended on a close knowledge of the creation accounts in the book of Genesis. The students got right to
work. They read sentences aloud to one another, pored carefully
over single words and phrases, asked each other questions, pointed
out anomalies and inconsistencies, and wondered. I couldn't help
myself, and sidled up to the pair of students nearest to me. When
they read about the creation of vegetation on the third day, they
noted the repetition of the word "seeds," and one of the students
connected the importance of seeds to something she had learned
in another class. When they came across the word "govern," they
pointed out how it implied order and control in the universe. And
so the conversations continued—a group of eighteen-to-twenty-
year-old students discussing and debating the meaning of the book
of Genesis in a New England classroom, the picture of attention.

After twenty to twenty-five minutes of this work, Fisher called
the group to attention and asked them what they had learned from
the experience, and especially what they had noticed that they
hadn't before. A student raised his hand immediately. "I've read

this a million times," he said, "and it never occurred to me what it means for the earth to be formless." Fisher asked him to read the appropriate passage out loud, and then asked other students—who were working from different versions of the Bible—to see if they had other translations of the word "formless." The class together tried to come up with some way for the language to express what a "formless" earth would be. This eventually led to another question about whether the language implied that some kind of formless world existed before God started shaping it. As they turned back to the text to consider this, the student who had made the first comment turned to his neighbor and used both hands to mime his head exploding, as if this text, which had become so mindlessly familiar to him, had suddenly turned his world upside down.

You should notice that Fisher's activity does not involve students sitting and focusing on the biblical passages in silence and isolation; the students worked together. Such collaboration can support the sense of community in the room, as well as make signature focus activities more productive. In *Now You See It*, Cathy Davidson argues for something called "collaboration by difference," by which she means that we all bring different perspectives to an experience, and we can gain the fullest possible picture of that experience when we combine our perspectives. Remember that one form of attention blindness occurs because we focus our attention so closely on one thing that we become blind to everything else. "Collaboration by difference," she writes, "is an antidote to attention blindness. . . . [It] respects and rewards different forms and levels of expertise, perspective, culture, age, ability, and insight, treating difference not as a deficit but as a point of distinction."[8] My attention might be blinded to one aspect of something I am trying to learn, while my peer is blinded to another aspect; when we talk and combine our perspectives, we expand each other's views to the full experience and deepen our learning and engagement. The collaborative element of Fisher's activity struck me as one of the keys to its success, in theory because of the way it draws on Davidson's notion of collaboration by difference. But in practice the social quality of the activity made it fun. This stuck out for me as I observed students doing their close readings, and reminded me of the flow theory of Mihaly Csikszentmihalyi: these students were deeply focused on their conversations with one another, and those conversations brought them the pleasures of attention.

Jessica Metzler, a senior associate director at Brown University's Sheridan Center for Teaching and Learning, offers a conceptual pathway for considering how any faculty member might develop activities like the one modeled by Kathleen Fisher. In November 2018, Metzler gave a workshop for faculty at a teaching conference on helping students develop new "ways of seeing" objects of study.[9] Although her focus was on helping people successfully teach with physical objects or in museum settings, her framework would work with anything we want students to pay close attention to, from objects to texts to problems. Drawing from research in object-based teaching, she had participants complete a process of analyzing an object that centered on three basic questions:

- **What?** For this first step, participants spent time observing an object and taking notes. In this case, as in Fisher's, staying focused and looking closely helped reveal unexpected new angles, perspectives, and ideas.
- **So what?** Metzler had participants write down questions based on their observations and then pass those questions around the room to one another and add new ones, giving everyone time to develop ideas or areas for further research. In the classroom, this second stage could take many forms, but it should involve Davidson's collaboration by difference.

- **Now what?** The final stage shifted into a more whole-class and teacher-centered discussion. What paths for research or future questions were raised? What questions were unanswered? What do the experts say? What does it mean, and what comes next?

These three broad questions can help teachers think about how to bring attention to any core element of the course material that needs to be defamiliarized, or even topics with which students might have no familiarity whatsoever. It begins with attention, expands to collaboration, and concludes with theorizing and reflection.

In my wife's kindergarten classroom, each student has a magnifying glass available to them, and at times they pull these focusing devices out and get a surprising new view of the everyday objects about which they are learning. In your classroom, what do students need to see under magnification? What teaching strategy can then help them collaborate and reflect on what they have seen?

Creating

Focusing cultivates the kind of attention we most often think about in relation to education. We sit, we concentrate, we ponder, we speak, we write. We view the whirring, distractible mind as the enemy of that kind of work. But that is a mistake. To the contrary, the mental pathways of distraction run parallel to—and sometimes overlap with—those of our most innovative and creative thinking. Our minds jump and skip in ways that can be annoying when we need singular focus for a task. But only a mind that drifts or leaps away from difficult problems occasionally can return to those problems with the insights gained from a few seconds, minutes, or hours in some distant place. Apple founder Steve Jobs once said something about creativity that caught my attention while working on this book: "Creativity is just connecting things. When you ask creative people how they did something, they feel a little guilty because they didn't really do it, they just saw something. It seemed obvious to them after a while. That's because they were able to connect experiences they've had and synthesize new things."[10]

His informal description of this process matches well with what experts in creativity tell us about how the creative mind works. In *Wired to Create: Unraveling the Mysteries of the Creative Mind*, Scott Barry Kaufman and Carolyn Gregoire write that "highly creative work blends together different elements and influences in the most novel, or unusual way."[11] What we often think of as original ideas, springing mysteriously from the head of a genius, are instead the product of accidental or deliberate pairings of existing (but seemingly unrelated) ideas. New artistic genres often arise this way: Irish punk music, the nonfiction novel, the television mockumentary.

The second form of signature attention activity that you might use in your classroom, then, involves putting your students in front of a task and encouraging them to use their distractible minds to create something concrete. One of the reasons that we sometimes find our minds unhelpful or unpleasant is because they jump around without any seeming purpose. But when we can get them to move in service of a specific outcome, we can harness them for both learning and creativity. Teachers often have students doing creative activities for out-of-class assessments. One could argue that research papers or presentations reward the kind of creative thinking I am describing, and they do. But here I am really arguing for brief, in-class activities that capture attention by providing space for creative thinking and that lead to a concrete outcome of some kind. You don't need to be the greatest pedagogical poet in the world to develop these kinds of activities; some very traditional active-learning strategies fall under this category. Here are four easy examples, at least one of which should be familiar to every experienced teacher:

The worksheet. This ancient teaching tool is one of my signature creation activities in literature courses. Students typically view poems as having hidden meanings; the author is concealing a life lesson of some kind, and their job is to crack open the shell of the poem and find the nut inside. Most of the poetry we teach in college courses, by contrast, has survived the test of time because of its multivalence—its capacity for holding multiple meanings. My creation activity in these classes involves presenting students with a printed copy of a poem, putting them in small groups, and asking them to annotate it as creatively as possible: identify any literary techniques we have discussed, make whatever connections they can see among the words of the poem, and then broaden out the potential connections between those words and other works, the poem's historical context, and their own lives. I encourage them to speculate with one another, to think creatively, to dream up whatever they can about what those words might be doing in the poem. Once they have completed this activity, which can take anywhere from five to twenty minutes, we get together as a class and they tell me what they have come up with. At that point, I can use my expertise and experience to guide them away from some connections (ones that don't fit well with other aspects of the poem, for example, or that are historically inaccurate) and toward the ones that are best supported by the poem as a whole and its historical context.

The concept map. Concept maps provide visual representations of a knowledge field, with word-filled bubbles, squares, or boxes organized spatially around core ideas. Lines of causality or relation connect the different items to one another; the final product of a concept map resembles a flat version of neurons connecting in our brains. The Center for Teaching and Learning at Brigham Young University has a nice overview of concept maps on its website, including a model example from a political scientist who wants his students to understand the sources of their values and beliefs.[12] The students begin creating their map by writing down a belief or value in a circle at the center. Then they draw lines out to other circles that contain their reasons for that belief or value, and from those circles they spin out another layer that identifies the sources of those convictions (for example, "media," "religion," or "grandparents"). Afterward the class as a whole analyzes their maps to identify the major sources of their beliefs and discusses what they learned about those sources. In this case the maps are completed individually, but a more common strategy is to ask students to work on them collaboratively on pieces of paper, poster boards, whiteboards, or through the various free online concept-mapping tools (which you can find with some quick searching). Concept maps are fascinating concrete products that can be used as a springboard for further debate, discussion, or creative work.

Short-answer polls. In Chapter Five, I described Eric Mazur's use of electronic polling, which focused on asking the kinds of questions that have right or wrong answers. But most electronic polling services allow students to respond to questions or prompts with short answers, and those can be displayed on the screen for review and discussion. To make this a creative activity, pose a question or problem that requires students to do some quick research on their phones or laptops, along the lines of Aisling Dugan's strategy of having students conduct quick research on the microbe of the day. For example, a criminologist who wants students to recognize the patchwork nature of our legal system, with its many variations from state to state, could certainly pick a legal area and show examples of legislation from five different states. But an easy signature creation activity would be to give the students the legal issue and pose the question to them: What are some of the variations we see in state laws? Students jump online and start searching. Give them slightly less time than they might need, to avoid them finishing early and checking out, and then ask everyone to write up short descriptions and submit them through the polling system. As their responses scroll across the screen at the front of the room, visible to all, ask students to elaborate on the examples they found.

Memes, tweets, Instagrams, and more. Put those sometimes maddening social media accounts to good use by giving students a task that requires intellectual engagement with them. This could take the form of searching and reporting, or collaborating and creating. Most teachers I know want their students to become more savvy about how the popular media reports on their subject or how the general public understands it. Pause during class to ask students to search for the most common or striking words and images of a concept—for example, supply and demand—on Twitter, Instagram, or Reddit, and then analyze with them the media and popular perceptions versus what they are learning with you. Invite students to critique what they have found, and use their critiques to help refine their understanding. Or ask them to become the creators. As every writer knows, the boundaries of a word count can be a source of great creativity. Ask students to condense the main idea of the class period into 280 characters, or create a meme that represents it as effectively as possible, and post the results to the course management system.

I have an inordinate fondness for learning about the specific things that teachers do in class, especially these kinds of in-class engagement activities, so examples could easily fill the rest of the book. To get you started in your search for signature creation activities, check out ABLConnect, a website of active and activity-based learning strategies housed at the Derek Bok Center of Harvard

University. You'll find a rich trove of practical examples there and links to other sources you can explore.

Connecting

Sarah Stein Lubrano is an instructional designer who has written eloquently about her life as a student and academic with attention deficit hyperactivity disorder. In an essay for *Aeon*, entitled "Living with ADHD: How I Learned to Make Distraction Work for Me," she makes a parallel argument to the one I am making in this book, explaining that, while attention might be especially challenging for people who share her diagnosis, it represents a challenge we all face on a regular basis. "These days," she writes, "I see my own distracted nature as a source of keen awareness for the fragility of *all* attention." She points to one aspect of instructional design that captures the focus of distracted learners of all kinds: a connection between the course content and the learner's personal experiences or aspirations. "Research increasingly suggests," she argues, "that people are more likely to take in new ideas and information when it relates to something they already care about. All of this is magnified for people diagnosed with ADHD, who lack focus, unless there's a strong and clear connection to their immediate concerns, but who can nonetheless focus profoundly when this element of deep interest is present."[13]

This statement mirrors what I heard in conversations I had with people about attention during the two years I spent researching and writing this book. "It's not that I *can't* focus," I would hear from people who told me they had troubles with attention. "I can focus just fine when something really matters to me." As Lubrano points out, that doesn't apply only to people with attention disorders; we are all more likely to wield our attention well when we are learning something that relates to our personal interests.

The final pathway toward signature attention activities is inviting students to create connections between your course content and the perspectives they bring into the room. Of course the attention of students will perk up when they can see how the content relates to their personal histories, their current experiences, or their future careers. Almost every teacher I have ever observed makes efforts to provide examples or cases that are designed to connect to the lives of their students. This is good practice, and we should do it whenever we can. But I think we make a mistake if we assume that this work depends entirely on *our* creative thinking. Saundra McGuire argues in her book *Teach Students How to Learn: Strategies You Can Incorporate Into Any Course to Improve Student Metacognition, Study Skills, and Motivation* that showing students connections might not be as effective as providing opportunities for them to make interesting new connections themselves:

> We don't have to make the connections for them; in fact it is much better if we don't. We can just throw a concept out there, like a ball, and ask, "What does this remind you of that you've encountered in your everyday life?" When students hit the ball back, they come up with the most wonderful examples and ideas that give them not only an efficient path to learning and mastery, but also *the most efficient path for them.*[14]

That final sentence reminds us that there are twenty or fifty or a hundred people in the room, and all of them bring their unique histories and aspirations to the course content. The connections we throw out to students are unlikely to work with every single one of them, which means we should supplement the connections we create with opportunities for them to make their own.

I have one signature attention activity for connecting that has become my most regular source of attention renewal in class, especially in the latter half of the class period. This activity was also described in my book *Small Teaching: Everyday Lessons from the Science of Learning*, and in presentations to faculty audiences it always captures their attention more than anything else I describe. This low-stakes assessment activity uses a blue exam book that students receive at the beginning of the semester and bring with them to class every day. Once or twice a week, they are asked to pull out that notebook in the latter half of the period and respond to a question I have posed about how the course material for that day or week connects to something in their own lives. Questions I have used in the past have included:

- How does something we talked about/read for today connect to an experience you have had in your own life?
- Can you think of a film, television show, or book that illustrates an idea that we have talked about thus far today?
- Can you connect something we have considered today with something you learned in another course? How did our discussion add to or change what you learned there?
- How could something we learned today be of use to you in whatever career you are envisioning for yourself right now? Or in a future course you might take here at the college?

My classroom is never more thoughtful and attentive than in those moments when students pull out their notebooks, stare off into space for a minute or two, and then settle in and write. The connections they make are always fascinating for me to read—and I do read them, although I only collect the notebooks two or three times per semester, and I don't provide much commentary on them. They are intended to help students see the relevance of the course material, but I will admit that the times when I read those notebooks are the most enjoyable hours of the semester. For every question I ask, at least one or two students write something that makes me think about the course material in an entirely new and thought-provoking way.

Although sometimes I only have time for students to write, whenever possible I will ask them to discuss their responses to these questions with one another in pairs, invite them to share in a whole-class discussion, or both. This activity has revitalized my teaching—and the attention of my students—more than anything else I have done in the past few years. I am fascinated by their responses to these questions. Saundra McGuire rightly argues that the connections the students create to your course material will be the most meaningful ones for them. Connection blue books might not work in your classroom, but what else could you develop that would enable students to make those meaningful links and reawaken their attention by helping them see striking new connections between the course material and their lives?

Quick Take

- Students may lose sight of the fascinating nature of your course material, as we all lose sight of the miracles of the everyday world. Think creatively about signature attention activities that could awaken students to the wonder of your discipline.
- Deploy those signature attention activities strategically throughout the semester. If you develop a great signature attention activity and use it every day, it will lose its power. When does attention flag in the rhythm of the semester? Can you schedule your signature attention activities in order to prevent that flagging, or to renew attention when it occurs?

- Develop your signature attention activities around the acts of focusing, creating, and connecting. These activities should be the most distinctive and engaging activities of your course. Other kinds of learning activities, such as lecture or discussion, can lead into them or emerge from them.

Conclusion

In this chapter and the previous one, I have argued that to sustain the limited attention of students throughout a class period, you have to think first like a playwright and then like a poet.

The playwright knows she has to maintain the attention of an audience for two hours, sitting in a darkened theater, expecting to be entertained. The play's construction reflects her efforts to keep the audience's attention. She might open with something confusing or disturbing, thus raising the viewers' curiosity about how a conundrum or conflict will be resolved. She shifts the action, scenery, and characters from scene to scene, act to act. The tension rises, falls, and rises again. She makes space for the intermission. All of these decisions reflect her awareness of the limits of the audience's attention. What lessons can you learn from her about how to sustain the attention of your audience? In the coming weeks and months, pay attention to the plays and performances you attend, the films and television shows you watch, and observe what the creators do to keep you hooked—and what is happening when you find yourself getting bored and itching for your phone.

At the heart of every play, every work of art, we should find some insight into the human condition, some experience that changes us. Our eyes, ears, and hearts are reopened to our own experiences, the experiences of others, or the everyday world around us. The poet and painter put new frames around the parts of the world that have become too familiar to us and help us see them with new attention. What activities can you develop that will have the same impact on your course material, your students, your classroom? Perhaps you don't have space for such activities in every class period; even a few per semester, placed at the right moments, might do the trick. Start next week, and let your store of signature attention activities grow and evolve over the course of the semester.

It's important to acknowledge that when you plan your classes like a playwright or a poet, you're going to create some messes. Students might check out during the transitions from one activity to the next, and your signature attention activities might fall flat. You might find that you have a signature attention activity that most of your students love, but a handful of them sit in the back corner and don't want to participate. On the one hand, that's teaching. For all of the reasons we have considered in this book, we should never expect perfect attention in class. If we want to have students actively engaged in their learning, we have to be willing to get a little messy. On the other hand, I don't want you to give up on those back-row students quite so easily. We have another strategy that we can mix into our efforts to support student attention and that might help get those students engaged in your course: the assessment process.

8

Assessed Attention

WHILE I WAS writing this book, I had the opportunity to present the ideas I was working on to faculty groups on different campuses. In those presentations, I would begin by describing some of the background research that you have read in Part One, designed to provide participants with the historical and biological contexts for distraction. I would argue that we can't hope to wall off distractions, which are endemic to the human condition. Then I would ask them to turn to their immediate neighbors to discuss a simple question, one that changed the focus from distraction to attention: When students were fully engaged and attentive in their classrooms, what was happening? In other words, what were they already doing in their teaching that captured their students' attention? The second time I posed this question to an audience of faculty members, at Cleveland State University, physicist Thijs Heus raised his hand from the back of the room and offered this simple explanation of when his students were most fully engaged in class: "When they are taking an exam!"

My immediate reaction to this comment was "Of course!" It had not occurred to me to consider an assessment as an attention-focusing experience, but a moment's reflection will likely confirm for you, as it did for me, that students are highly attentive to the course material when they are taking an exam or completing almost any assessment that contributes to their course grade. That includes when they are giving presentations or taking quizzes, and even when they are completing a low-stakes activity like a worksheet that will count toward their participation grade. Activities that contribute to students' grades usually have the powerful effect of focusing their attention on the course material.

At least those were my thoughts in the immediate wake of Heus's comments. After the workshop, when I had time to reflect on the experience, a different reaction followed. Many smart thinkers in higher education over the course of the past several decades—people whose work I deeply admire—have been arguing that we should de-emphasize the role that grading plays in the learning process. Some of those thinkers trace their concerns back to the research of psychologist Edward Deci, who conducted some seminal experiments on motivation in the latter half of the twentieth century. Deci and his colleagues had students complete tasks that they could either pursue for their own interests (which meant they were driven by intrinsic motivation) or for an external reward (which meant they were driven by extrinsic motivation). They found consistently that giving people an external reward for the completion of a task could damage their initial, self-generated interest in that task. In other words, let's say I invite you to kick some soccer balls into a goal, an activity you find satisfying and enjoyable. If I pause you midway through the process and offer you a reward for every ball you get in, it turns out that, at least according to some research, your motivation to score goals will actually decrease. The conclusion drawn from this research is that external rewards, and the extrinsic motivation they foster, can damage deeper, internal motivation. As a result, many educational thinkers and teachers have argued that we need to eliminate extrinsic motivators like grades in our teaching, as they can harm the intrinsic motivations that students might bring to their learning.[1]

In what follows, I will draw from research on grades, motivation, and attention—not in order to make the case that graded assessments focus attention, as that should be obvious enough to anyone who has ever taught a credit-bearing course of any kind. Instead, I will focus here on the ways we can take advantage of the attention-focusing power of graded assessments without the collateral damage that grades can cause. To do that, we have to make a distinction between assessments and grades. Assessments are those activities that students complete in order for you to measure their learning progress. They provide both you and the students with information about that progress, and create opportunities for you to give feedback to the students on how they can continue to improve. Assessments typically (though not always) contribute to student grades. The positive effect of putting a grade on an assessment is that it can amp up attention, which in turn can heighten learning.

But it will only do so if we fully understand the potentially negative effects of grades, and build in structures that mitigate those effects.

A Balanced Perspective on Grades

Graded work is ubiquitous in higher education, in spite of the fact that most teachers would likely prefer to teach without it. I had a colleague who used to quip at departmental meetings that he taught for free but got paid for grading. The discomfort that many of us feel around the enterprise of grading may arise from an instinct that aligns with what educational theorists like Alfie Kohn have argued about grades. In his books and essays about the detrimental effects of grading, Kohn asserts that many decades of research have produced three core findings that should make us skeptical about grading our students. In an overview of that research, "The Case Against Grades," he explains:

- *Grades tend to diminish students' interest in whatever they're learning.* A "grading orientation" and a "learning orientation" have been shown to be inversely related and, as far as I can tell, every study that has ever investigated the impact on intrinsic motivation of receiving grades (or instructions that emphasize the importance of getting good grades) has found a negative effect.
- *Grades create a preference for the easiest possible task.* Impress upon students that what they're doing will count toward their grade, and their response will likely be to avoid taking any unnecessary intellectual risks.
- *Grades tend to reduce the quality of students' thinking.* They may skim books for what they'll "need to know." They're less likely to wonder, say, "How can we be sure that's true?" than to ask "Is this going to be on the test?"[2]

These are serious criticisms that will likely resonate with anyone who has ever wielded a red pen, spoken with students about grades, or fielded requests for one extra point that will improve a student's grade from a B- to a B. Grades absolutely have the power to narrow students' focus to performing well on tasks, rather than encouraging them to learn.

Cathy Davidson's overview of the history of grades, in her book *Now You See It*, can help us resee the strangeness of our standard practice of stamping letters of the alphabet on documents as a way of measuring the quality of someone's learning. The omnipresence of this practice in American schools makes invisible the fact that in earlier decades and centuries, and in many other cultures, students were evaluated in more personalized ways, with teachers assessing their learning as a result of direct interaction. As schooling became the norm (and often mandatory) in Western countries and students were packed into increasingly large classrooms, teachers needed more efficient ways to assess learning. At the same time, a corporatizing world wanted mechanisms for sorting children according to their intellectual abilities, and grades became a language that communicated skill levels not only to the student, but to future employers. But while grades can help teachers manage workloads and communicate student achievement to the outside world, stamping a letter on a complex piece of writing, or project, or even a test has always been a blunt way of assessing what someone has learned. The impact of that bluntness, according to Davidson, is that "our classrooms are generally among the most intellectually straitjacketed environments our students enter."[3] Davidson echoes Kohn's arguments that grading narrows the focus of students to performing well on tasks, rather than encouraging them to learn.

In response to these arguments, creative teachers have developed an array of alternative ways to think about grading. All of them acknowledge that, in the end, institutions ask us to assign letters or numbers to student performance at the end of the class. But what happens prior to that final imposition of the grade doesn't have to look the way it always has. For example, in "specifications grading," the instructor articulates clear standards that tie each grade mark (A, B, C) to a specific quantity and quality of work, and students decide which grade marker they wish to work toward. The responsibility then falls entirely on the student to complete that level of work, and they have as many opportunities as they want or need to get there. If their first effort at a paper does not meet the specifications for the grade they are seeking, they take it back, revise it, and keep trying until they reach the level they have identified as their goal. Some teachers might know this system as "contract grading," in which students contract to produce a certain amount of work and receive a specific grade in return. One important feature of these systems is that they reduce the pressure students might feel to perform perfectly on any individual assessment; if the students' performance does not meet the standard on any given assessment, they can keep trying until they achieve the goal they have set for themselves. Such systems also make very clear the standards according to which student work will be evaluated, something that teachers are not always great at articulating. Overall, alternative grading models like these encourage individual responsibility, ask students to take ownership of their grades, and put the emphasis on achieving long-term mastery of course content over short-term performance.

Teachers who use these systems advocate for them passionately, and I always encourage faculty members who are frustrated with grading to explore them and see whether they might fit in their courses. But I will once again pronounce myself an agnostic when it comes to grading systems, because I have never quite been convinced by the arguments of Kohn and others who view grades as universally antithetical to learning. In my view, that argument represents what I believe is a partial reading of the full literature on this subject. There is no doubt that grades should not be our primary method of motivating students or providing feedback on their work. We should inspire them with curiosity and purpose, and we should provide them with plenty of substantive feedback in both oral and written forms. This chapter assumes you do those things. But as we guide students toward the deeper goals of our courses, they will need smaller incentives along the way, to nudge them to stay on track when they hit roadblocks, get frustrated or bored, or become distracted by their lives outside of the course. Graded work can keep them on track or get them back when they falter. Grades can also orient students toward fundamental learning tasks that are necessary but hard. I have never met a writing student, or a student in any course, who loves to do the hard work of mastering the grammar and mechanics of formal writing. Much of the writing we do in class can be informal and doesn't need to follow those rules. But at least some of the writing does, since mastery of those rules will enable them to succeed at college and professional writing tasks. Grades can keep the attention of students on whatever the equivalent of grammar might be in your discipline.

In contrast to the single-minded view that grades always damage student motivation, other research suggests that the ideal approach to motivating students is a mix of intrinsic motivators (like deep goals) and extrinsic ones (like grades). It should be noted here as well that the simplistic dichotomy of intrinsic versus extrinsic motivation offers only one way to understand the relationship between motivation and learning. The authors of *How Learning Works: Seven Research-Based Principles for Smart Teaching*, for example, identify the key sources of motivation as triangular: goals (which include both performance and learning targets), values (the importance of the goals to the student), and expectancies (the extent to which the student believes the goals are achievable). The authors' conclusions about these different elements of motivation would apply to almost any theoretical scheme we could imagine: "No single variable is universally deterministic with regard to motivating students."[4] In other words, nothing works—or doesn't work—for everybody. This, of course, matches very well what we know about teaching in general: that no particular strategy works for every student. We're humans. We are all different. Some students love listening to lectures, and some love having discussions. Some love group work, and some hate it. In the end, this leads to the only teaching principle that I have tried to put into practice over the course of my entire career: vary your methods. Sometimes students should love what you are doing, and sometimes they should be challenged by it. The same is true for motivation. If teachers try to lean too heavily on one form of motivation (intrinsic or extrinsic, values or expectancies), we will always be orienting our courses toward a subset of students. Mixing different motivational approaches provides us with the most comprehensive approach toward inspiring our students to join us on a learning journey, stick with it when times get rough, and leave with substantive new knowledge, skills, or values.

I'll finish by noting that at least some research demonstrates a positive link between extrinsic motivation and the kind of sustained attention we want in the classroom. Researchers from the Boston Attention and Learning Lab have a standard test that they have developed to measure how long people can sustain their attention to a computer-based task. In an article that featured the lab's work, cognitive psychologist Mike Esterman explains that he and his colleagues ran an experiment with that test in which they told college students that the better they performed on the attention tasks, the more quickly they would be finished with them—at which point they could leave the lab and get on with their day. The promise of finishing the experiment as quickly as possible is a classic example of extrinsic motivation (by contrast, a participant would be intrinsically motivated if she found the attention tasks fascinating and wanted to learn from them). The result of this experiment showed that the presence of an extrinsic motivator substantially increased people's attention to the experimental tasks. As Esterman explains, "The extra motivation increased the person's ability to sustain attention by more than 50 percent. . . . We were kind of blown away by the size of these effects."[5] Esterman's lab mate, cognitive neuroscientist Joseph DeGutis, argues that "one of the things we've realized is that it's hard to separate motivation from sustained attention. . . . If we're not looking at motivation, then we're really missing the boat in terms of attention." The conclusion of these researchers supports the notion that extrinsic motivators (like grades) should take their place among the strategies that we use to sustain attention in the classroom, even though we should be using them in conjunction with strategies like building community and cultivating curiosity.

The three recommendations of this section argue for a mixed motivational approach to sustained attention in the classroom, one that includes the use of graded assessments. What unites these recommendations is that they draw on the power that grades have to foster attention in the classroom, and to orient students toward the course material and intellectual skills that will prove most helpful to them in earning the grades they seek. In other words, I'm not advocating for these strategies just because they focus attention; I'm advocating for them because they focus the attention of students in ways that will help them learn.

Low-Stakes Assessments

In Chapter Six, I argued for a modular approach to the classroom experience, in which you are doing several different kinds of teaching activities throughout the period. In Chapter Seven, I argued that signature attention activities should have a regular place in your rotation. Some of those activities, whether they are signature attention ones or more conventional classroom activities like writing or problem-solving, will produce a concrete outcome: a piece of paper, a slice of the whiteboard, a poll response, a post to the learning management system. My experience has taught me that students don't always engage willingly in these kinds of activities; some view active-learning moments as opportunities for distraction. One of the most frequent comments I get from faculty at workshops concerns this problem: "I design these great learning activities for my students, but they don't want to participate. They just sit there and don't do anything. They would rather sit and listen to me lecture." We could spend a long time discussing why this happens, but here I am going to offer a very simple solution: identify the most important engagement activity that you want your students to complete each day or each week—such as your signature attention activity—collect it on paper or electronically, and have it make a minimal contribution toward the students' grades.

These kinds of activities should be the intellectual sandbox in which your students get to play, or the rehearsals where they warm up for the higher-stakes performances. Allocating a very low-stakes grade on such activities sends a signal to students that exploration and rehearsal are important to their learning. You can view the use of grades on such activities as infantilizing, forcing students to do work in class, and I understand how some teachers and students might take that view. But if the activities are well-designed ones that promote learning, you can instead view the grades as rewarding students for doing the work that will prove most helpful to their studies. Think of all the extrinsic motivators that people give themselves to exercise—online badges and stickers, reporting their results on social media, joining communities of support, signing up for a 5K—even though everyone knows perfectly well that exercise is good for you and you shouldn't need such extrinsic motivators to undertake it. But those small incentives seem to give people the extra nudges they need. Low-stakes grades on in-class activities do the same. Without that incentive, some students might check out and angle toward their distractions. Those students are likely to be the ones who have trouble in class, or are disconnected from it, and are more likely to fail. With the small incentive of the grade to motivate participation, those same students might decide to attend more carefully, and their work on that activity might connect them to their fellow students, help them see the course material as worthy of their attention, and give them the practice they need to succeed on the upcoming exam. Your most prepared students don't need the incentive of a low-stakes grade to participate in your engagement activities. They'll do just fine without it. Adding the grade provides an incentive for those students who are less well prepared or academically oriented to engage with the valuable learning activities you have created for them.

These kinds of low-stakes graded activities can also be used in lieu of participation grades, which are frequently given to students on an eyeball basis and hence are subject to all kinds of biases. You might be more likely to give a high participation grade to a student who spoke recently, or the students you like, or the students who remind you of yourself, and so forth. Open-ended participation grades also tend to incentivize and reward a few dominant students who like to raise their hands and talk, which can shut out those who need more time to process and think, or who might not be as confident in their abilities in the classroom. Sociologist Jay Howard has documented this well-known phenomenon in the college classroom, referring to it as the "consolidation of responsibility."[6] A few vocal students do most of the participating in class, shutting out others, and those students earn the participation points that others are then denied. By contrast, when you incentivize participation with a low-stakes grade on signature attention activities (or other in-class work), you are drawing everyone into the conversation, even students who might be initially reluctant, or who would prefer to check out. You might well find, as I have, that sometimes those students have terrific insights and ideas, and that they were checked out or distracted less from laziness or boredom and more from the feeling that they did not see a meaningful way to enter the class conversation. Low-stakes grading on classroom activities provides them precisely the entry point they need.

As a final practical point, whatever grades you put on in-class activities should fall into the category of what composition theorist

Peter Elbow calls "minimal grading."[7] Give full credit for good faith efforts, or step it up occasionally with slightly higher stakes (for example, Excellent, Satisfactory, or Incomplete). You'll need to keep it minimal if you don't want to add lots of new grading time to your schedule. If I have students complete the kind of poetry worksheet I described in the last chapter, working in groups of three in a class of thirty, I get ten worksheets that I can scan quickly for completion in five minutes or less. I don't need to comment on them because we would have followed the worksheet activity with a whole-class discussion in which they told me what they wrote and I recorded and evaluated their ideas with them in class. I can't say that using this low-stakes, minimal grading approach won't add any extra grading time to your workload, but you should find that the small extra effort is more than repaid with a greater expenditure of attention from your students.

The Testing Effect

Higher-stakes assessments, especially in the form of tests and quizzes, can play an equally important role in promoting both attention and learning in your course, in spite of the negative perceptions that many of us have toward them. Teachers usually see their job as introducing new content to students and helping them process or encode it. But a long line of research, dating back more than a hundred years, argues that the challenge of long-term learning is retrieving knowledge or skills from our brains after our initial exposure to them. According to this research, we are very good at "learning" something new for a very short period of time, and then forgetting it. But to count something as truly learned, we should be able to retrieve it from our long-term memories weeks, months, or years after our encounter with it. "We typically focus on getting information *into* students' heads," write Pooja K. Agarwal and Patrice M. Bain in *Powerful Teaching*. "On the contrary, one of the most robust findings from cognitive science research is the importance of getting information *out* of students' heads."[8] When students have truly mastered something, they can recall it in different contexts and use it to tackle novel problems or challenges. You wouldn't count your students as having learned your course material if they did well on a test on Friday and couldn't recollect any of it, or use it in the service of some task, on Monday. But we all know how often that happens with students who spend all of their learning time trying to cram knowledge into their brains.

What they should be doing instead is engaging in retrieval practice, which means that they are repeatedly forcing themselves to draw newly learned material from their memories and put it to work. The power of this kind of practice is perhaps the most thoroughly researched subject we have in education. The more times students engage in retrieval practice with something they have studied, the better they are able to call up that material from their memories in the future. You might object at this point that you want students to do more than be able to retrieve stuff from their memories. In that case, I have good news for you: the more students have mastered foundational knowledge and skills with retrieval practice, the better they are able to do the kind of higher-order thinking we all want from our students. In *Powerful Teaching*, Agarwal and Bain summarize multiple research studies that demonstrate that "retrieval practice boosts students' higher-order thinking, application of knowledge, and skills like writing and math."[9] Teachers are sometimes concerned that the kind of knowledge students learn for exams doesn't transfer beyond the context of the test itself, but several studies on learning transfer show that knowledge learned for tests can and does transfer meaningfully to other contexts.[10]

This quick overview of the research on the power of retrieval practice helps explain why tests and quizzes not only measure learning but actually produce it. Although we don't often think of them this way, tests and quizzes are practice memory exercises. They force students to retrieve what they have learned and articulate it or apply it. In so doing, they are strengthening their ability to repeat those steps in the future. So we should not by any means apologize for, or shy away from, tests and quizzes. They engage the attention of students and promote learning. In-class engagement activities can also be oriented toward retrieval practice; for a wealth of ideas about how to incorporate retrieval into activities like the ones described in the last section, see books like *Powerful Teaching* or my own *Small Teaching*.

My physicist friend Thijs Heus was correct in noting that students are highly attentive when they are taking an exam, but I am sure that most of us have seen that students are also highly attentive when we link classroom material and activities to upcoming assessments, whether tests or papers or anything else. Nothing tends to make students perk up in class more than when I introduce some new poem or theory with a statement that they are likely to see it return on the midterm or final exam. We should thus be as transparent as possible, letting students know when what we are doing in class will link directly to an assessment. Teachers sometimes deride this kind of thinking as "teaching to the test." As I have argued elsewhere, though, we should of course teach to the test—or the paper, or whatever else you have created to assess their learning at the end of the semester. If we design great assessments—ones that have been carefully constructed to allow students to demonstrate their learning in significant ways—then what else should we be doing but helping them develop the knowledge and skills they need to succeed on them? Tests and other high-stakes assessments thus become an opportunity for frequent spurs to attention in your classroom. The language and attitude with which we explain it makes all the difference. I can threaten students with reminders about the upcoming exam, or I can call them to attention by pointing out that engaging in this next activity, or paying special attention to these next slides, will give them the knowledge or skills they need to succeed on next week's exam.

One great way to capture attention and orient students toward an upcoming exam or assessment is by asking them to help you create it. An exam-review day is likely to be a peak attention moment in the semester, but you can also make it an excellent learning activity by having students write questions that you will use on the test. One group of food scientists experimented with having students write exam questions for a course and reported on the results in a 2018 publication. Their experiment was inspired by prior research that had demonstrated that student performance on exams improved when they had the opportunity to write questions or create exam prompts.[11] In the food-science course, two of the three exams were created by the instructors; one was created largely from a question bank generated by the students. Importantly, the instructors gave students guidelines about constructing effective exam questions before they started, including exposure to Bloom's taxonomy and encouragement to ask questions that promoted higher-order thinking. The students performed significantly better on the exams they helped generate the questions for—and that difference did not simply occur because they were answering their own questions. Twenty questions were chosen from a bank of six hundred generated by the entire course.[12] After all, explained one of the authors in an interview with the *Chronicle of Higher Education*, "we figured if they had 600 questions and they sat down and memorized answers to all of them . . . then how different is that from really studying?" The process of learning from exams can thus begin when you involve students in the construction of the test, which can serve as an excellent review or in-class activity to complete in groups. I have done this myself and seen student attention perk up, and exam anxiety decrease, when they are invited to cocreate the assessments that will determine their grades.

Of course, tests and quizzes have potentially negative effects on student learning and your classroom climate. If you are constantly quizzing and testing students, they won't have the opportunity to encode and process the course material. Tests and quizzes can also inspire fear and anxiety in students, and those emotions can interfere with their learning. To achieve the positive effects of testing and quizzing—and the engaged attention that accompanies these activities—without the negative consequences, consider offering what Flower Darby, the author of *Small Teaching Online*, calls an "Oops Token."[13] This conceptual token means that students have the opportunity to fail or do poorly at least one time without having it included in their final grade calculations. For example, an instructor can give four tests and count three, or give weekly quizzes and count the best ten. Remember, well-designed tests and quizzes promote learning, so you are not doing anything wrong by adding one that can be dropped if something goes awry for a student. If you don't want to drop one, instead allow students to retake their lowest-scoring test. Whatever route you might take, this type of thinking makes your exam-giving as compassionate as possible, allowing room for the kinds of failures that we all experience from time to time.

After the workshop in which that physicist first introduced me to the role that tests can play in promoting attention, I mentioned his comment to an academic friend. A wistful look crossed her face. "I loved taking tests," she said. "They were one of my favorite parts of school. I loved sitting down, getting in the test-taking zone, and knowing that I had a task to complete, a certain amount of time to complete it, and that afterward I would find out how I did." She sighed. "Sometimes I wish I could still take tests." Both she and that physicist recognized the way that tests and quizzes can fully absorb our attention and put us in that flow state. If that were all they did, they would still be worth incorporating into our teaching. But the literature on retrieval practice demonstrates that they can also be a potent tool to support learning, and as such deserve an important place in the strategies we use to capture attention in the service of our students' education.

Attention-Getting Assessments

The final strategy for connecting attention and assessment hearkens back to the last chapter, in which we considered how defamiliarization can help create and renew attention. The first two recommendations of this chapter connect to in-class activities and tests and quizzes. It's very likely that many readers either supplement such activities with other, out-of-class assessments—like papers, presentations, and projects—or that they rely more heavily on those kinds of assessments. In this section, I want to recommend a strategy for thinking in new ways about out-of-class assessments, which of course can become overly familiar to students, as we ask them to go through the paces of writing a paper of literary analysis, or giving a presentation on a topic of their choosing, or some variation of this kind of work. The more creative approach—one that will defamiliarize these assessments for your students and present them with intriguing new challenges designed to spark their attention—involves shifting one key feature: the audience.

One of the most innovative examples I have seen of this approach comes from David Crowley, a professor of biology who began his teaching career helping students master the basics of his courses, and did so effectively enough to earn tenure at my college at the end of his sixth year. Shortly after he had done so, however, he took a leave from the college to pursue another degree, an experience that returned him to teaching with a greater sense of purpose for both himself and his students. When he returned to his biology courses, new degree in hand, he enrolled in an academy that runs out of the Center for Teaching Excellence that I direct, and that gives faculty the time and resources to think newly and deeply about their teaching. The combination of his time away from the classroom and his work in the academy inspired him to develop a new assessment for his students, one that specifically asks them to notice what has captured their attention in the course and to bring it to the attention of others.

To accomplish this, Crowley presents the assessment to his students as having three core tasks:

- First, the students identify some aspect of the course that has fascinated or intrigued them, or that they have come to care about. What, in other words, has captured their attention?
- Next, they have to define an audience that should pay greater attention to this subject. That audience can be their family members, a sports team, their dorm mates, the local community, or even a single political representative.
- Finally, they complete the project by bringing their course interest to the attention of their defined audience.

The form that the finished project can take is completely open, and the assignment has manifested a range of creative and fascinating projects. One group of students, for example, became interested in the role that water plays in sustaining life and decided that they wanted to educate their fellow students about their water usage. They created a poster campaign that provided key facts about the amount of water used in showers and hung them in the dorm bathrooms around campus. In addition to the actual work they do in the creation of such a campaign, the students write a reflection paper about their work, which provides a comparable product that Crowley can grade.

A similarly inspiring project that made creative use of audience was created by biologist Stan Eisen, a faculty member at Christian Brothers University, who has students in his upper-level courses write a children's book about complex subjects. Eisen's work was described in an article in the *Chronicle of Higher Education*, in which he explained that he views the assignment "as a tool to get students engaged so they see the topic as interesting, fascinating, and worthwhile"—and, I would add, it tackles the intriguing challenge of making that topic interesting, fascinating, and worthwhile to a very challenging audience with a short attention span. The first book produced, *Don't Get Sick, Stan!*, was from students in a parasitology course, and focused on the parasites that might sicken students in a school cafeteria. Students in a zoology course produced a coloring book called *All Creatures Small and Smaller: The World of Invertebrates*. Eisen has a faculty member from the education department present to his students about writing for children, which provides them with needed support for this unusual assignment.[14]

I argued above that we can view teaching as primarily an exercise in joint attention: calling the attention of our students to the aspects of our discipline that matter. These projects have a similar purpose, now displaced to the students. Having identified what in the course has captured their attention, the students think creatively about how to capture the attention of others. Many kinds of innovative projects in higher education take this form, although we might not explicitly frame them in attentional terms. But when we ask students to write or communicate to public audiences, build websites or create podcasts, record YouTube videos or design pamphlets or brochures—in short, whenever we ask them to create a product that will have a life outside of our classroom—we are charging them with the task of capturing the attention of others and directing it to our course material. So much of the work that students do in higher education is oriented toward what my colleague Carl Robert Keyes once called "an audience of one"—the professor. But if we want students to think critically and creatively about attention and distraction, as we all likely do, we should instead invite them at least once to take on the difficult task of designing a project that identifies something important in our discipline and works to capture the attention of a distracted world.

Quick Take

- Create a category of graded work that consists of in-class, low-stakes activities, and use those activities to hold students' attention on work that will help them succeed in the course. That work could be writing, solving problems, collaborating on online documents, or whatever else fits your discipline and teaching approach. Grade these assessments minimally, and remind students that they are being rewarded for showing up and practicing, just as they are on their sports teams and in other pursuits.

- The literature on retrieval practice, sometimes known as the testing effect, tells us that the more times students attempt to retrieve knowledge from memory, the more firmly they will establish that knowledge in their minds. Use tests and quizzes (low stakes whenever possible) to help ensure that students have mastery of the basics in your course. Remind students of the value of these assessments, and provide students with opportunities to fail occasionally and still succeed in the course.

- Displace the work of attention to your students in at least one major assessment for the semester. Ask them to identify the aspect of the course that has most captured their attention and to bring it to the attention of others. You can still use your normal suite of tests, quizzes, papers, and so on, but offer at least one opportunity for students to think about why your course material deserves the attention of a wider audience.

Conclusion

Early in my career, I believed it was possible to use teaching wizardry to motivate every student to pay full attention in my courses. I just had to find the perfect combination of intriguing activities that would widen their eyes in awe, engage their brains with curiosity, and incentivize them to engage in challenging intellectual work. I thought I could motivate them all to love English literature and writing if I devised the perfect course. In those years, I avoided things like tests, quizzes, and low-stakes grades in class, thinking I shouldn't need them to incentivize participation and attention. My students should want to attend and participate because we're doing amazing stuff in here! But semester after semester, course after course, those ideals bumped up against students who seemed checked out no matter what I did. It took me a long time to realize that not all students had it in them to love literature and writing, that not all students really loved college or learning, and that not all students were going to love everything we did in class. But many of those students, even though they weren't passionate devotees of British literature, still wanted to succeed in my courses and in college. In recent years, I have come to recognize that grades and assessments, with all of their attendant extrinsic motivation, have an important role to play in ensuring the success of those students.

Assessments have an equally important function in the lives of students who might wish to dedicate more time and resources to my class, or to college in general, but who don't have the bandwidth for it. We all know that students are increasingly juggling many different obligations and commitments. Their attention is being pulled in a thousand different directions, and not only by their social media accounts and digital devices. They are dealing with family obligations, jobs, sports and clubs, personal relationships, mental health issues, and more. We can't and shouldn't expect all of our students to come into our classes with the energy and motivation to just explore and learn. We should do everything we can to cultivate that attitude, but everything we can do will never be enough for every student in the room. What grades do for students is help them recognize what they should pay attention to in a course. When we assign a grade to a piece of work, it intensifies it in the context of the entire course, and thereby piques the attention of students. If they have limited resources—cognitive, emotional, or otherwise—graded assessments can help them identify where to direct their energy. If we do our jobs as we are supposed to, and design our graded assessments so that they promote learning, we are drawing the attention of students to the aspects of the course that will help them succeed.

9

Mindful Attention

THE INCREASED ANXIETY we have about distraction in education today (and in our lives more generally) means that interest has spiked in techniques designed to help us focus our monkey minds more effectively. Mindfulness has perhaps been the most bally-hooed technique in this respect, with research in both mental health and education purporting to demonstrate its ability to gain more control over our distractible minds. Naturally, a practice that could improve our focusing capabilities has a special appeal to educators, and educators at every level have indeed shown a strong interest in mindfulness. My wife has heard about its benefits at her professional development days; I have attended workshops about it on my campus. I sat down to wait my turn at the barbershop recently, and on a shelf next to me were brightly colored postcards advertising a local yoga studio with the following headline: "Change the World: Mindfulness and Movement for Classroom, Home, and Studio." When you are learning about the potential power of an educational technique at the barbershop, you know that cultural saturation has been achieved.

At the earliest talks I gave on distraction and attention—at which stage I was not addressing mindfulness in my presentations—I was invariably approached by people who wanted to talk to me about mindfulness, most frequently because they were using it or experimenting with it in their own teaching. In these conversations, I always asked them to describe for me how they were incorporating it into their classes, and was struck by the similarities among their approaches. Almost everyone I met who used mindfulness did so in the opening minutes of class, guiding their students through a meditation activity of some sort, such as focused breathing. Although very few of those faculty members were doing any kind of formal evaluation of the impact of this strategy on their students, they all reported anecdotal positive results for themselves and their students. They were sure that these activities benefited learning, the climate of the room, or both. Given the general research on the ability of mindfulness to improve people's lives in many areas, it didn't surprise me at all to hear about its positive effects in the classroom.

In response to these conversations, I dove into the research literature on mindfulness in higher education, hoping to discover that brief mindfulness activities in the classroom could indeed fulfill the promise of improving student attention. What I found was little, if any, solid evidence that classroom mindfulness activities could positively impact either long-term learning or student attentional capacities. My initial response was that mindfulness was a false lead, but this conclusion was premature. I do believe mindfulness has the potential to help both faculty and students manage distractions in the classroom, but I believe it has more power to do so if we focus on the mindful attitudes and actions of the teacher, and not attempt to impose mindfulness practices on our students. In other words, in this chapter I am going to flip the standard script on mindfulness in the classroom, and encourage you to think about it more in relation to your work than to the work of your students. I'll do so first by reviewing some of the research on student mindfulness practices, and then by making recommendations for how a mindful approach to your teaching can support better attention in the classroom.

The Mixed Messages on Mindfulness

The philosophy of mindfulness takes many forms, but most educators draw from a model developed in the work of Jon Kabat-Zinn, a molecular biologist who founded the Stress Reduction Program at the University of Massachusetts Medical School. Although mindfulness has its origins in Buddhism, Kabat-Zinn and other medically based practitioners offer a secular version, one that intersects very clearly with questions of attention and distraction. The core work of mindfulness involves training attention on some aspect of your experience of the present moment—such as the rhythm of your breathing or the sensations in your body—and thereby reducing the amount of time you spend distracted by your whirring monkey mind.[1] The more you can orient your attention toward your experience in the present moment, the less you find yourself distracted by everything that is not the present, from your everyday fears and anxieties to the promise of fun times on your phone. As we learned in Part One, attention is a limited-capacity resource; the more you attend to the present moment, therefore, the less cognitive space you have for potential distractors. The practice of mindfulness—which often takes the form of guided breathing exercises, but can include other activities—leads to a more mindful awareness of the world around us, where we embrace the present moment in all of its glorious plenitude.

I have been an irregular practitioner of mindfulness for more than a decade now. My mindfulness work—which has included everything from readings by gurus like Jon Kabat-Zinn and Thich Nhat Hanh to group meditation sessions and meditation smartphone apps—has led me to focus on three elements. The first is the core lesson that mindfulness teaches: we must learn to embrace the present moment. That embrace works against the kind of mindlessness that I wrote about in Chapter Seven—when we are going through life on automatic pilot, not noticing the wonders of the world around us—and the way we can become lost in our distractions and ignore the people right in front of us. Second, most mindfulness teachers, Kabat-Zinn included, teach their students to practice mindfulness not only through meditation, but also by identifying and setting an intention for certain daily activities that can be completed mindfully. For example, you might decide that when you are washing dishes every day, you will do it mindfully, by concentrating your attention as much as possible on the experience of washing the dishes: the sound of the running faucet, the feel of the warm and soapy water, the movement of your wrists and fingers as you carefully place a clean dish in the rack.

As anyone who has ever attempted meditation will tell you, one of the first things you discover when you try to focus attention on the present moment is how easily and often the mind becomes distracted from it; mindfulness thus also teaches its practitioners not to judge themselves (or others) for their distractibility. They are instructed instead simply to notice that the distraction has occurred, and then gently pull their focus back to the present moment, over and over again. One group of mindfulness researchers describes the core work of mindfulness as entailing both attention and acceptance, by which they mean that in mindfulness we accept the present moment as we find it, distractions and all.[2] From this, we take our third and final feature of mindfulness: a compassionate acknowledgement of our distractibility. We should be compassionate toward ourselves and our own inattentive minds, which should lead us to have compassion for the inattention of others.

A solid body of research demonstrates that when people are able to absorb these lessons into their daily lives, mindfulness can offer significant improvements to their health, both physical and mental. Experiments have demonstrated the ability of mindfulness practice to lower blood pressure, reduce chronic pain, improve anxiety and depression, help people with addictions, and more.[3] Other experiments have shown that regular practitioners of mindfulness have a better ability to control their attention and regulate their emotions.[4] Given the research-based promises of mindfulness, educators at every level have experimented with using these techniques to help students develop better powers of attention. But only a small minority of teachers have ten, fifteen, or thirty minutes that they are willing to devote to non-content-related activities in every class period. Most teachers I know feel they are already squeezed for time in their courses, and they aren't willing to devote significant amounts of time to something like mindfulness practice. This leads to the question that has been posed by a small but growing group of research teams: Can guiding students through brief mindfulness activities in class, no more than five or ten minutes long, help reduce distractions and improve their learning throughout the subsequent class period? Or, more idealistically, can such brief but regular exercises improve their attentional capacities?

The researchers who have tackled this question have produced mixed results at best. Destany Calma-Birling and Regan A. R. Gurung from the University of Wisconsin–Green Bay, for example, tested whether a five-minute mindfulness activity at the beginning of a class period would improve student learning.[5] They had one group of students in a course on human development listen to a lecture about mindfulness and then practice a mindfulness technique for five minutes; a second group of students watched a video related to course content and instead spent the five minutes reviewing their notes. This happened during the tenth week of the semester, and was repeated a second time in a subsequent class period. It was repeated a third time, but in the third iteration both groups received the mindfulness intervention. At the end of the semester, the researchers compared all three sets of quiz scores for groups one and two. The scores of the mindfulness group were significantly higher than those of the content-review group for the first two quizzes, but they evened out for the third quiz, when both groups had the mindfulness intervention. These results suggest that the five minutes of mindfulness practice had indeed made a difference in helping students learn throughout the sixty-minute lectures.

Unfortunately, however, these results did not seem to carry into the long-term learning of the students, even when the mindfulness practice was extended beyond the quiz days. In the mindfulness group in the experiment above, the students actually continued to practice five minutes of mindfulness at the beginning of every class period for the remainder of the semester. To see whether the mindfulness group gained any long-term advantage from this extended practice, the experimenters compared the results with the control group on two exams that the students took after the experiment had begun. For both of those exams, the control group slightly (but not significantly) outperformed the mindfulness group. "Our results," the researchers conclude, "show that five minutes of mindfulness practice does not lead to improvements in exam scores, suggesting that the enhancements in students' knowledge retention are transitory."[6] In other words, although a few minutes of mindfulness seemed to provide an initial boost to the attentional capacities of the students, leading to an increase in short-term learning, it did not produce the kind of longer-term boost that the experimenters hypothesized they might see.

A different group of researchers tested whether extended engagement with mindfulness in a college course could improve the "executive functions" of their students' brains.[7] Executive functions, they explain, are "the complex, cognitive abilities necessary for planning, self-monitoring, goal setting, and strategic behavior."[8] Surely all teachers would love to have in their pockets an educational strategy that could promise such improvements. In this experiment, students in two different courses were given tests at the beginning of the semester designed to measure their executive-function capacities. One of those courses then proceeded as usual. In the second course, the students learned about mindfulness from their instructor, an experienced meditation trainer, and then spent the first ten minutes of every class period (meeting twice per week) engaged in a meditation activity. They were also encouraged to practice mindfulness outside the course, and to keep journals about their experiences. At the end of the semester, students from both courses were given the executive-function tests again, and the results were compared. No significant differences between them emerged. Students from both classes improved on the tests in equal measure, which the researchers speculate was due to the fact that the tests were easier for them the second time around.

Multiple other studies have shown results like these, suggesting that mindfulness, in the common ways we are seeing teachers attempt to apply it in the classroom—for example, short meditation practices at the beginning of the class period—has not yet been shown to produce a measurable, long-term impact on learning.[9] Likewise, we are not yet seeing mindfulness experiments in the classroom that are producing long-term gains in the general attentional capacities of students. I remain open to the possibility that future experiments on mindfulness might yet yield such results, but we have nothing definitive thus far.

But that doesn't mean mindfulness, or perhaps more accurately the lessons that mindfulness teaches, does not have a role to play in the classroom, and in our work of supporting student attention. I take seriously the comments I have heard, and opinion essays I have read, from teachers expressing the benefits of mindfulness in their classrooms.[10] Their experiences certainly run parallel to the extensive research that has been done on the positive impact of mindfulness in other areas of life, especially physical and mental health. While the research on mindfulness in education has not convinced me that imposing such a practice on students produces concrete results, I believe we have much to learn as teachers from the theory of mindfulness if we consider our work in light of the three core lessons I outlined above, which we will consider more fully below. Both teachers and students can benefit when teachers take a more mindful approach to their teaching, a position I have been stealthily advocating for throughout this entire book.

To understand what I mean by that last statement, we have to remember the distinction between *mindfulness practice* and *mindful awareness*. When most people think about mindfulness, they think about meditation, a technique often used by researchers in the kinds of experiments I've just described. Meditation is a common method of mindfulness practice. But as we are reminded by Harvard psychologist Ellen Langer, the author of *Mindfulness*, "Meditation is a *tool* to achieve post-meditative mindfulness." That state of post-meditative mindfulness, or mindful awareness, puts us "in the present, noticing all the wonders that we didn't realize were right in front of us."[11] That state can exist when we are strolling down the street, talking with friends, or teaching or learning in the classroom. To be mindfully aware means to break through the mindless way we normally experience the world and embrace the present moment. It means attuning ourselves deeply to a conversation with a student, noticing and accepting the rhythms of attention in our classrooms, and making deliberate changes to our teaching practice to shake ourselves out of our usual routines and see the classroom anew. These are all activities that can lead to a mindful classroom, even if you never engage in the formal work of meditation or mindfulness practice.

In the recommendations of this chapter, I am thus going to turn the lens of mindfulness from student to teacher. I invite you now to reflect on the ways the three features of mindfulness—having compassion for your mind and the minds of your students, setting a concrete intention for mindfulness in the classroom, and embracing each classroom moment in all of its unique glory—can make you a mindful educational practitioner. This doesn't mean that you can't or shouldn't practice mindfulness with your students. If you have established such a practice in the classroom and are seeing positive results, by all means you should continue it—and if you are measuring those results, please let the rest of us know about them. But for those of us who are not yet ready to meditate with our students, I'll advocate instead for strategies to make yourself a more mindful educator, especially as it relates to attention and distraction.

Cultivate Compassion

A friend at another university contacted me one summer to ask if I would hold a virtual Q&A with a group of new faculty, who had been reading one of my previous books. When the day and time came, I waved to them through the computer and then sat back to see what questions they had. A woman raised her hand and posed the following question to me: "I teach an evening class that meets from 7:00 to 10:00 p.m. Many of the students work during the day, and are already tired by the time they get to my classroom. How can I keep them focused and engaged for three hours at the end of the day?" I write this first recommendation for that faculty member, for all of us who are feeling more distracted than we used to, and for our students, who are tempted by the allure of their devices while we are asking them to do the hard work of learning.

The primary lesson I hope you have taken from this book is that attention is an achievement; if we want students to achieve attention in our classroom, then we have to cultivate it deliberately. But I can't imagine anything a teacher could do—truly, nothing—that would keep a group of students spellbound for three hours in the evening after a full day's worth of work. So the second lesson I hope you will take away is that, when it comes to attention and distraction, we need to treat ourselves and our students with compassion. The attention that we ask of students in the classroom is an especially challenging achievement: it requires sustained focus over an extended period of time, it asks them to struggle and work, and the payoffs for that struggle are often not immediately visible. The temptation to turn away from that hard work, and default to more immediate pleasures or pursuits, has always been strong and has intensified in recent years.

Have compassion first for yourself. You feel distracted at times because we all feel distracted at times, and some researchers in this area would argue that we feel distracted most of the time. This doesn't mean that you, like your students, should not work to harness your attention toward your research, teaching, family, and other pursuits. Of course you should, and plenty of books and resources are out there if you are looking for assistance in managing your relationship to distractions. I read those books, I practice mindfulness, and I have set certain boundaries around my work and family spaces to ensure that I bring my attention to them as much as I can. But in spite of all those efforts, I fail all the time. I am plenty distracted. I am as likely as you are to stop in my work and see what's happening on Twitter or Instagram, to pull out my phone in idle moments (and even not-so-idle moments) and allow its easy distraction to ward off boredom, frustration, and anxiety. This is how we are, and this is how we live today. Recognize that the temptations around you are strong, and fight them as best as you can—but recognize as well that you have a brain that was built to focus and disperse, to attend and distract, just like the brains of your early human ancestors.

The compassion that you afford to yourself, when it comes to attention and distraction, should extend to your students as well. Like you, they are working with distractible brains, in the midst of many enticing technologies, and their attention strays. As we devise techniques to return it to the classroom, we should do so with empathy for their struggle. We know these challenges ourselves, just as humans have for as long as we have been writing about attention and distraction. When we see student attention ebbing away from us in the classroom, we can wag our fingers and threaten consequences, or we can pause and invite: "I see I am losing some of you. This is hard stuff. Let's see what we can do to get ourselves back on track here." And then, as we walk back to our offices and reflect on the day's teaching, as we post on social media and talk with our colleagues, we can remember that the vast majority of our students work very hard to succeed in our courses, and that supporting them in that work is our core mission.

Make Mindful Moments

Paula Fitzpatrick, a psychologist and the dean of the College of Liberal Arts and Sciences at my university, teaches courses in positive psychology, in which her students both learn about and practice mindfulness. She has also been trained in the mindfulness-based stress reduction technique developed by Jon Kabat-Zinn, giving her the formal credentials to teach mindfulness to others. In the spring of 2019, Fitzpatrick offered a lunchtime session on mindfulness for faculty members, which featured a mix of practice and lecture. She guided us through two short presentations, discussed the origins of mindfulness, and offered some practical recommendations for working, teaching, and living mindfully. Like other mindfulness teachers I have read or heard, she encouraged us to start small with our thinking about mindfulness. Rather than just trying to make our lives more mindful in a general way, she suggested we identify key moments in the classroom when we might try to bring a more mindful embrace of the present moment.

One moment that she described in this respect was our arrival in the room. She encouraged us to reflect on the fact that when we and our students come into the classroom, everyone arrives trailing clouds of distraction from whatever prior activities and thoughts have been occupying our attention. We might be obsessing over a text from a loved one, indignant about the latest outrage perpetrated by our least favorite politician, or thinking about the lunch we just ate or the one we'll be having after class. Students are talking to their peers, swiping through their Instagram feeds, and worrying about their dwindling bank accounts. From this state of minds in motion, we expect students to grind the spinning wheels to a sudden halt and focus on string theory, or institutional racism, or existentialism. We should not wonder that they have difficulty drawing the class into focus—or that we have the same difficulties.

Although Fitzpatrick offered a quick meditation activity to use as an option at the opening of class, she emphasized in a much more general way the importance of arriving mindfully in the room, both for teachers and for students. In other words, we should be deliberate in how we open the class period—and that most certainly does not have to take the form of focused breathing. For my entire teaching career, I have been opening most of my class sessions with a brief writing activity based on the homework reading. These exercises, in which students write freely in response to a discussion question, take just five minutes and help us transition into the class session. You could envision almost any kind of work that students could do individually or in conjunction with you to mark a mindful transition into the class period. In my book *Small Teaching*, I described the work of astronomer Peter Newbury, who puts up an image and invites his student to notice and wonder about it.[12] I know a number of faculty members who play music at the start of class. Fitzpatrick herself reviews the plans for the day and guides her students through a minute of focused breathing. A colleague in philosophy told me that he uses roll call to mark the opening of his class mindfully; for him, the calling of student names at the beginning of class is less about tracking their absences and more about calling everyone deliberately into the room. In all of these cases, a brief opening activity encourages students to funnel the turbulent water of their minds into a calmer pool. If you listen to a mindfulness app on your phone or attend a mindfulness session in person, you'll notice that they frequently begin with the sound of three gongs. Those gongs mark the transition into mindful awareness, just as these kinds of opening activities are designed to mark the transition into that day's learning.

If you're not convinced that a few minutes of breathing exercises carry much benefit for your students, consider instead identifying a short engagement activity and using it to mark a mindful transition into the classroom every day. Activities like Aisling Dugan's microbe of the day internet searches, described in Chapter Five, or like my writing exercises, serve a dual purpose: they bring students mindfully into the class period, but they also support their learning in some way. Having students engage in mindful breathing might work for you and your students, in which case go for it; but if that doesn't appeal to you, consider how you can take some familiar or existing teaching strategy in your repertoire and use it to create a ritual transition into your class period each day, ensuring that each class contains at least a few mindful minutes.

If the opening of the period doesn't work for you, pick the closing few minutes instead, and create some activity that will send your students out into the world in a more mindful state. Or do it in the middle of class. The details don't matter. What matters is that you select one concrete aspect of your daily classroom routine and turn it into an opportunity for mindful awareness for both you and your students. Even if it doesn't create some measurable difference in their long-term learning or attentional capacities, it might give everyone in the room a few moments of respite from their distractions, and that will make for a better classroom experience for everyone.

Embrace the Present Moment

Outside of formal mindfulness practice, I fall most effortlessly into a mindful embrace of the present moment when I am traveling somewhere new and unusual. Twenty years later, I can remember to this day the moment when I stepped off the plane for the first time in another country, to visit my brother then living in Cairo. My senses were jolted into new life in that airport terminal, and I reveled in amazement at every experience I had over the course of the week, from a crawling descent into the heart of a Giza pyramid to my first taste of hummus. That initial international trip has spurred in me an intense desire to continue my travels to new and unusual places, largely because of the way I am shaken from my daily routines and expectations and forced into a raw and exhilarating experience of the present. I find not only that my embrace of the present moment grows more firm when I am abroad, but that it can last for days, weeks, or months after I have returned—when I relish anew the moments when I can settle into a chair in the backyard and savor the simple joys of a New England summer day.

In Chapter Seven, I argued for the importance of jolting students from the familiar routines of their learning through the development of signature attention activities. Outside of formal mindfulness practice, I know of nothing more potent for awakening humans to the present moment than the disruption of a routine or a confrontation with something new and unexpected. Such disruptions and confrontations shouldn't just be imposed on your students; they should become one of the ways you regularly renew your own attention to your teaching and remind yourself to embrace the present moment of the classroom. I make it a habit to change at least one thing each semester in every course I teach, not because anything necessarily needs fixing, but because I know that, if I don't, I will slip into habits that will dull my own interest in the course and the material, and that dullness will ripple out to my students. In this book, I have offered you a series of recommendations for ways you might experiment in your course design and classroom practice, and I would encourage you to identify one or two and try them tomorrow, next week, or next semester. Make yourself just a little bit uncomfortable in the classroom, and your renewed attention to the course, and to your students, will help you embrace that moment.

For my final recommendation of this chapter, then, I offer a handy summary of the recommendations I have made in the previous chapters, to which you can return when you are looking for quick reminders about how to cultivate attention in the classroom:

- Cultivate **community** in your classroom. Begin by inviting students to share their values and strengths, and affirm the assets they bring, rather than their deficits. Continue your commitment to community by learning their names. Use their names throughout the semester (and ask them to do so as well); in large classes, use name placards to support your efforts. Finally, arrange the space of your classroom, or attend to the positioning of bodies in the room, in ways that are designed to support attention. Opt for flexible classrooms whenever possible, arrange furnishings in ways that support attention and build community, and use your own movement around the room as a lever to hold the attention of your students.
- Build your course around **curiosity** and seek opportunities throughout the semester to pique the curiosity of your

students. Attention is the bridge between curiosity and learning, and your course design can take advantage of that connection. Questions create curiosity, so begin thinking about its role in your teaching by including in your course description the big questions that will make students curious about the material. On the first day of the semester, design an activity that engages them with those questions and with the mysteries or puzzles of your course. Consider ways to use questions to drive your teaching throughout the semester, informally or with peer instruction. Finally, work actively to solicit the questions that your students might bring into the room or that your course raises for them.

- Recognize that change renews attention, and build in regular changes to your classroom **structure**: shifts from one activity to the next, from passive to active, from thinking to writing to speaking. Think about your teaching strategies as modules that you can deploy strategically throughout the class period, with a specific focus on attention. Make sure your organization of these modules is visible to your students, using oral or written signposts and structures to guide them through the class period. Have some quick attention-renewal activities in your pocket, which you can use when student attention flags. Finally, jazz up those slides with images and graphics that will help sustain the attention of students during your slide-based lectures.

- Include **signature attention activities**—designed specifically to cultivate students' attention and help them see the material with fresh and fascinated eyes—in your modules. Focusing, creating, and connecting all provide conceptual pathways to the development of signature attention activities. Through these pathways, you are seeking to jolt students from their mindless routines in the classroom or their overly familiar expectations about your subject matter or their educational experience.

- Use **assessments** to help overworked students, who are struggling to master the material and activities of five courses, understand where to focus their attention. Low-stakes graded activities in the classroom nudge students to attend to the work that will benefit them. Tests and quizzes will assist them in strengthening the core knowledge of your course. You can also design creative assessments with which they help bring the course material to the attention of others.

I probably don't need to convince a good and conscientious teacher like you to continue to experiment with your teaching, to try new things each semester or year in support of your students and their learning. But I do hope this book has convinced you that such small, continuous experimentation has the potential to reawaken *your* attention in the classroom, which may be just as important as devising techniques to awaken the attention of your students. We can't embrace the present moment when we are sleepwalking through it, and we can fall into sleepwalking easily in our daily work lives. Breaking and reshaping your teaching routines, one semester at a time, may be your best path to embracing each day in the classroom and becoming a more mindful teacher.

Quick Take

- Recognize that distractibility is an architectural feature of the human brain, and have compassion for yourself and your students. Assume that your students are doing their best to be attentive in the challenging environment of the classroom, and that they need your support and understanding more than they need your scolding. Find in your own moments of distraction the reserves of compassion you need for your students.

- Design a ritual or activity that helps students arrive in the room. Use that ritual as a way to draw them from their distractions and into the course for that session. You can do something similar at other marked points throughout the class period, such as the halfway point—when their minds might especially crave distraction—or in the closing moments.

- Use your reading of this book to make a commitment to renewing your attention to the present moment of the classroom. Experiment with new course designs or teaching practices in the coming days, weeks, and months. Break free from your normal patterns and routines, open yourself to novelty and uncertainty, and embrace the attention to the present that these disruptions can bring.

Conclusion

While the evidence that mindfulness practice can have a positive impact on student learning or attention is mixed, a more solid evidence base exists for the positive impact it can have on teachers. The practice of mindfulness can help people learn to regulate their emotions more effectively, becoming less reactive to stress, frustration, anger, and more. To teach young people is an incredibly rewarding experience, but it can also be emotionally challenging. Researchers have thus explored whether mindfulness can help teachers manage their emotions more effectively. In her book *The Spark of Learning: Energizing the College Classroom with the Science of Emotion*, psychologist Sarah Cavanagh reviews some of those studies, including one that she describes as a "gold-standard controlled study" in which the researchers compared teachers who had completed a mindfulness training with those who had not. Looking at self-reports from the two groups of teachers, as well as their actual classroom behaviors, the experiment showed striking results. As Cavanagh summarizes them, "The teachers [who had been trained in mindfulness] were more satisfied with their work, better able to manage their attention to emotional matters, felt better, and conducted more organized classes."[13] The study supports the argument I have been making in this chapter: that when the teacher becomes more mindful, it ultimately benefits the students. I have felt this in my own experience with mindfulness and teaching, and thus want to conclude this chapter with a brief description of how mindfulness practice has changed my own life.

At the end of a difficult spring semester more than ten years ago, I came home from campus early and lay down on the couch for a nap, exhausted from the end-of-semester crush, and fell instantly asleep. A short while later, something startled me awake and I bolted to a sitting position. The sudden waking and physical exertion set my heart racing in a way that frightened me. Not knowing much about what a heart attack actually was, and feeling unusual activity in my heart, I assumed I was about to die. I called 911 and was very soon in an ambulance on the way to the hospital before the kids arrived home. At the hospital, they explained to me that I was not having a heart attack; this was an anxiety attack, something I had never experienced before, and I am still not sure why it occurred on that day. But as anyone who has experienced anxiety or panic attacks will know, they forge pathways in your brain that don't close down as easily as you would like. An association had been created between a panicky feeling and a racing heart, and that association began to creep into my life in unexpected ways. For example, the normal elevation of my heart rate during exercise would reanimate that panicky feeling, causing my heart to race even more and sometimes even palpitate with fear. When I found myself in situations that provoked normal, everyday anxiety, my heart would be sent galloping in ways that would escalate those normal feelings into uncomfortable excess. I spoke to my doctor, read books and websites, talked with anyone I knew who had experienced anxiety or panic attacks, and learned that what I was experiencing was pretty typical. But none of that knowledge made the problem disappear. No matter how much I tried to dissect and think away the problem, it persisted.

It was at that point, long before I had reflected on any of what you have just read in this chapter, that I committed myself to experimenting with mindfulness. Jon Kabat-Zinn's *Full Catastrophe Living* had been given to me by a psychologist friend, along with a dozen recorded meditations, of twenty to forty minutes in length, that aligned with ideas from the book. For a few weeks or months, I read Kabat-Zinn's book and dabbled around in the tapes, feeling excited by what I was learning and definitely seeing some benefits from my occasional practice. But it was not until I completed a full eight weeks of practice on a daily basis that I finally felt the full power of mindfulness. Over the course of those eight weeks, as the result of twenty minutes of mindful practice per day, I finally was able to weaken the unhappy connections my brain had made and free myself from the effects of my mysterious anxiety attack.

But I also experienced myriad other benefits from my mindfulness practice. Even though I still had plenty of work piled on my desk and all of the cares and concerns of a spouse and father of five children, I found that those stressors had lost much of their power over me. I relaxed in the classroom, and I was more interested and curious in my teaching than I had been in years. I felt a greater sense of compassion and understanding for my students. Outside of school, I became much more attuned to the joys of everyday life, from the taste of food to the feel of leaves crunching beneath my feet on a hike through the woods. I realized how much of my everyday stress and anxiety came from worrying about future events that might never occur. Whenever I felt my mind running down some pathway toward worry, I was able to stop myself and hear the voice of Kabat-Zinn asking me: Is the thing you are worrying about happening right now? The answer was almost always no, and I was able to let go and recapture my peace of mind.

In short, mindfulness changed my life for the better in many ways, and I continue to practice it, though not quite as regularly as I want to or should. I thus can't resist, while I have you here at the end of a chapter on mindfulness, recommending that, if you have ever felt inclined to explore it in a more formal way, I would encourage you to give it a try. You might know about or discover resources on your campus that can help you. We have a room in our campus ministry center set aside for prayer or meditation, and many educational institutions have formal programs on mindfulness for faculty and staff, or regular opportunities to pause during the middle of the day and engage in a brief mindfulness practice. For that matter, you might even find opportunities to practice mindfulness at the barbershop. But whatever the venue might be, if you have the time and inclination, take the plunge. You might not suddenly be able to ward off all distractions and concentrate like a monk, but you might well find an increased ability to focus on the present moment, which will bring you greater joy and peace in your life, both as a teacher and as a human.

Conclusion

The Classroom as
Attention Retreat

ROLLO MAY was an American psychologist whose life and career spanned most of the twentieth century, and whose wide-ranging intellect produced more than a dozen books on subjects from love and beauty to anxiety and violence. His work crosses many disciplines and trades in big ideas. In 1975, he published *The Courage to Create*, a slim volume of reflections based on a series of lectures he had delivered about the sources and meanings of human creativity. In that book, he tells a detailed story about a time when he was working on a difficult problem for his doctoral dissertation, and was stuck at a theoretical impasse that had him completely stymied. Exhausted and frustrated, he left behind his books and papers for the day and walked out into the streets of New York City. "About fifty feet away from the entrance to the Eighth Street station," he explains, the solution to the problem leaped into his mind. The intellectual floodgates then opened up for him:

And as quickly as that idea struck me, other ideas poured out. I think I had not taken another step on the sidewalk when a whole new hypothesis broke loose in my mind. I realized my entire theory would have to be changed. . . . I was convinced there, on the street—and later thought and experience only convinced me the more—that this [was] a better, more accurate, and more elegant theory, than my first.[1]

May's explanation for this experience draws from language about the role that the unconscious takes in breaking through the barriers of our conscious mind, a theoretical construct that doesn't match very well with the way psychologists understand and talk about the brain today. But the story he tells should be familiar to almost anyone who does intellectual or creative work: stepping away from external sources and into some space where the mind can wander freely leads to a productive breakthrough. All of my own intellectual insights come in these moments: standing idly in the shower, hiking in the woods near my home, washing dishes at the sink, pulling up weeds in the yard.

In Part One of this book, I argued that time spent with our digital devices has not architecturally diminished our attention span. But that doesn't mean that the hours we spend scrolling through feeds might not be having an impact on our lives that deserves careful consideration—including potentially depriving us of light-bulb discoveries like the one described by Rollo May, and perhaps experienced by you as well. Neuroscientist Moheb Costandi argues that our brains have tremendous capacity for change over the course of our lifetimes, as they respond and adapt to our individual experiences and our environment. "Your brain is, to a large extent, unique," he writes, "custom-built from the life experiences you have had since being in your mother's womb, to meet the demands you place on it today."[2] (He also echoes Daniel Willingham in noting that such changes occur within the constraints of what he calls our "neurological substrates," or core features and functions of the brain, such as our memories or attention systems.) The challenge we face in the age of omnipresent digital distractions is that we are narrowing the kinds of life experiences we are giving to our brain and reducing the demands we make of it. We no longer ask it to grapple with idle time (in which we turn to our social media), or navigate our way through the built environment around us (for which we use our GPS), or memorize basic knowledge (for which we use Google). We limit our opportunities for connection with the physical people around us when we immediately turn to our phones in public settings (such as a classroom), and we limit our opportunities for creative thinking if we expect it to come only through digital work (such as internet searching).

We have gained much from the role that our devices play in our lives. But even as we recognize the productive power of our time in the digital world, we should also recognize that gains sometimes bring losses. The learning of our students will be most effective when we expand the context in which they do their thinking; it should include engagement with digital resources, dialogue with the students around them, and times when their brains have the opportunity to work quietly behind the scenes, as Rollo May's brain did on the streets of New York City. Our role as educators should thus include providing a full range of opportunities for thinking, especially when so much of our students' time outside of the classroom is spent with screens. Their plastic brains are being shaped largely in the presence of those screens; we should view this as negative not because screens are bad, but because excessive time with them is limiting their access to other forms of thinking. A parallel argument is made about the extent to which screen time may be harmful for younger children: not because screens are necessarily bad, but because they eclipse the time that children could be spending outdoors, engaging in imaginative play, and socializing with one another.

Outside of the classroom, both we and our students swim in a sea of digital devices, instant news, social media connections, and digitally mediated conversations. Inside the classroom, we have the opportunity to give students another kind of experience—one in which they engage fully with one another and with the experiences we have created for them, forcing their brains into the kinds of unexpected and unfamiliar spaces that lead to new learning. In a 2013 essay in *Harvard Magazine*, art historian Jennifer L. Roberts explains that the pace of life in the digital era means that she feels compelled to think more about the pace of her students' learning experiences. In doing so, she is drawn especially to "the slow end of this tempo spectrum . . . creating opportunities for students to engage in deceleration, patience, and immersive attention." She articulates her reasoning for this by pointing to the ways the student experience outside of the classroom moves with increasing rapidity:

> I would argue that these are the kind of practices that now most need to be actively engineered by faculty, because they simply are no longer available "in nature," as it were. Every external pressure, social and technological, is pushing students in the other direction, toward immediacy, rapidity, and spontaneity—and against this other kind of opportunity. I want to give them the permission and the structures to slow down.[3]

Just like Joanna E. Ziegler, whose teaching practice I cited in the Introduction, Roberts not only wishes for increased attention from her students, but she also provides the structures that support their attention. Prior to completing a research project on a painting of their choosing, students spend three hours viewing the work—a time span even Roberts acknowledges is "painfully long." But that long and painful immersion in a painting, she explains, can lead to startling new insights, both for her and her students.

My colleague Esteban Loustaunau, an inspiring teacher of Spanish language and literature, wrote an essay a few years back for *Inside Higher Ed*, in which he argued that teachers have to be willing to allow their classrooms, at least at times, to become a "retreat space" where we step away from our scripted behaviors and become fully present to one another.[4] In a similar way, I have been arguing in this book for a conception of the classroom as a retreat space from distraction, where we make deliberate efforts to do the hard work of using our attention in support of our learning. Retreats are often challenging at first, as people find themselves unmoored from their usual surroundings and connections. But slowly, gradually, they settle in and learn to see the world, and their lives, with new clarity and insight.

The classrooms of the twenty-first century have the power to bring such insight and clarity to the lives of our students by giving them safe and supported spaces where they can pause from their distractions and engage with us, with one another, and with the fascinating questions of our disciplines. Teachers today have to think creatively about how we educate students in a world of rapid transformation, which seems likely to continue. Like the poet, we invite our listeners to step back from their unthinking routines and habits and look more closely, pause and attend, reflect and respond.

"To pay attention," writes Mary Oliver, in a phrase that captures well the vocation of the teacher today, "this is our endless and proper work."[5]

Acknowledgments

FOR THE PAST several years, I have been part of a small writers' group, which has made everything I write much better than it would be otherwise. Mike Land has a storyteller's ear, which helps me see more clearly how to provide engaging descriptions of both scholarly research and classroom experiences. Sarah Cavanagh provides feedback on everything from single word choices to large conceptual matters, and is almost always right. Thanks to her disciplinary expertise, she also pointed me to dozens of studies, experiments, and resources on attention and distraction that I might have overlooked, for which I am incredibly grateful.

Thanks to my agent, John Wright, for connecting me with Basic Books. Special thanks to my editor, Eric Henney, for providing generous and helpful feedback on the manuscript. What you hold in your hands is a much better book as a result of his careful and supportive reading.

During the two years I spent thinking about and drafting this book, I was teaching literature or writing classes every semester. I learned much from my students about when and how humans pay attention in school and when they are distracted. I had my moments of frustration with them, as surely they had with me. But in the end, I am grateful for the privilege of being in a room with them two or three days a week, thinking and talking about literature and writing. I can't imagine a better life than that. Thanks to all of the students who have made that life possible.

Acknowledgments

Assumption College has always been supportive of my work, and I am grateful to Provost Greg Weiner and all of the administrators and colleagues who have cheered on my writing, said a kind word about it, and been supportive and helpful friends and conversation partners.

My children—Katie, Madeleine, Jillian, Lucie, and Jack—amiably tolerated a father distracted by book writing. They also helped me think more clearly about the challenges faced by young people today, especially with respect to this grand human experiment we are undertaking of putting screens everywhere in our lives. If my children are any indication, we'll be fine.

Readers will see in this book how much of my thinking about anything related to education is informed by my wife, Anne. Her dedication to her students and their families is a source of constant inspiration. We are all lucky to have her in our lives.

Appendix

Our Device Policy
British Literature Survey II

In this class we will spend the majority of our time engaged in activities that depend upon you being present and attentive to one another, and of course to the works of literature we will study. We are all challenged these days by the ways in which our digital devices—including laptops, tablets, and phones—can steal our attention away from our immediate surroundings. In this class we will have a technology policy that is designed to support your attention to one another and to the course material. I have developed this policy for three reasons.

1. A significant body of research demonstrates that when students engage in off-task behavior on their devices, **it hurts the learning of the peers sitting near them.** In one study, students who were *not* using a device in a class lecture, but were seated *within view of a peer with a device*, performed 17 percent worse on an exam based on that lecture material than students who were not within view of someone else's device. Hence the first purpose of this policy is to ensure that your devices are not harming the learning of your peers.

2. This class depends upon everyone's active engagement. My job is to provide you with exposure to the course material and organize class so that you develop your own ideas about what that material means. Your ideas will become richer when they are articulated and engaged in dialogue with the ideas of your peers. If you are focused on your device, instead of our work, **you are depriving the entire class of your ideas and questions—both of which we all want to hear.** Your attention contributes to *all* of our learning.

3. Finally, since so much of the course depends upon discussion, I want to make sure that we all **show respect for one another by listening to each other.** We all have likely had the demoralizing experience of trying to speak with someone who was focused on their phone, and feeling hurt by their lack of attention to us. In this class I want us to respect everyone's voices by being present and listening to each other.

In order to achieve all of these objectives, the device policy for the course is as follows:

1. You *may* use laptops to read the texts and take notes in the course as you wish and as needed. If you use a laptop, **close any tabs that are not related to the course.** Remember, off-task behaviors can hurt the learning of your peers.

2. If you choose to read the works online and use your laptop in class, **get an app or program that can help you take and save notes directly on the texts themselves.** You can use the online tool Hypothes.is to do this, but I can provide you with other ideas, depending upon how you are getting access to the works.

3. You *may* have your phone out on your desk, but **keep it facedown so you are not continually seeing new notifications that steal away your attention.** Those continued flashes of light have been engineered to hijack your attention, and can hurt both your learning and the learning of your peers.

4. There will be times in class when I want everyone to put their devices away and focus on some activity: a quick writing exercise, a discussion circle, a worksheet. In those activities, we will all be device free.

5. Finally, in order to show everyone that we are listening respectfully to one another, please remove any AirPods or earbuds at the start of class.

If anyone has an accommodation that would make any of these policy items challenging in any way, please let me know by e-mail prior to Wednesday's class. I will make sure I modify the policy accordingly. *I am very happy to do this.* If you have any other hesitations or concerns about the policy, for any reason at all, please let me know that as well. I want to ensure that this policy supports our work while meeting your needs as a student.

We will revisit this policy at the midterm, to check and see whether it is still working for everyone. For now, please indicate that you understand the policy and agree to abide by it with your signature below.

Signed: _____ Date: _____

Notes

Introduction

1 E. M. Delafield, *The Diary of a Provincial Lady* (London: Virago Modern Classics, 2008).

2 E. M. Delafield, *The Provincial Lady in London* (New York: Harper and Brothers, 1933), 31.

3 James Zull, *The Art of Changing the Brain: Enriching the Practice of Teaching by Exploring the Biology of Learning* (Sterling, VA: Stylus, 2002).

4 Yves Citton, *The Ecology of Attention*, trans. Barnaby Norman (Cambridge: Polity Press, 2017), 98.

5 Michelle D. Miller, *Minds Online: Teaching Effectively with Technology* (Cambridge, MA: Harvard University Press, 2014), 87.

6 Susan Dynarski, "Laptops Are Great. But Not During a Lecture or a Meeting," *New York Times*, November 22, 2017, www.nytimes.com/2017/11/22/business/laptops-not-during-lecture-or-meeting.html.

7 Pam A. Mueller and Daniel M. Oppenheimer, "The Pen Is Mightier than the Keyboard: Advantages of Longhand over Laptop Note Taking," *Psychological Science* 25, no. 6 (June 2014): 1159–1168. While I was finishing the revisions for this book, a newer study attempting to replicate this experiment was published, and did not find the same level of superiority for longhand notes. See Kayla Morehead, John Dunlosky, and Katherine A. Rawson, "How Much Mightier Is the Pen than the Keyboard for Note-Taking? A Replication and Extension of Mueller and Oppenheimer (2014)," *Educational Psychology Review* 31 (2019): 753–780.

8 Jessica Ferronetti, "Technology and Your Students," D'Amour Center for Teaching Excellence, www1.assumption.edu/cte/damour-student -fellows/2017-2018-student-fellow-essays/jessica-ferronetti-technol ogy-and-your-students/.

9 Beckie Supiano, "Digital Distraction Is a Problem Far Beyond the Classroom. But Professors Can Still Help," *Chronicle of Higher Education*, April 7, 2019, www.chronicle.com/article/Digital-Distraction -Is-a/246074.

10 Adam Gazzaley and Larry Rosen, *The Distracted Mind: Ancient Brains in a High-Tech World* (Cambridge, MA: MIT Press, 2016). This scenario is first introduced on page 30.

11 For a subtle consideration of such evolutionary arguments, see Marlene Zuk, "The Evolutionary Search for Our Perfect Past," *New York Times*, January 19, 2009, www.nytimes.com/2009/01/20/health/views /20essa.html.

12 Ian McGilchrist, "The Divided Brain," RSA Animate, October 2011, video, 11:48, www.ted.com/talks/iain_mcgilchrist_the_divided_brain.

13 Gazzaley and Rosen, *Distracted Mind*, 13.

14 Nir Eyal, *Hooked: How to Build Habit-Forming Products* (New York: Penguin, 2014), 2. Five years later, Eyal turned around and published *Indistractable: How to Control Your Attention and Choose Your Life* (Dallas: BenBella Books, 2019), a book designed to help people resist those same habit-forming products.

15 Tim Wu, *The Attention Merchants: The Epic Scramble to Get Inside Our Heads* (New York: Vintage Books, 2016), 6.

16 I take this same problem-based approach to educational improvement in my book *Cheating Lessons: Learning from Academic Dishonesty* (Cambridge, MA: Harvard University Press, 2013).

17 The extent to which we should blame the explosion of smartphones for teenage mental-health problems remains for me an open question. Too many news stories seem to be pushing us toward some certain conclusion on this question, usually landing on the idea that rising rates of anxiety and depression among teens stem from their phone and social media use. For two informed and research-based perspectives on the potential causes of these rising rates of mental-health problems among young people, see Sarah Rose Cavanagh, *Hivemind: The New Science of Tribalism in Our Divided World* (New York:

Grand Central, 2019); and B. Janet Hibbs and Anthony Rostain, *The Stressed Years of Their Lives: Helping Your Kid Survive and Thrive During Their College Years* (New York: St. Martin's Press, 2019).

18 Daniel Reisberg, *Cognition: Exploring the Science of the Mind*, 6th ed. (New York: W. W. Norton and Company, 2016), 168.

19 Carlos Montemayor and Harry Haroutioun Haladjian argue that "the many components of attention cannot be described by a single mechanism, but rather constitute a collection of cognitive processes that produce the ability to be attentive." Carlos Montemayor and Harry Haroutioun Haladjian, *Consciousness, Attention, and Conscious Attention* (Cambridge, MA: MIT Press, 2015), 26.

20 Ellen Langer, *The Power of Mindful Learning* (Boston: Da Capo Press, 1997).

21 Joanna E. Ziegler, "The Role of Contemplative Ritual in Approaching Art," in *Becoming Beholders: Cultivating Sacramental Imagination and Actions in College Classrooms*, eds. Karen E. Eifler and Thomas M. Landy (Collegeville, MN: Liturgical Press, 2014), 52.

Chapter One

1 Aristotle, *Nicomachean Ethics*, trans. Joe Sachs (Newburyport, MA: Focus Publishing, 2002), 188.

2 Saint Augustine, *Confessions* (Peabody, MA: Hendrickson Publishing, 2004), 223.

3 Huston Smith and Philip Novak, *Buddhism: A Concise Introduction* (New York: HarperCollins, 2003), 48.

4 Cited in David Marno, *Death Be Not Proud: The Art of Holy Attention* (Chicago: University of Chicago Press, 2016), 98.

5 Brian Cowan, *The Social Life of Coffee: The Emergence of the British Coffee House* (New Haven, CT: Yale University Press, 2015). See also Melvyn Bragg, "Coffee," December 12, 2019, in *In Our Time*, produced by BBC4, podcast, 55:00, www.bbc.co.uk/programmes /m000c4x1.

6 Tom Standage, *Writing on the Wall: Social Media—The First 2,000 Years* (New York: Bloomsbury, 2013), 111.

7 Standage, *Writing on the Wall*, 112.

8 Isaac Watts, *The Improvement of the Mind* (Boston: Hickling, Swan, and Brown, 1855), 143.

9 Cited in Natalie M. Phillips, *Distraction: Problems of Attention in Eighteenth-Century Literature* (Baltimore: Johns Hopkins University Press, 2016), 41. Phillips provides an excellent overview of growing fears about attention and distraction in the eighteenth century.

10 Reproduced in Melissa Dickson, "The Victorians Had the Same Concerns About Technology as We Do," *The Conversation*, June 21, 2016, http://theconversation.com/the-victorians-had-the-same-concerns -about-technology-as-we-do-60476.

11 Luke Fernandez and Susan J. Matt, *Bored, Lonely, Angry, Stupid: Changing Feelings About Technology, from the Telegraph to Twitter* (Cambridge, MA: Harvard University Press, 2019), 213.

12 D. A. Christakis et al., "Early Television Exposure and Subsequent Attentional Problems in Children," *Pediatrics* 113 (2004), 708–713.

13 Children's Hospital and Regional Medical Center, "Study Finds Link Between Television Viewing and Attention Problems in Children," news release, *Science Daily*, April 6, 2004, www.sciencedaily.com /releases/2004/04/040406090140.htm.

14 T. Stevens and M. Mulsow, "There Is No Meaningful Relationship Between Television Exposure and Symptoms of Attention-Deficit /Hyperactivity Disorder," *Pediatrics* 117 (2006), 665–672.

15 Michael Z. Newman, "Children of the 80s Never Fear: Video Games Did Not Ruin Your Life," *Smithsonian Magazine*, May 25, 2017, www.smithsonianmag.com/history/children-80s-never-fear-video -games-did-not-ruin-your-life-180963452/.

16 Edward L. Swing, Douglas A. Gentile, Craig A. Anderson, and David A. Walsh, "Television and Video Game Exposure and the Development of Attention Problems," *Pediatrics* 126 (2010), 214–221.

17 "Video Games Threaten Kids' Attention Span," CBC, July 5, 2010, www.cbc.ca/news/technology/video-games-threaten-kids-attention -span-1.939917.

18 Nicholas Carr, *The Shallows: What the Internet Is Doing to Our Brains* (New York: W. W. Norton, 2010), 10.

19 Carr, *The Shallows*, 129.

20 Carr, *The Shallows*, 31.

21 Carr, *The Shallows*, 63.

22 Brian Resnick, Julia Belluz, and Eliza Barclay, "Is Our Constant Use of Digital Technologies Affecting Our Brain Health? We Asked

11 Experts," *Vox*, February 26, 2019, www.vox.com/science-and
-health/2018/11/28/18102745/cellphone-distraction-brain-health
-screens-kids.

23 Daniel Willingham, "Smartphones Don't Make Us Dumb," *New York
Times*, January 20, 2015, www.nytimes.com/2015/01/21/opinion
/smartphones-dont-make-us-dumb.html.

24 Henry Wilmer, Lauren E. Sherman, and Jason M. Chein, "Smartphones
and Cognition: A Review of Research Exploring the Links Between
Mobile Technology Habits and Cognitive Functioning," *Frontiers in
Psychology* 8 (April 25, 2017), www.frontiersin.org/articles/10.3389
/fpsyg.2017.00605/full.

25 This is not to say, however, that excessive exposure to screens at a
very young age might not shape people's brains for better or worse—
that's true of many things that can happen to us as infants. But even if
we see problems arising from excessive screen use from a young age,
it still might not be the screens themselves—instead the screen time
could be substituting for healthy behaviors in which children should
engage, like physical activity and imaginative play and socializing.
The problem may arise less from the screen itself, in other words, than
from what the screen crowds out.

Chapter Two

1 This three-part scheme is my own; there are many competing schemes
to describe how humans learn. My recommended titles would include
Joshua R. Eyler, *How Humans Learn: The Science and Stories Be-
hind Effective College Teaching* (Morgantown, WV: West Virginia
University Press, 2018); Susan A. Ambrose et al., *How Learning
Works: Seven Research-Based Principles for Smart Teaching* (San
Francisco: Jossey-Bass, 2010); Yana Weinstein and Megan Sumer-
acki with Oliver Caviglioli, *Understanding How We Learn: A Visual
Guide* (New York: Routledge, 2019); and Peter C. Brown, Henry
L. Roediger III, and Mark A. McDaniel, *Make It Stick: The Science
of Successful Learning* (Cambridge, MA: Harvard University Press,
2014).

2 Pooja K. Agarwal and Patrice M. Bain, *Powerful Teaching: Unleash
the Science of Learning* (San Francisco: Jossey-Bass, 2019), 11.

3 Montemayor and Haladjian, *Consciousness*, 25.

4 Michelle Miller, "Tweet and You'll Miss It," *Inside Higher Ed*, December 2, 2014, www.insidehighered.com/views/2014/12/02/essay-calls-professors-start-teaching-students-about-distraction-and-attention.

5 Weinstein, Sumeracki, and Caviglioli, *Understanding How We Learn*, 53.

6 Larry D. Rosen, L. Mark Carrier, and Nancy A. Cheever, "Facebook and Texting Made Me Do It: Media-Induced Task-Switching While Studying," *Computers in Human Behavior* 29, no. 3 (May 2013): 948–958.

7 Charles Calderwood, Phillip L. Ackerman, and Erin Marie Conklin, "What Else Do College Students 'Do' While Studying? An Investigation of Multitasking," *Computers and Education* 75 (June 2014): 19–29.

8 Bernard R. McCoy, "Digital Distractions in the Classroom: Student Classroom Use of Digital Devices for Non-Class Related Purposes," *Journal of Media Education* 4, no. 4 (2013): 5–14, http://en.calameo.com/read/000091789af53ca4e647f. Bernard R. McCoy, "Digital Distractions in the Classroom Phase II: Student Classroom Use of Digital Devices for Non-Class Related Purposes," *Journal of Media Education* 7, no. 1 (2016): 5–32, http://nwmet.org/wp-content/uploads/Digital-Distraction_Research_-Bernard-R.-McCoy.pdf.

9 Yvonne Ellis, Bobbie Daniels, and Andres Jauregui, "The Effect of Multitasking on the Grade Performance of Business Students," *Research in Higher Education Journal* 8 (2010), https://papers.ssrn.com/sol3/papers.cfm?abstract_id=1595375.

10 Arnold L. Glass and Mengxue Kang, "Dividing Attention in the Classroom Reduces Exam Performance," *Educational Psychology* 39, no. 3 (2019): 395–408.

11 Andrew Lepp et al., "College Students' Multitasking Behavior in Online Versus Face-to-Face Courses," *SAGE Open* (January–March 2019): 1–9, https://journals.sagepub.com/doi/pdf/10.1177/2158244018824505.

12 N. Katherine Hayles, "Hyper and Deep Attention: The Generational Divide in Cognitive Modes," *Profession* (2007): 187.

13 Mihaly Csikszentmihalyi, *Flow: The Psychology of Optimal Experience* (New York: Harper Perennial, 1990), 3.

14 Csikszentmihalyi, *Flow*, 4.

15 Mihaly Csikszentmihalyi, *Finding Flow: The Psychology of Engagement with Everyday Life* (New York: Basic Books, 1997), 26.

16 Csikszentmihalyi, *Flow*, 10.

17 For a summary of this research, and some qualifications of it, see William C. Compton and Edward Hoffman, *Positive Psychology: The Science of Happiness and Flourishing* (Belmont, CA: Wadsworth, 2013), 86–90.

Chapter Three

1 Dynarski, "Laptops Are Great."

2 Jonathan Zimmerman, "Welcome, Freshmen. Look at Me When I Talk to You," *Chronicle of Higher Education*, September 11, 2016, www.chronicle.com/article/Welcome-Freshmen-Look-at-Me/237751.

3 Matthew Numer, "Don't Insult Your Class by Banning Laptops," *Chronicle of Higher Education*, December 4, 2017, www.chronicle.com/article/Don-t-Insult-Your-Class-by/241972.

4 Karen Costa, "The Nuance of Note Taking," *Inside Higher Ed*, July 30, 2019, www.insidehighered.com/advice/2019/07/30/why-professors-shouldnt-ban-laptops-and-other-note-taking-devices-classrooms.

5 Lee Skallerup Bessette, "Rethinking Laptop Bans (AGAIN) and Note Taking," *Chronicle of Higher Education*, March 19, 2018, www.chronicle.com/blogs/profhacker/rethinking-laptop-bans-again-and-note-taking/65223 (site discontinued).

6 Elena Neiterman and Christine Zaza, "A Mixed Blessing? Students' and Instructors' Perspectives About Off-Task Technology Use in the Academic Classroom," *Canadian Journal for the Scholarship of Teaching and Learning* 10, no. 1 (Spring 2019), https://ojs.lib.uwo.ca/index.php/cjsotl_rcacea/article/view/8002/6577.

7 Jesse Stommel has been the most vocal advocate of the admirable idea that we should err on the side of trust in our students, which seems traceable back to a tweet and subsequent blog post in which he argued that our pedagogy should "start by trusting students." Jesse Stommel, "Why I Don't Grade," October 26, 2017, www.jessestommel.com/why-i-dont-grade/.

8 Adam Alter, *Irresistible: The Rise of Addictive Technology and the Business of Keeping Us Hooked* (New York: Penguin, 2017), 5.

9 Lindsay McKenzie, "Professor Bans Laptops, Sees Grades Rise," *Inside Higher Ed*, May 11, 2018, www.insidehighered.com/news/2018/05/11 /ohio-state-professors-technology-ban-finds-positive-reaction-and -results.

10 Rick Godden and Anne-Marie Womack, "Making Disability Part of the Conversation: Combatting Inaccessible Spaces and Logics," *Hybrid Pedagogy*, May 12, 2016, http://hybridpedagogy.org/making-disability -part-of-the-conversation/.

11 Michael T. Luongo, "Screens in the Classroom: Tool or Temptation?," *New York Times*, December 11, 2019, www.nytimes.com/2019/12/11 /education/screens-classroom-tool-temptation.html.

12 Godden and Womack, "Making Disability Part of the Conversation."

13 Daniel H. Pink, *Drive: The Surprising Truth About What Motivates Us* (Edinburgh: Canongate, 2010), 90–91.

14 Barry Schwartz, *The Paradox of Choice: Why More Is Less* (New York: HarperCollins, 2016), 3.

15 Schwartz, *The Paradox of Choice*, 5.

16 See Cathy Davidson, "Getting Started 5: First Class: Collectively Writing a Constitution," HASTAC, August 13, 2015, www.hastac.org/blogs /cathy-davidson/2015/08/13/getting-started-5-first-classcollectively -writing-constitution.

17 Ashley Waggoner Denton, "Smartphones, Laptops, and Learning: A PowerPoint Resource," *Teach, Reflect, Repeat* (blog), August 15, 2018, https://teachreflectrepeat.com/smartphones-laptops-and-learning -a-powerpoint-resource/.

18 Richard J. Harnish and K. Robert Bridges, "Effect of Syllabus Tone: Students' Perception of Instructor and Course," *Social Psychology of Education* 14, no. 3 (September 2011): 319–330.

19 Aviva Bower, "Disconnect to Connect: Empowering Students with the Research on Multitasking" (presentation), Professional and Organizational Development Network in Higher Education 44th Annual Conference, Pittsburgh, PA, November 18, 2019.

20 Flower Darby, "How to Be a Better Online Teacher," *Chronicle of Higher Education*, www.chronicle.com/interactives/advice-online-teaching.

21 Matt Reed, "Device Etiquette," *Inside Higher Ed*, November 13, 2019, www.insidehighered.com/blogs/confessions-community-college-dean /device-etiquette.

Chapter Four

1 "Important Milestones: Your Baby by Two Months," Centers for Disease Control and Prevention, October 24, 2019, www.cdc.gov /ncbddd/actearly/milestones/milestones-2mo.html.

2 Michael C. Frank, Edward Vul, and Scott P. Johnson, "Development of Infants' Attention to Faces During the First Year," *Cognition* 110, no. 2 (2009): 160–170.

3 Aristotle, *Nicomachean Ethics*, 175.

4 Harriet L. Schwartz, *Connected Teaching: Relationship, Power, and Mattering in Higher Education* (Sterling, VA: Stylus, 2019), 13.

5 See Cia Verschelden and Lynn Pasquerella, *Bandwidth Recovery: Helping Students Reclaim Cognitive Resources Lost to Poverty, Racism, and Social Marginalization* (Sterling, VA: Stylus, 2017).

6 Akira Miyake et al., "Reducing the Gender Achievement Gap in College Science: A Classroom Study of Values Affirmation," *Science* 330, no. 6008 (November 2010): 1234–1237.

7 Judith M. Harackiewicz et al., "Closing the Social Achievement Gap for First-Generation Students in Undergraduate Biology," *Journal of Educational Psychology* 106, no. 2 (2014): 375–389.

8 Yoi Tibbetts et al., "Affirming Independence: Exploring Mechanisms Underlying a Values Affirmation Intervention for First-Generation Students," *Journal of Personal Social Psychology* 110, no. 5 (May 2016): 635–659.

9 Eugenio Parise, Angela D. Friederici, and Tricia Striano, "'Did You Call Me?' 5-Month-Old Infants Own Name Guides Their Attention," *PLOS One* 5, no. 12, (December 3, 2010), https://journals.plos.org /plosone/article?id=10.1371/journal.pone.0014208.

10 Hongsheng Yang et al., "The Cognitive Advantage for One's Own Name Is Not Simply Familiarity: An Eye-Tracking Study," *Psychonomic Bulletin and Review* 20, no. 6 (2013): 1176–1180.

11 See James M. Lang, *Small Teaching: Everyday Lessons from the Science of Learning* (San Francisco: Jossey-Bass, 2016), esp. the second and fourth chapters.

12 For an excellent and ongoing compendium of the research on this learning principle, see Pooja K. Agarwal's website Retrieval Practice (retrievalpractice.org).

13 Katelyn M. Cooper et al., "What's in a Name? The Importance of Students Perceiving that an Instructor Knows Their Names in a High-Enrollment Biology Classroom," *CBE: Life Sciences Education* 16, no. 1 (2017): 7.

14 See, for example, resource pages from the Eberly Center at Carnegie Mellon University (www.cmu.edu/teaching/solveproblem/strat-cheating/tips-studentnames.html).

15 Carol E. Holstead, "Want to Improve Your Teaching? Start with the Basics: Learn Students' Names," *Chronicle of Higher Education*, August 29, 2019, www.chronicle.com/article/Want-to-Improve-Your-Teaching-/247098.

16 Derek Bruff, *Intentional Tech: Principles to Guide the Use of Educational Technology in College Teaching* (Morgantown: West Virginia University Press, 2019).

17 Melissa Rands and Ann M. Gansemer-Topf, "'The Room Itself Is Active': How Classroom Design Impacts Student Engagement," *Journal of Learning Spaces* 6, no. 1 (2017): 31.

18 Doug Lemov, "Notes on Circulating: Break the Plane and Engage When You Circulate," *Doug Lemov's Field Notes* (blog), Teach Like a Champion, September 29, 2014, https://teachlikeachampion.com/blog/notes-circulating-break-plane-engage-circulate/.

19 I describe Woodworth's insights into classroom performance in more detail in my book *On Course: A Week-by-Week Guide to Your First Semester of College Teaching* (Cambridge, MA: Harvard University Press, 2008), 69–73.

Chapter Five

1 Eyler, *How Humans Learn*, 24.

2 Eyler, *How Humans Learn*, 29.

3 Mario Livio, *Why? What Makes Us Curious* (New York: Simon & Schuster, 2017), 114.

4 Livio, *Why?*, 58.

5 This experiment and others are nicely summarized in Sarah Cavanagh, *The Spark of Learning: Energizing the College Classroom with the Science of Emotion* (Morgantown: West Virginia University Press, 2016), 120–124.

6 Weinstein, Sumeracki, and Caviglioli, *Understanding How We Learn*, 55.

7 Weinstein, Sumeracki, and Caviglioli, *Understanding How We Learn*, 55.

8 Daniel Willingham, *Why Don't Students Like School? A Cognitive Scientist Answers Questions About How the Mind Works and What It Means for the Classroom* (San Francisco: Jossey-Bass, 2009), 75.

9 Ian Leslie, *Curious: The Desire to Know and Why Your Future Depends on It* (New York: Basic Books, 2014).

10 Jessica Lahey, "Teaching: Just Like Performing Magic," *The Atlantic*, January 21, 2016, www.theatlantic.com/education/archive/2016/01 /what-classrooms-can-learn-from-magic/425100/.

11 Rebecca Zambrano, "The 'Big Bang' of Motivation: Questions that Evoke Wonder in Our Students," *Faculty Focus*, February 18, 2019, www.facultyfocus.com/articles/teaching-and-learning/the-big -bang-of-motivation-questions-that-evoke-wonder-in-our-students/.

12 Description and quotes in this section from Cate Denial, "Making the First Day Matter," August 3, 2016, https://catherinedenial.org/blog /uncategorized/making-the-first-day-matter/.

13 I wrote more fully about this in James M. Lang, "Small Changes in Teaching: The First Five Minutes of Class," *Chronicle of Higher Education*, January 11, 2016, www.chronicle.com/article/Small-Changes-in -Teaching-The/234869.

14 For the published version of Mazur's journey and practice, see Eric Mazur, *Peer Instruction: A User's Manual* (New York: Pearson, 1996). Another excellent resource for the use of peer instruction is Derek Bruff, *Teaching with Classroom Response Systems: Creating Active Learning Environments* (San Francisco: Jossey-Bass, 2009).

15 John Dunlosky et al., "Improving Students' Learning with Effective Learning Techniques: Promising Directions from Cognitive and Educational Psychology," *Psychological Science in the Public Interest* 14, no. 1 (2013): 4–58. And if you made it to this footnote, you're curious to know what they found, right? The full text of the article is available for free online: https://pcl.sitehost.iu.edu/rgoldsto/courses/dunlosky improvinglearning.pdf.

16 Christine Chin and Jonathan Osborne, "Students' Questions: A Potential Resource for Teaching and Learning Science," *Studies in Science Education* 44, no. 1 (2008): 1–39.

17 Meriah L. Crawford, "A Simple Trick for Getting Students to Ask Questions in Class," *Faculty Focus*, October 13, 2017, www.facul tyfocus.com/articles/effective-teaching-strategies/a-simple-trick-for -getting-students-to-ask-questions-in-class/.

18 Gazzaley and Rosen, *Distracted Mind*, 8.

Chapter Six

1 Karen Wilson and James H. Korn, "Attention During Lectures: Beyond Ten Minutes," *Teaching of Psychology* 34, no. 2 (2007): 85–89.

2 Diane M. Bunce, Elizabeth A. Flens, and Kelly Y. Neiles, "How Long Can Students Pay Attention in Class? A Study of Student Attention Decline Using Clickers," *Journal of Chemical Education* 87, no. 12 (2010): 1438–1443.

3 Stephen Kaplan, "The Restorative Benefits of Nature: Toward an Integrative Framework," *Journal of Environmental Psychology* 15 (1995): 170. Kaplan argues that exposure to nature is the most impactful way to renew attention (and obtain other cognitive benefits). A more comprehensive treatment of this idea, and application of it to the college environment, can be found in Donald A. Rakow and Gregory T. Eells, *Nature RX: Improving College-Student Mental Health* (Ithaca, NY: Cornell University Press, 2019).

4 Kaplan, "Restorative Benefits," 170.

5 Bunce, Flens, and Neiles, "How Long."

6 Kathleen M. Quinlan, "What Triggers Students' Interest During Higher Education Lectures? Personal and Situational Variables Associated with Situational Interest," *Studies in Higher Education* 44, no. 10 (2019): 1781–1792.

7 See Gail Taylor Rice, *Hitting Pause for Learning: 65 Lecture Breaks to Refresh and Reinforce Learning* (Sterling, VA: Stylus, 2018), 34–36.

8 Lemons described the intellectual provenance of this workshop in an e-mail to me as follows: "That presentation was based on the '5E' model, which was described to me by Kimberly Tanner. I met Kim at a case study workshop in upstate NY. She is a Professor of Biology and Director of the Science Education Partnership and Assessment Laboratory (SEPAL) at San Francisco State University. Kim gave a presentation at the case study workshop in NY, and her presentation was primarily based on her publication entitled, 'Order Matters: Using the

5E Model to Align Teaching with How People Learn' in *CBE-Life Sciences Education*, vol 9, 159-164, Fall 2010."

9 Daniel Rosenn, "Is It Asperger's or ADHD?," Asperger/Autism Network, www.aane.org/is-it-aspergers-or-adhd/.

10 Christine Harrington and Todd Zakrajsek, *Dynamic Lecturing: Research-Based Strategies to Enhance Lecture Effectiveness* (Sterling, VA: Stylus, 2017), 56.

11 Christopher Emdin, *For White Folks Who Teach in the Hood…and the Rest of Y'all Too: Reality Pedagogy and Urban Education* (Boston: Beacon Press, 2016).

12 On reading aloud and its impact on attention, see Meghan Cox Gurdon, *The Enchanted Hour: The Miraculous Power of Reading Aloud in the Age of Distraction* (New York: Harper, 2019).

13 John Medina, *Brain Rules: 12 Principles for Surviving and Thriving at Work, Home, and School* (Seattle, WA: Pear Press, 2014), 190.

14 Miller, *Minds Online*, 95.

15 Miller, *Minds Online*, 154–155.

16 Chris Drew, "Using Colors, Images, and Cartoons to Support Learning," Learning Scientists, www.learningscientists.org/blog/2019/10/31-1.

17 Drew, "Using Colors."

Chapter Seven

1 Mary Oliver, *Devotions: The Selected Poems of Mary Oliver* (New York: Penguin, 2017), 173–174.

2 Oliver, *Devotions*, 105.

3 Christopher Chabris and Daniel Simons, *The Invisible Gorilla: How Our Intuitions Deceive Us* (New York: Crown, 2010), 55.

4 Chabris and Simons, *Invisible Gorilla*, 55.

5 Davidson, *Now You See It*, 49.

6 Langer, *Mindful Learning*, 43.

7 Here's how Fisher described the origins of this activity to me in an e-mail: "This approach has long been used in the study of the Talmud in a traditional study pair called a 'havruta' (also spelled 'hevruta') which I'm told means 'friendship' or 'partner.' The idea is that you unravel the multiple meanings of a text by being in dialogue with it and with each other. Meaning is constructed rather than simply received. I learned this from Devorah Schoenfield at Loyola University

of Chicago in a workshop on religious pluralism sponsored by the American Academy of Religion and then adapted it to some of my course readings."

8 Davidson, *Now You See It*, 100.

9 Jessica Metzler, "Ways of Seeing: Building Center-Museum Partnerships to Support Teaching" (presentation, POD Conference, Portland, OR, November 15, 2018). I did not attend this session; it was brought to my attention in Susan Hrach's book *Minding Student Bodies*, which was in the production stage at West Virginia University Press at the time of this writing. I subsequently conducted a brief phone interview about the approach with Jessica Metzler on January 10, 2020.

10 Gary Wolf, "Steve Jobs: The Next Insanely Great Thing," *Wired*, February 1, 1996, www.wired.com/1996/02/jobs-2/.

11 Scott Barry Kaufman and Carolyn Gregoire, *Wired to Create: Unraveling the Mysteries of the Creative Mind* (New York: Perigee, 2015).

12 "Concept Mapping." Center for Teaching and Learning, Brigham Young University, https://ctl.byu.edu/tip/concept-mapping.

13 Sarah Stein Lubrano, "Living with ADHD: How I Learned to Make Distraction Work for Me," *Aeon*, October 18, 2019, https://aeon.co/ideas/living-with-adhd-how-i-learned-to-make-distraction-work-for-me.

14 Saundra Yancy McGuire and Stephanie McGuire, *Teach Students How to Learn: Strategies You Can Incorporate into Any Course to Improve Student Metacognition, Study Skills, and Motivation* (Sterling, VA: Stylus, 2015), 26.

Chapter Eight

1 You can find an overview of Deci's research and ideas in Edward L. Deci, *Why We Do What We Do: Understanding Self-Motivation* (New York: Penguin, 1996).

2 Alfie Kohn, "The Case Against Grades," November 2011, www.alfiekohn.org/article/case-grades/.

3 Davidson, *Now You See It*, 159.

4 Ambrose et al., *How Learning Works*, 82.

5 Michaeleen Doucleff, "How to Get Kids to Pay Attention," *Mindshift* (blog), KQED, June 21, 2018, www.kqed.org/mindshift/51509/how-to-get-kids-to-pay-attention.

6 Jay R. Howard, *Discussion in the College Classroom: Getting Your Students Engaged and Participating in Person and Online* (San Francisco: Jossey-Bass, 2015).

7 Elbow has produced a two-page handout that provides his guide to minimal grading, available on his personal website. Peter Elbow, "Grading: Do It Less, Do It Better," http://peterelbow.com/pdfs/Grading_Less_Grading_Better.pdf.

8 Agarwal and Bain, *Powerful Teaching*, 28.

9 Agarwal and Bain, *Powerful Teaching*, 39.

10 Shana K. Carpenter, "Testing Enhances the Transfer of Learning," *Current Directions in Psychological Science*, October 1, 2012, https://journals.sagepub.com/doi/full/10.1177/0963721412452728. Carpenter's essay reviews multiple studies demonstrating this effect.

11 See B. Rosenshine, C. Meister, and S. Chapman, "Teaching Students to Generate Questions: a Review of the Intervention Studies," *Review of Educational Research* 66, no. 2 (1996): 181–221.

12 Max Teplitski et al., "Student-Generated Pre-Exam Questions Is an Effective Tool for Participatory Learning: A Case Study from Ecology of Waterborne Pathogens Course," *Journal of Food Science Education* 17, no. 3 (2018): 76–84.

13 Flower Darby with James M. Lang, *Small Teaching Online: Applying Learning Science in Online Classes* (San Francisco: Jossey-Bass, 2019), 98–99.

14 "Why One Science Professor Has Students Write a Children's Book," *Chronicle of Higher Education*, October 18, 2018, www.chronicle.com/article/Why-One-Science-Professor-Has/244844.

Chapter Nine

1 Kabat-Zinn's most comprehensive presentation of the theory and practice of mindfulness comes in Jon Kabat-Zinn, *Full Catastrophe Living: Using the Wisdom of Your Body and Mind to Face Stress, Pain, and Illness* (New York: Bantam Books, 2013).

2 Scott R. Bishop et al., "Mindfulness: A Proposed Operational Definition," *Clinical Psychology: Science and Practice* 11, no. 3 (2004): 232.

3 For an overview of these studies, see Daphne M. Davis and Jeffrey A. Hayes, "What Are the Benefits of Mindfulness," *Monitor on Psychology* 43, no. 7 (2012), www.apa.org/monitor/2012/07-08/ce-corner.

4 For an overview of these studies, see Daniel P. Barbezat and Mirabai Bush, *Contemplative Practices in Higher Education: Powerful Methods to Transform Teaching and Learning* (San Francisco: Jossey-Bass, 2014), 24–27.

5 Destany Calma-Birling and Regan A. R. Gurung, "Does a Brief Mindfulness Intervention Impact Quiz Performance?," *Psychology Learning and Teaching* 16, no. 1 (June 2017): 323–335.

6 Calma-Birling and Gurung, "Brief Mindfulness Intervention," 330.

7 Casey Helber, Nancy A. Zook, and Matthew Immergut, "Meditation in Higher Education: Does It Enhance Cognition?," *Innovations in Higher Education* 37 (2012): 349–358.

8 Helber, Zook, and Immergut, "Meditation," 351.

9 See, for example, Jian-Wei Lin and Li Jung Mai, "Impact of Mindfulness Meditation Intervention on Academic Performance," *Innovations in Education and Teaching International* 55, no. 3 (2018): 366–375. Some studies that do claim to show positive results for mindfulness in education base them on laboratory experiments or on short-term learning only, as in Rebecca Iranzo Bennett et al., "Mindfulness as an Intervention for Recalling Information from a Lecture as a Measure of Academic Performance in Higher Education: A Randomized Experiment," *Higher Education for the Future* 5, no. 1 (2018): 75–88. For an example of a study that does report some positive impact, see Jacquelyn J. Lee and Sarah A. Himmelheber, "Field Education in the Present Moment: Evaluating a 14-Week Pedagogical Model to Increase Mindfulness Practice," *Journal of Social Work Education* 52, no. 4 (2016): 473–483. In this case, though, mindfulness was very thoroughly integrated into the entire course. In addition to the brief meditations, the students learned about mindfulness, discussed it regularly in class, and wrote journal entries about it. I'm prepared to believe that such a full commitment to mindfulness in a course could have lasting impact, but I also don't believe most faculty members are willing to make that kind of commitment.

10 See, for example, Moira Martin, "Mindfulness and Transformation in a College Classroom," *Adult Learning* 29, no. 1 (2018): 5–10; or Keith Kroll, "On Paying Attention: Flagpoles, Mindfulness, and Teaching Writing," *Teaching English in the Two-Year College* 36, no. 1 (2008): 69–78.

11 Ellen Langer, *Mindfulness: 25th Anniversary Edition* (Boston: Da Capo Press, 2014), xxv.

12 Lang, *Small Teaching*, 179.

13 Cavanagh, *Spark of Learning*, 70–71.

Conclusion

1 Rollo May, *The Courage to Create* (New York: W. W. Norton, 1975), 57–58.

2 Moheb Costandi, *Neuroplasticity* (Cambridge, MA: MIT Press, 2016), 155.

3 Jennifer L. Roberts, "The Power of Patience," *Harvard Magazine* (November–December 2013), https://harvardmagazine.com/2013/11/the-power-of-patience.

4 Esteban Loustaunau, "The Classroom as Retreat Space," *Inside Higher Ed*, December 6, 2016, www.insidehighered.com/advice/2016/12/06/benefits-stepping-outside-regular-habits-classroom-essay.

5 Oliver, *Devotions*, 264.

Index

Index

Index

Index

Index

Index

Index

Index

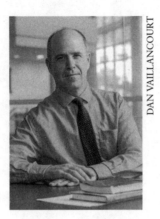

DAN VAILLANCOURT

JAMES M. LANG is a professor of English and director of the D'Amour Center for Teaching Excellence at Assumption University. He is the author of three previous books on higher education teaching and learning: *Small Teaching*, *Cheating Lessons*, and *On Course*. He is also a longtime monthly columnist for the *Chronicle of Higher Education*. He lives in Worcester, Massachusetts. Visit his website at www.jamesmlang.com.